PETER PARKER: THE SPECTACULAR SPIDER-MAN

SPIDER-GEDDON

SEAN RYAN
WRITER

JUAN FRIGERI
ARTIST

JASON KEITH
COLOR ARTIST

PHILIP TAN [#311-312] & **MORRY HOLLOWELL** [#311],
RAIN BEREDO [#312] AND **JEFF DEKAL** [#313]
COVER ART

VC's TRAVIS LANHAM
LETTERER

KATHLEEN WISNESKI
ASSISTANT EDITOR

NICK LOWE
EDITOR

SPIDER-GEDDON: NOIR VIDEO COMIC

DAVID HINE & FABRICE SAPOLSKY
WRITERS

PACO DIAZ
ARTIST

ANDRES MOSSA
COLOR ARTIST

SPIDER-GEDDON: ANIMATED VIDEO COMIC

KEVIN SHINICK
WRITER

DARIO BRIZUELA
ARTIST

RACHELLE ROSENBERG
COLOR ARTIST

JEFF ECKLEBERRY
LETTERER

PACO DIAZ
COVER ART

ANNIE CHENG
PRODUCTION

TIM SMITH 3
PRODUCTION MANAGER

TIM ELDRED
LAYOUTS

MARK BASSO & JACOB THOMAS
EDITORS

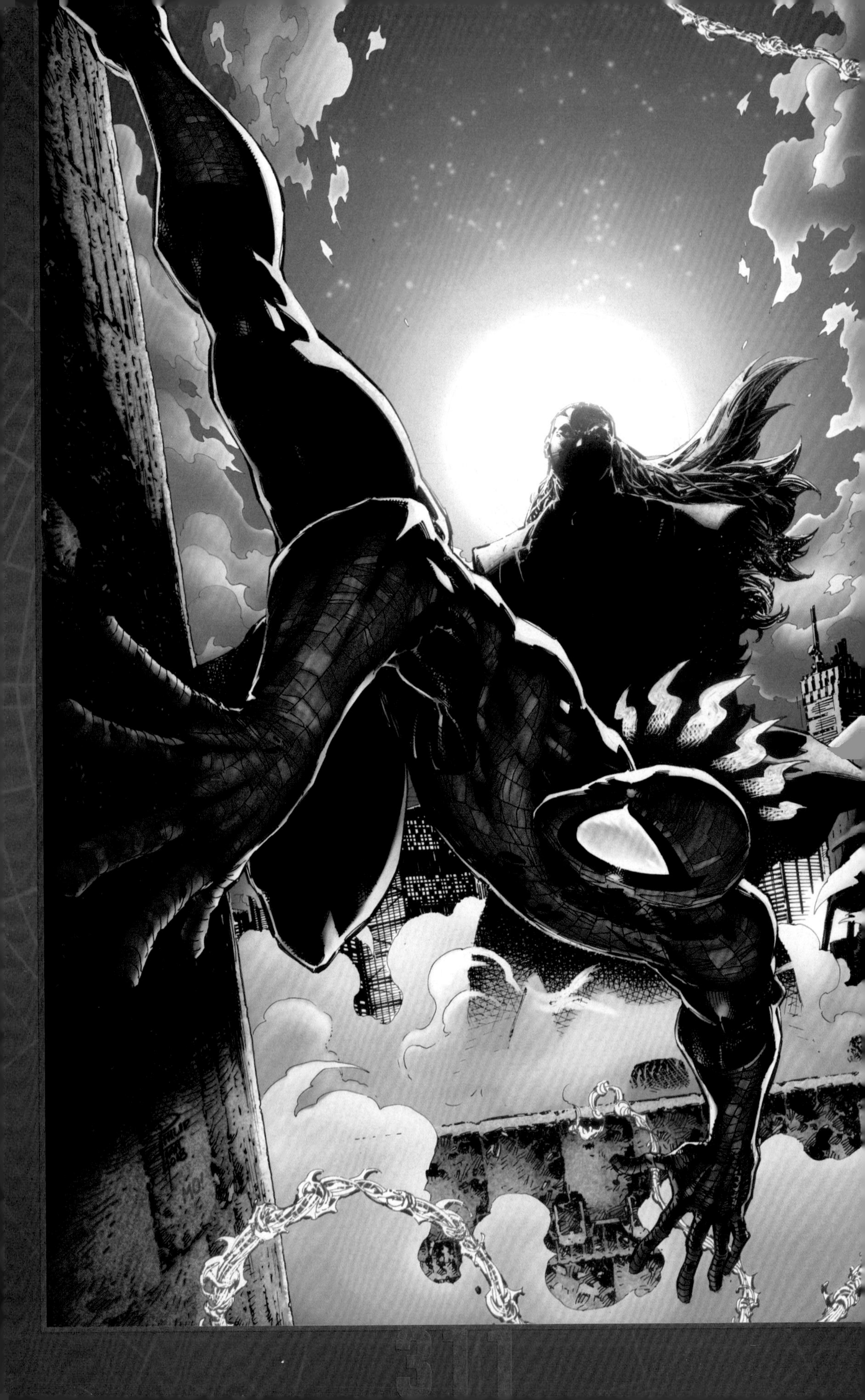
311

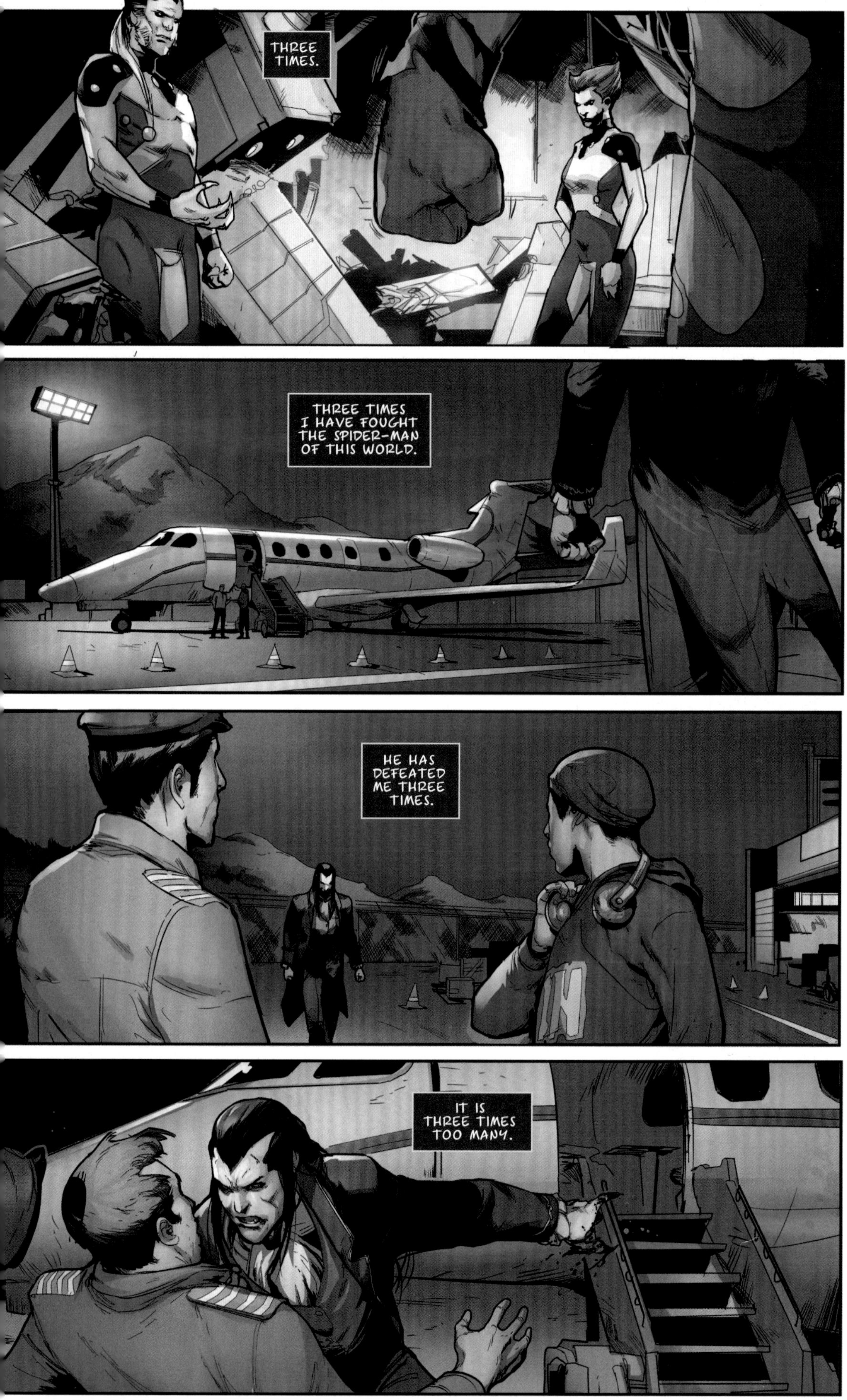
THREE TIMES.
THREE TIMES I HAVE FOUGHT THE SPIDER-MAN OF THIS WORLD.
HE HAS DEFEATED ME THREE TIMES.
IT IS THREE TIMES TOO MANY.

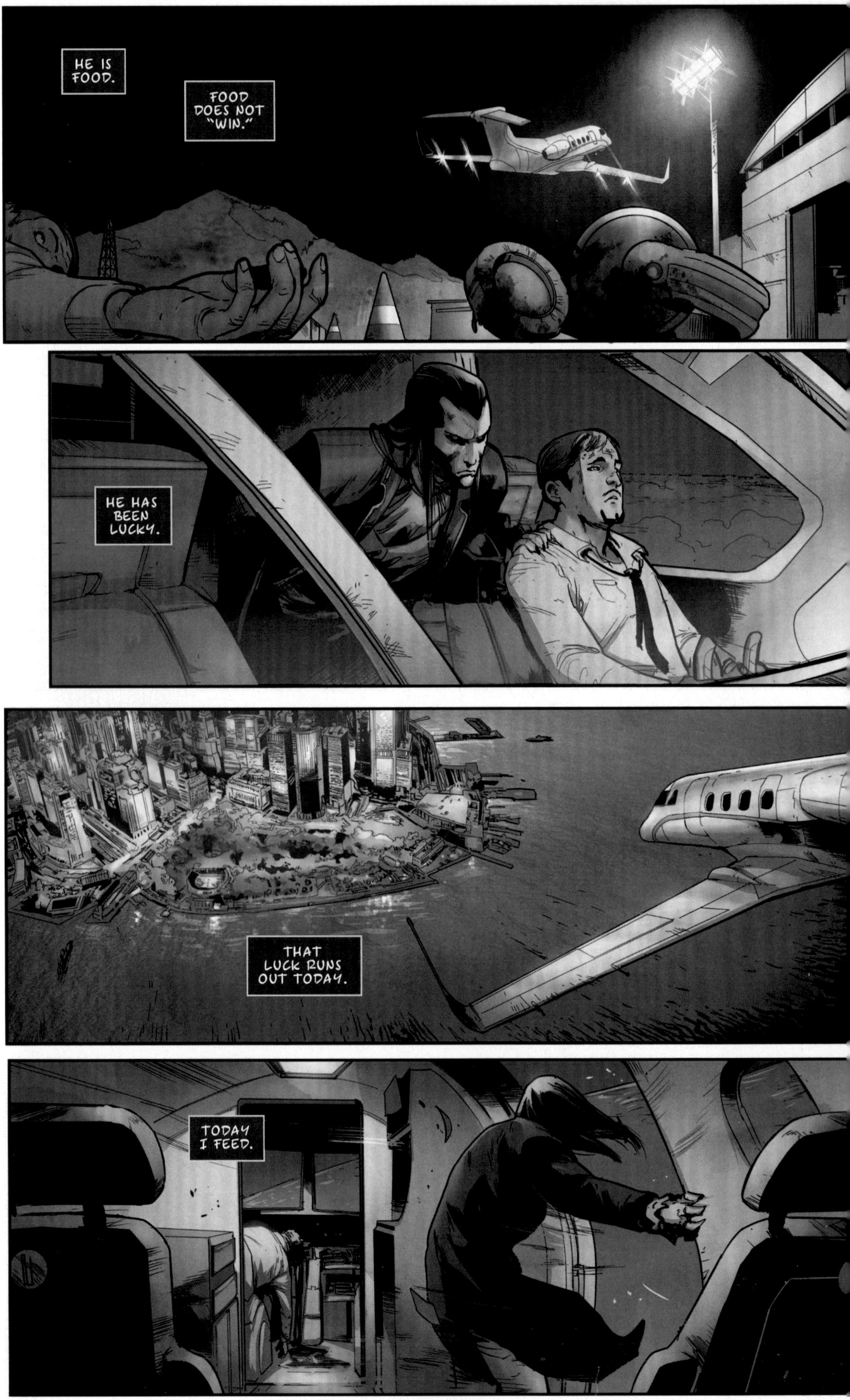
HE IS FOOD.
FOOD DOES NOT "WIN."
HE HAS BEEN LUCKY.
THAT LUCK RUNS OUT TODAY.
TODAY I FEED.

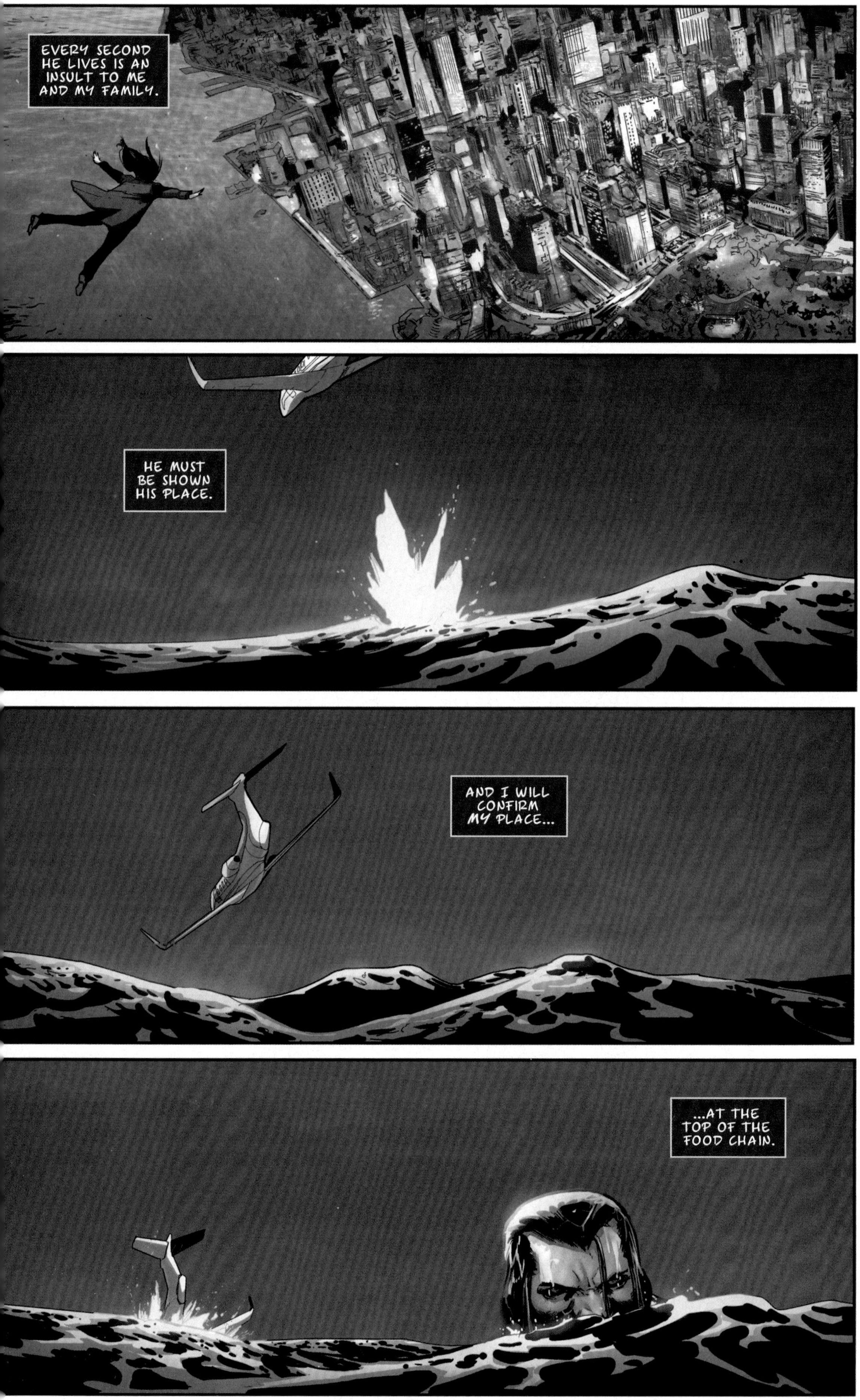
EVERY SECOND HE LIVES IS AN INSULT TO ME AND MY FAMILY.
HE MUST BE SHOWN HIS PLACE.
AND I WILL CONFIRM MY PLACE...
...AT THE TOP OF THE FOOD CHAIN.

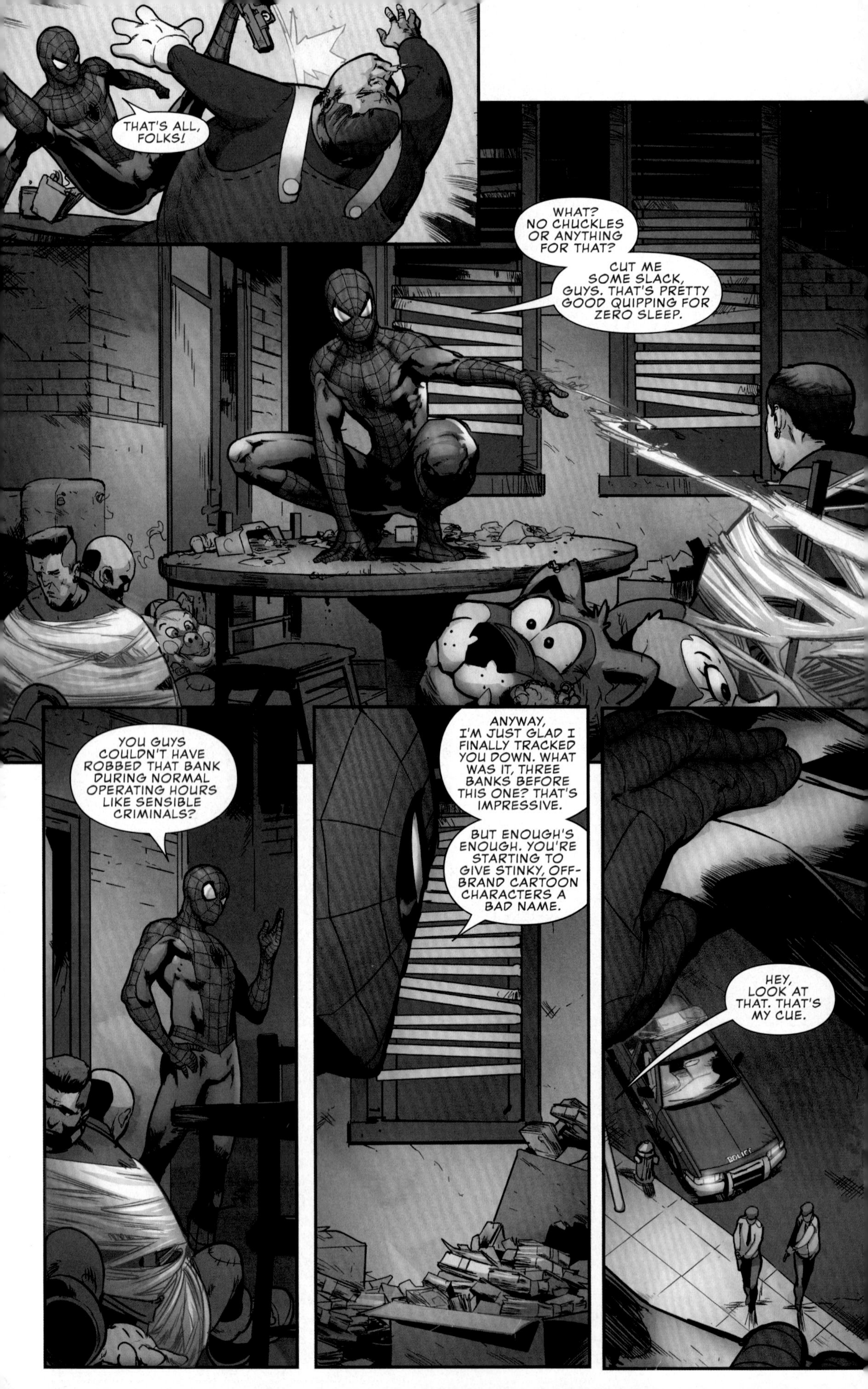
THAT'S ALL, FOLKS!
WHAT? NO CHUCKLES OR ANYTHING FOR THAT?
CUT ME SOME SLACK, GUYS. THAT'S PRETTY GOOD QUIPPING FOR ZERO SLEEP.
YOU GUYS COULDN'T HAVE ROBBED THAT BANK DURING NORMAL OPERATING HOURS LIKE SENSIBLE CRIMINALS?
ANYWAY, I'M JUST GLAD I FINALLY TRACKED YOU DOWN. WHAT WAS IT, THREE BANKS BEFORE THIS ONE? THAT'S IMPRESSIVE.
BUT ENOUGH'S ENOUGH. YOU'RE STARTING TO GIVE STINKY, OFF-BRAND CARTOON CHARACTERS A BAD NAME.
HEY, LOOK AT THAT. THAT'S MY CUE.

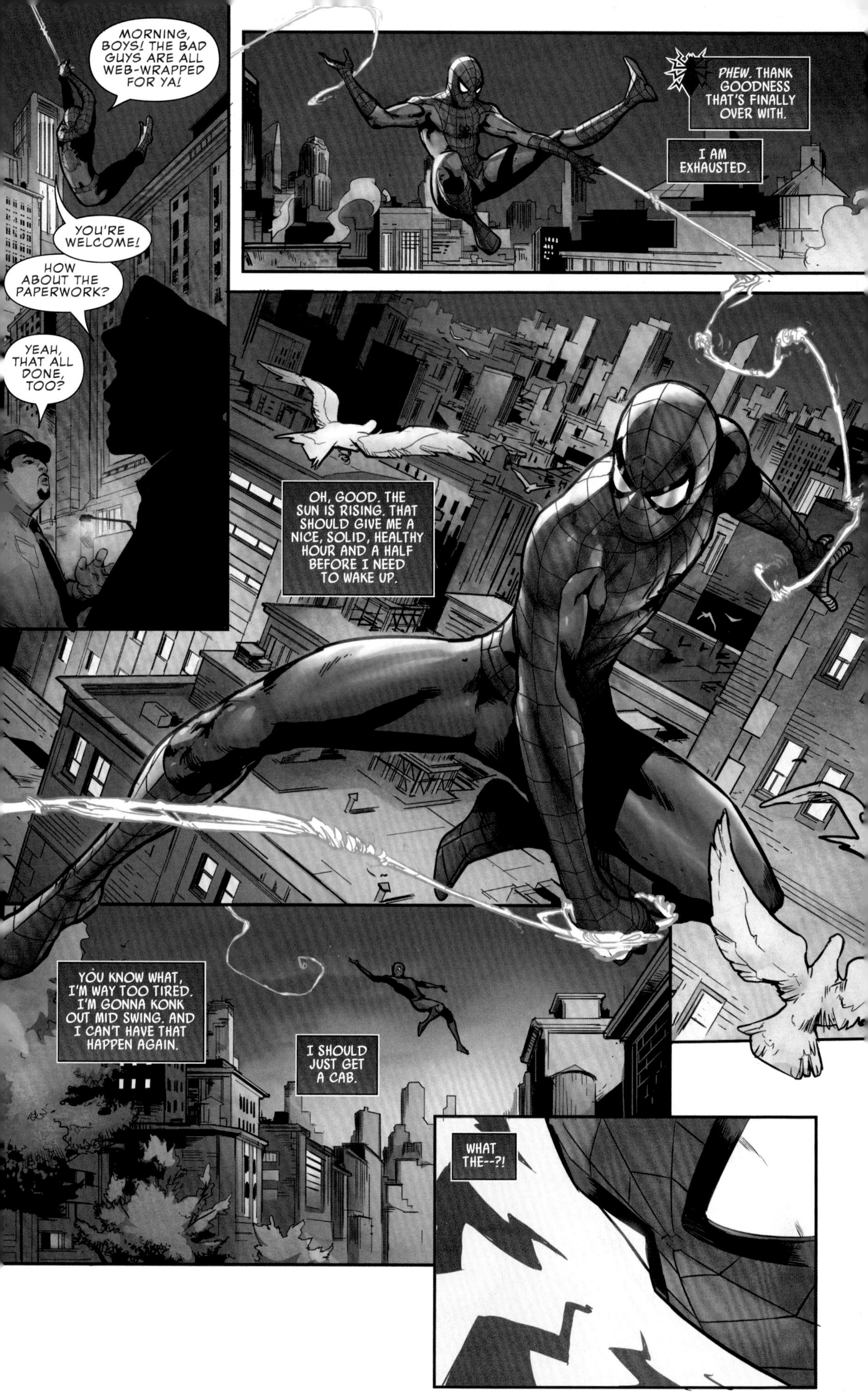
MORNING, BOYS! THE BAD GUYS ARE ALL WEB-WRAPPED FOR YA!
YOU'RE WELCOME!
HOW ABOUT THE PAPERWORK?
YEAH, THAT ALL DONE, TOO?
PHEW. THANK GOODNESS THAT'S FINALLY OVER WITH.
I AM EXHAUSTED.
OH, GOOD. THE SUN IS RISING. THAT SHOULD GIVE ME A NICE, SOLID, HEALTHY HOUR AND A HALF BEFORE I NEED TO WAKE UP.
YOU KNOW WHAT, I'M WAY TOO TIRED. I'M GONNA KONK OUT MID SWING. AND I CAN'T HAVE THAT HAPPEN AGAIN.
I SHOULD JUST GET A CAB.
WHAT THE--?!

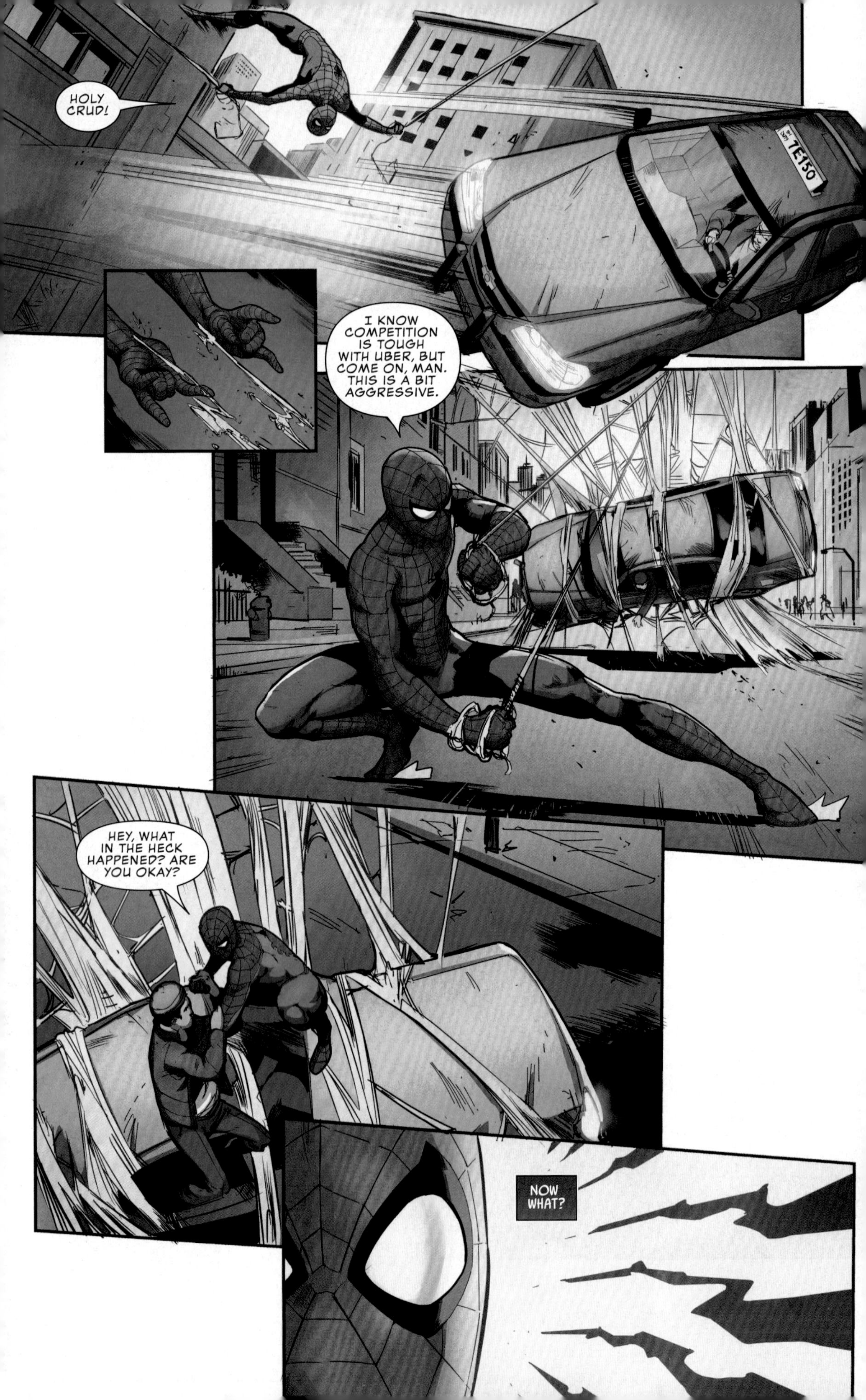
HOLY CRUD!
I KNOW COMPETITION IS TOUGH WITH UBER, BUT COME ON, MAN. THIS IS A BIT AGGRESSIVE.
HEY, WHAT IN THE HECK HAPPENED? ARE YOU OKAY?
NOW WHAT?

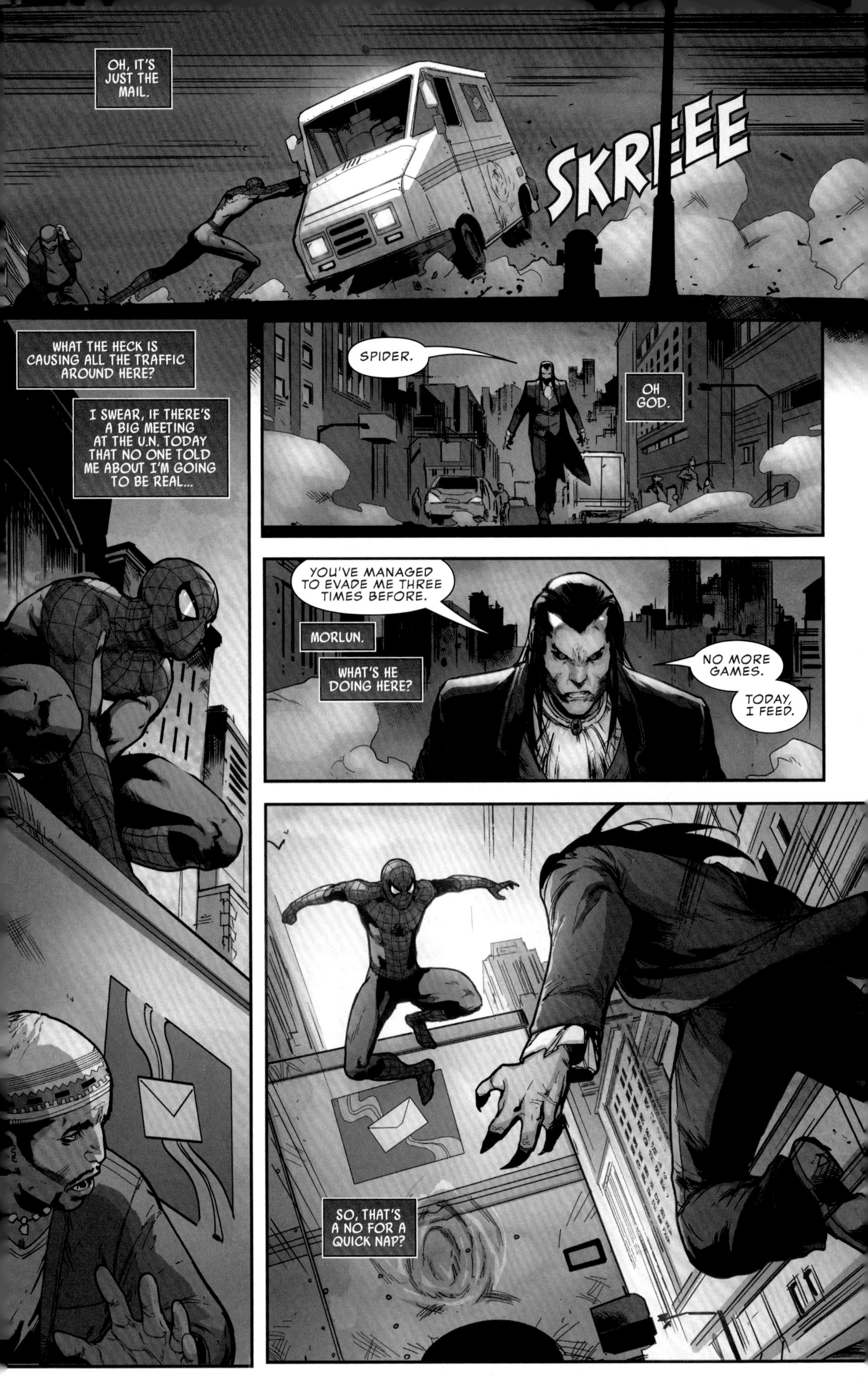

OH, IT'S JUST THE MAIL.
SKREEE
WHAT THE HECK IS CAUSING ALL THE TRAFFIC AROUND HERE?
I SWEAR, IF THERE'S A BIG MEETING AT THE U.N. TODAY THAT NO ONE TOLD ME ABOUT I'M GOING TO BE REAL...
SPIDER.
OH GOD.
YOU'VE MANAGED TO EVADE ME THREE TIMES BEFORE.
MORLUN.
WHAT'S HE DOING HERE?
NO MORE GAMES.
TODAY, I FEED.
SO, THAT'S A NO FOR A QUICK NAP?

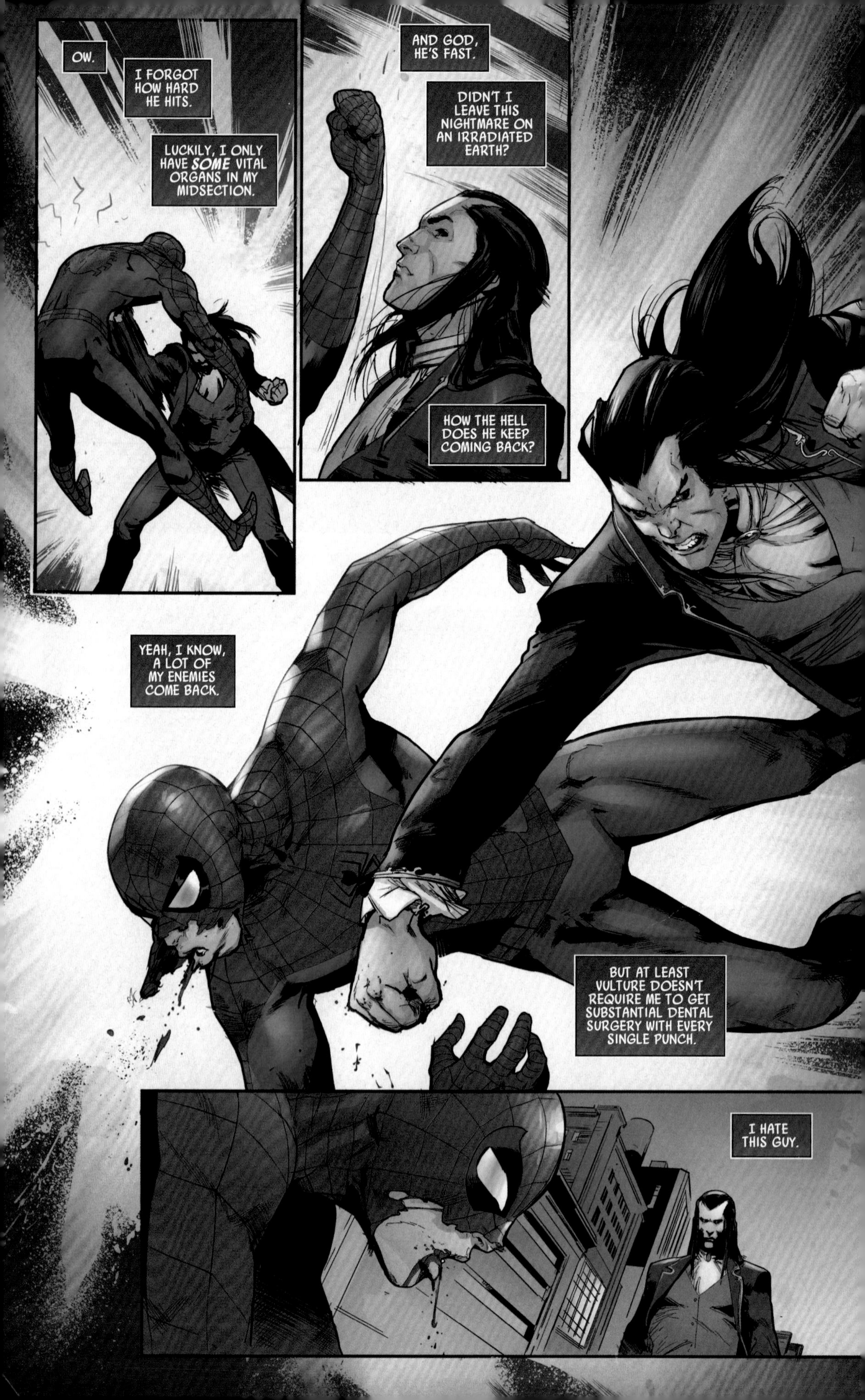
OW.
I FORGOT HOW HARD HE HITS.
LUCKILY, I ONLY HAVE SOME VITAL ORGANS IN MY MIDSECTION.
AND GOD, HE'S FAST.
DIDN'T I LEAVE THIS NIGHTMARE ON AN IRRADIATED EARTH?
HOW THE HELL DOES HE KEEP COMING BACK?
YEAH, I KNOW, A LOT OF MY ENEMIES COME BACK.
BUT AT LEAST VULTURE DOESN'T REQUIRE ME TO GET SUBSTANTIAL DENTAL SURGERY WITH EVERY SINGLE PUNCH.
I HATE THIS GUY.

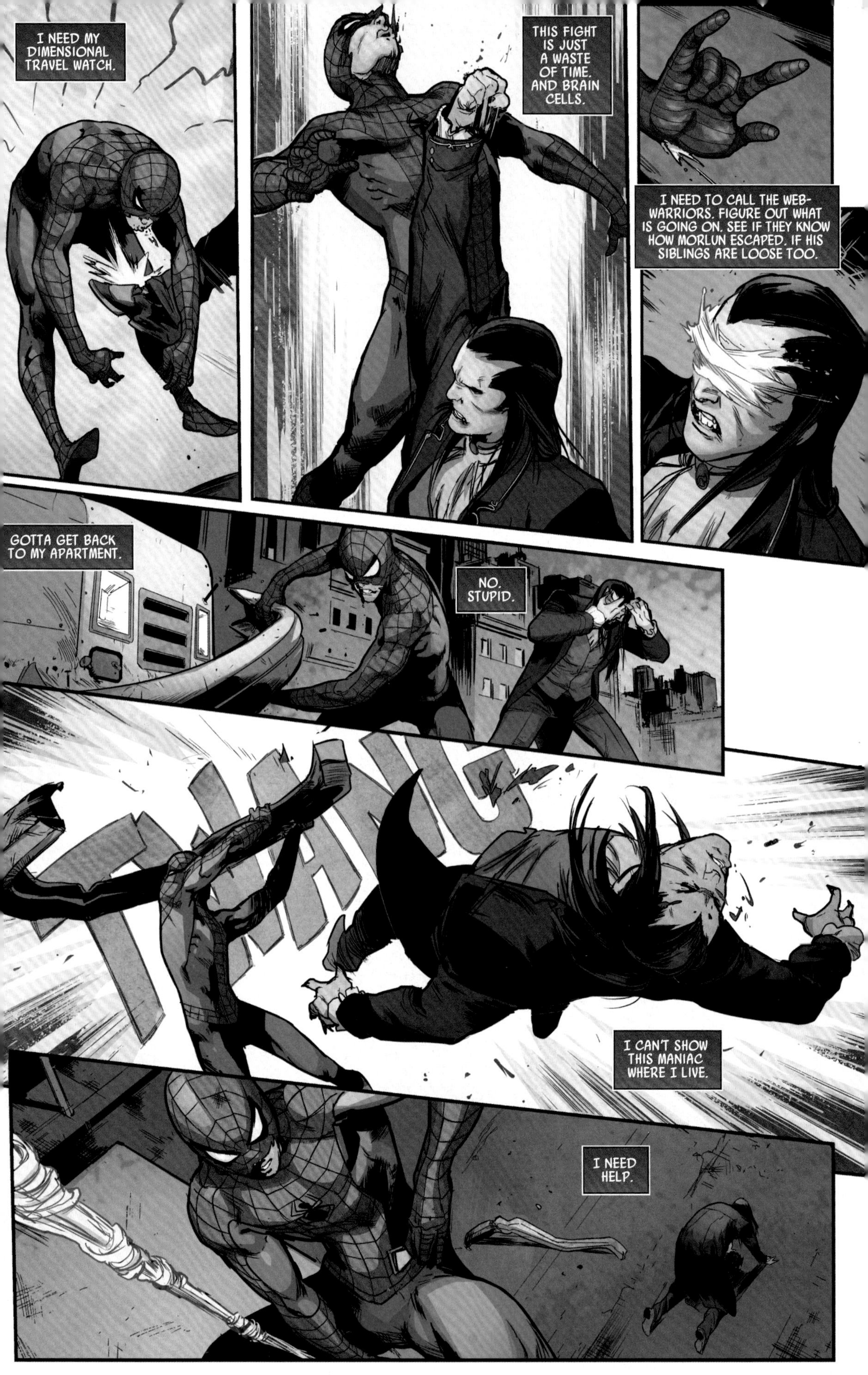
I NEED MY DIMENSIONAL TRAVEL WATCH.
THIS FIGHT IS JUST A WASTE OF TIME. AND BRAIN CELLS.
I NEED TO CALL THE WEB-WARRIORS. FIGURE OUT WHAT IS GOING ON. SEE IF THEY KNOW HOW MORLUN ESCAPED. IF HIS SIBLINGS ARE LOOSE TOO.
GOTTA GET BACK TO MY APARTMENT.
NO. STUPID.
I CAN'T SHOW THIS MANIAC WHERE I LIVE.
I NEED HELP.

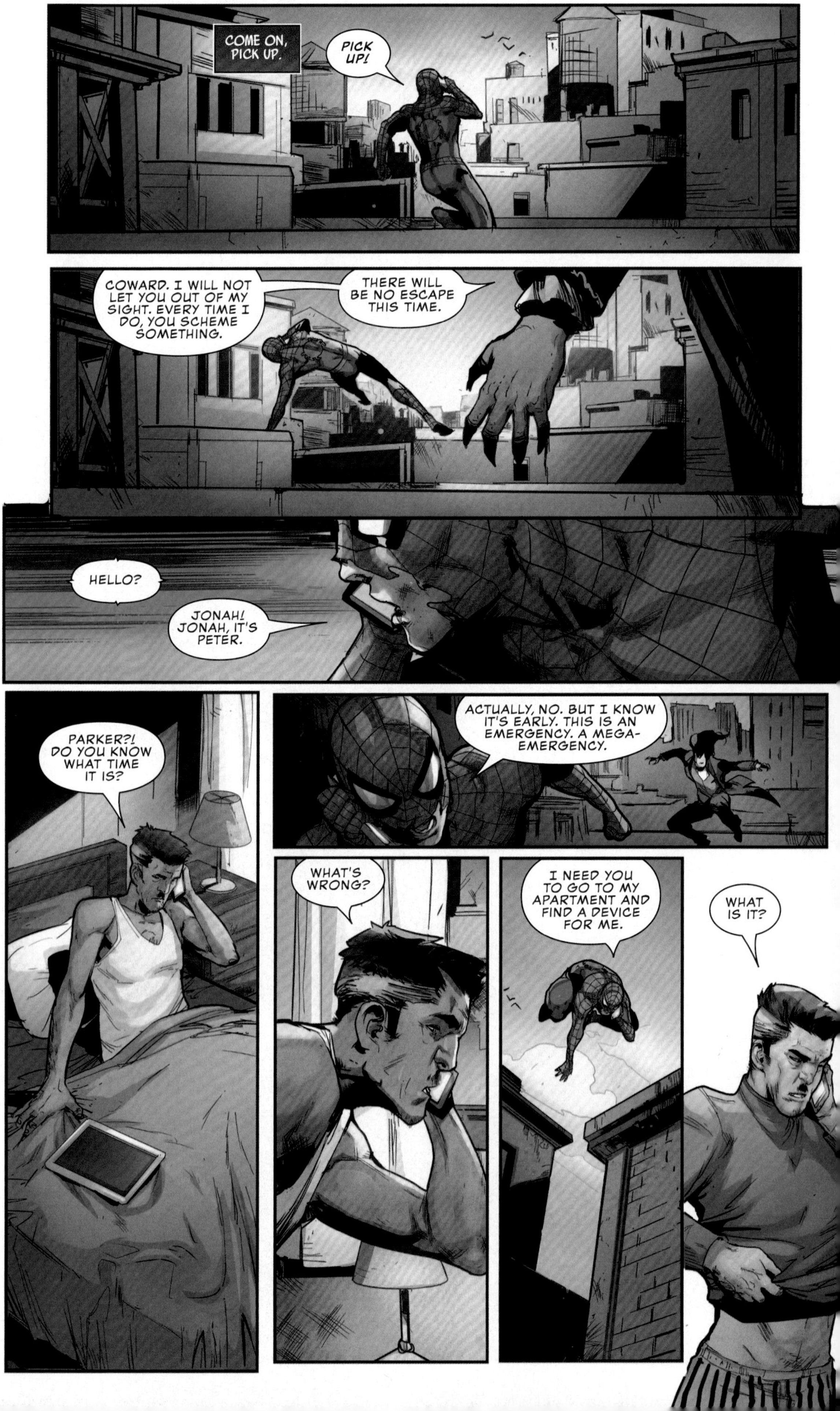
COME ON, PICK UP.
PICK UP!
COWARD. I WILL NOT LET YOU OUT OF MY SIGHT. EVERY TIME I DO, YOU SCHEME SOMETHING.
THERE WILL BE NO ESCAPE THIS TIME.
HELLO?
JONAH! JONAH, IT'S PETER.
PARKER?! DO YOU KNOW WHAT TIME IT IS?
ACTUALLY, NO. BUT I KNOW IT'S EARLY. THIS IS AN EMERGENCY. A MEGA-EMERGENCY.
WHAT'S WRONG?
I NEED YOU TO GO TO MY APARTMENT AND FIND A DEVICE FOR ME.
WHAT IS IT?

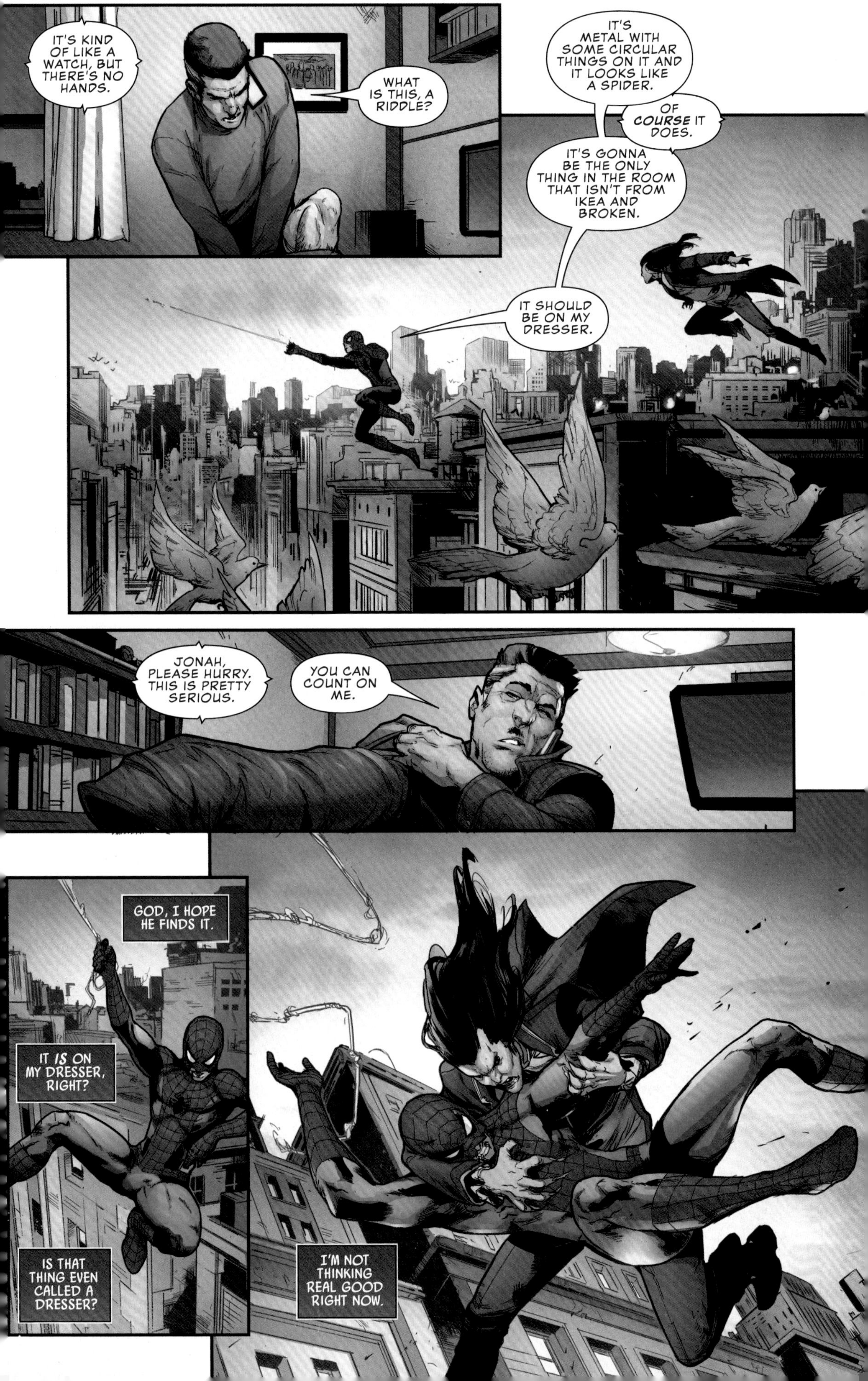
IT'S KIND OF LIKE A WATCH, BUT THERE'S NO HANDS.
WHAT IS THIS, A RIDDLE?
IT'S METAL WITH SOME CIRCULAR THINGS ON IT AND IT LOOKS LIKE A SPIDER.
OF COURSE IT DOES.
IT'S GONNA BE THE ONLY THING IN THE ROOM THAT ISN'T FROM IKEA AND BROKEN.
IT SHOULD BE ON MY DRESSER.
JONAH, PLEASE HURRY. THIS IS PRETTY SERIOUS.
YOU CAN COUNT ON ME.
GOD, I HOPE HE FINDS IT.
IT IS ON MY DRESSER, RIGHT?
IS THAT THING EVEN CALLED A DRESSER?
I'M NOT THINKING REAL GOOD RIGHT NOW.

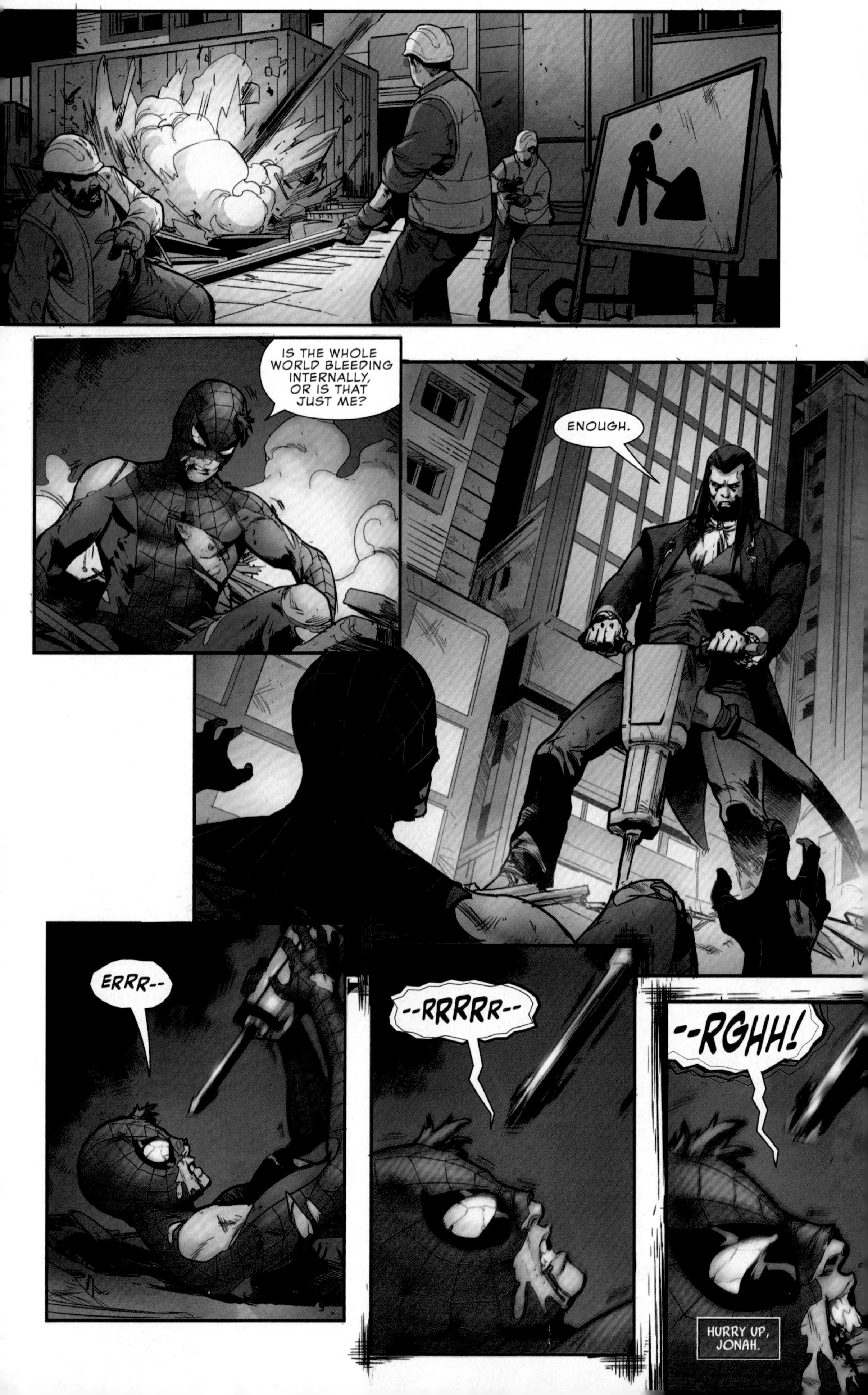
IS THE WHOLE WORLD BLEEDING INTERNALLY, OR IS THAT JUST ME?
ENOUGH.
ERRR--
--RRRRR--
--RGHH!
HURRY UP, JONAH.

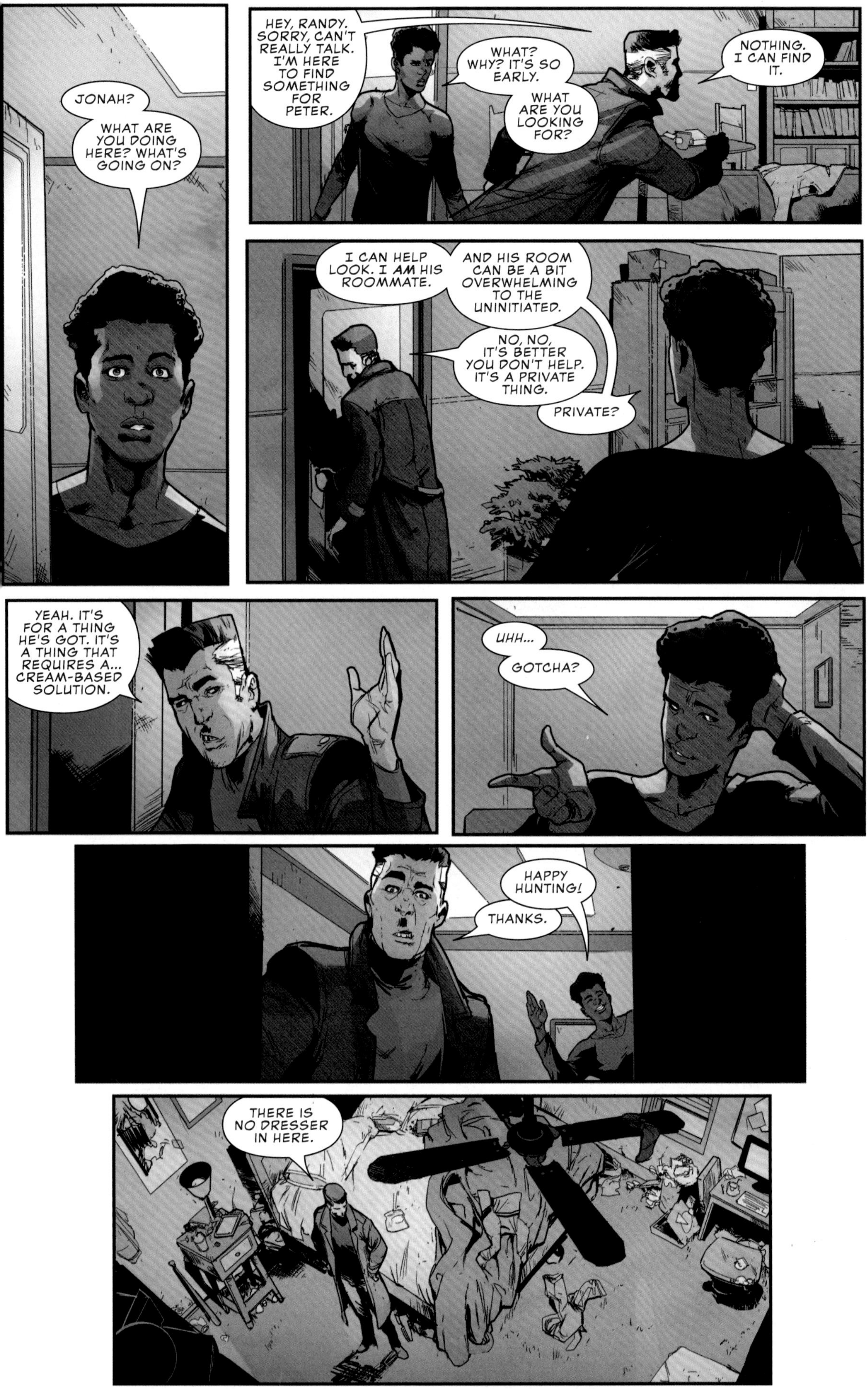

JONAH?
WHAT ARE YOU DOING HERE? WHAT'S GOING ON?
HEY, RANDY. SORRY, CAN'T REALLY TALK. I'M HERE TO FIND SOMETHING FOR PETER.
WHAT? WHY? IT'S SO EARLY.
WHAT ARE YOU LOOKING FOR?
NOTHING. I CAN FIND IT.
I CAN HELP LOOK. I AM HIS ROOMMATE.
AND HIS ROOM CAN BE A BIT OVERWHELMING TO THE UNINITIATED.
NO, NO, IT'S BETTER YOU DON'T HELP. IT'S A PRIVATE THING.
PRIVATE?
YEAH. IT'S FOR A THING HE'S GOT. IT'S A THING THAT REQUIRES A... CREAM-BASED SOLUTION.
UHH...
GOTCHA?
HAPPY HUNTING!
THANKS.
THERE IS NO DRESSER IN HERE.

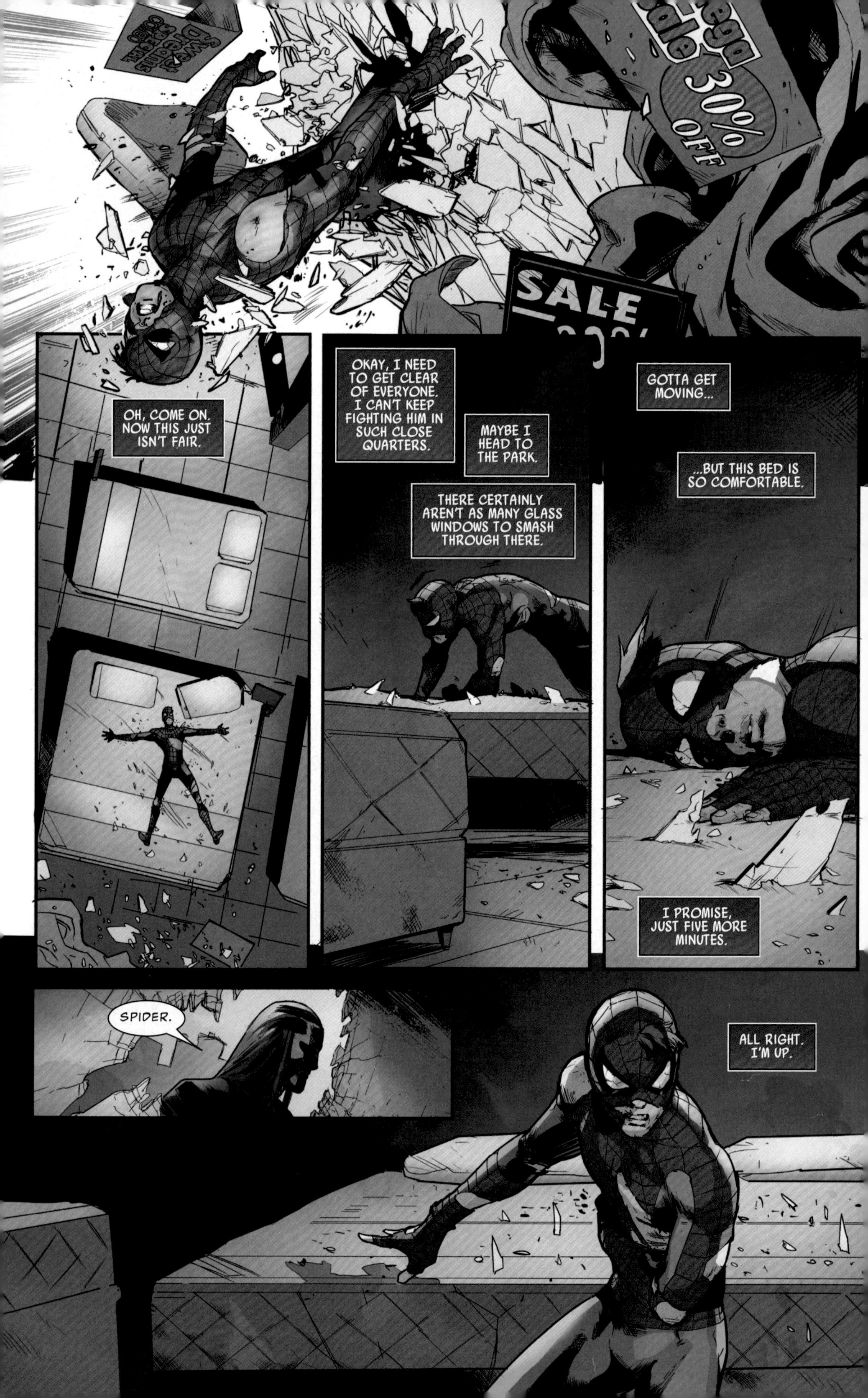
Mega Sale 30% OFF
SALE
OH, COME ON. NOW THIS JUST ISN'T FAIR.
OKAY, I NEED TO GET CLEAR OF EVERYONE. I CAN'T KEEP FIGHTING HIM IN SUCH CLOSE QUARTERS.
MAYBE I HEAD TO THE PARK.
THERE CERTAINLY AREN'T AS MANY GLASS WINDOWS TO SMASH THROUGH THERE.
GOTTA GET MOVING...
...BUT THIS BED IS SO COMFORTABLE.
I PROMISE, JUST FIVE MORE MINUTES.
SPIDER.
ALL RIGHT. I'M UP.

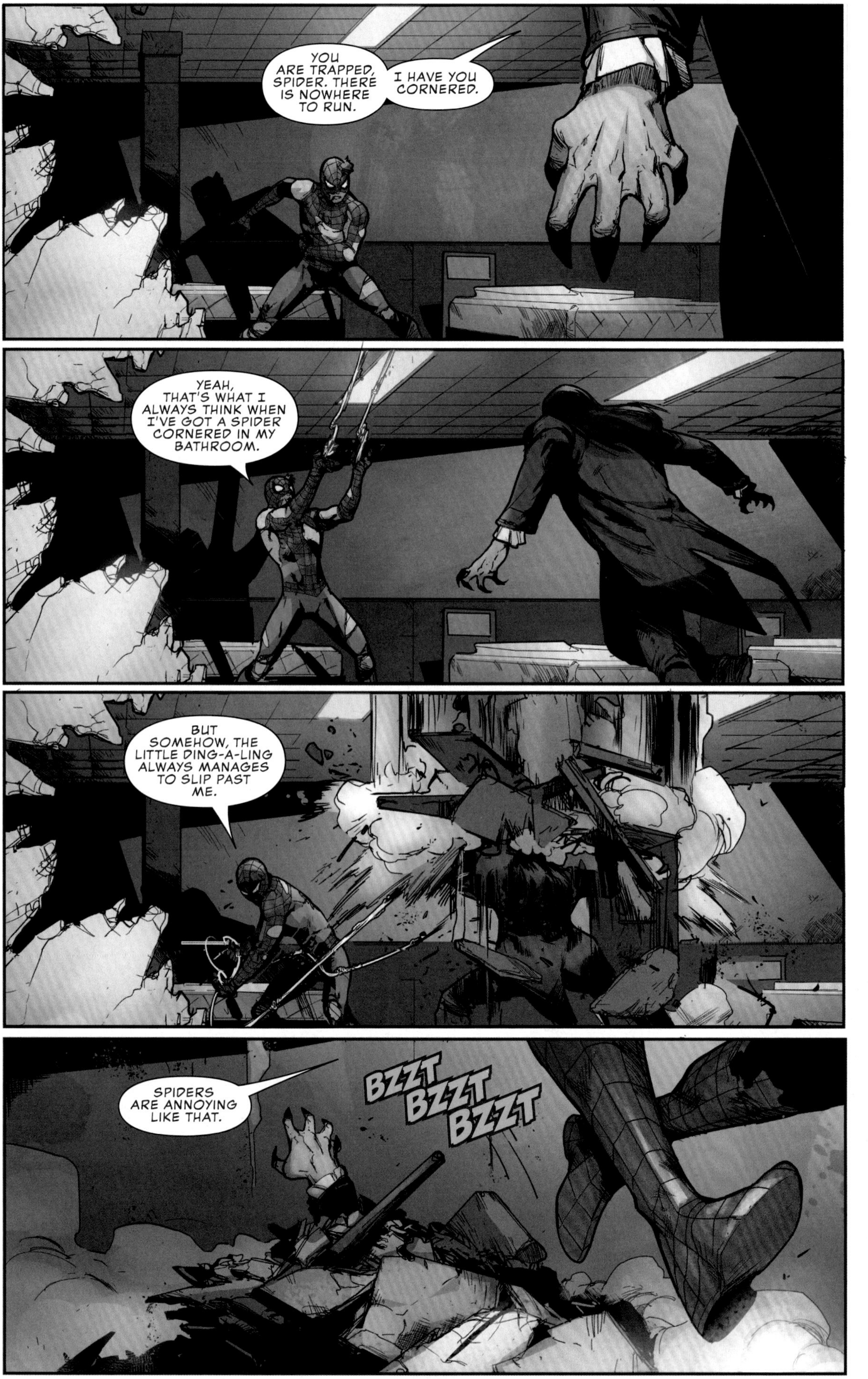
YOU ARE TRAPPED, SPIDER. THERE IS NOWHERE TO RUN.
I HAVE YOU CORNERED.
YEAH, THAT'S WHAT I ALWAYS THINK WHEN I'VE GOT A SPIDER CORNERED IN MY BATHROOM.
BUT SOMEHOW, THE LITTLE DING-A-LING ALWAYS MANAGES TO SLIP PAST ME.
SPIDERS ARE ANNOYING LIKE THAT.
BZZT BZZT BZZT

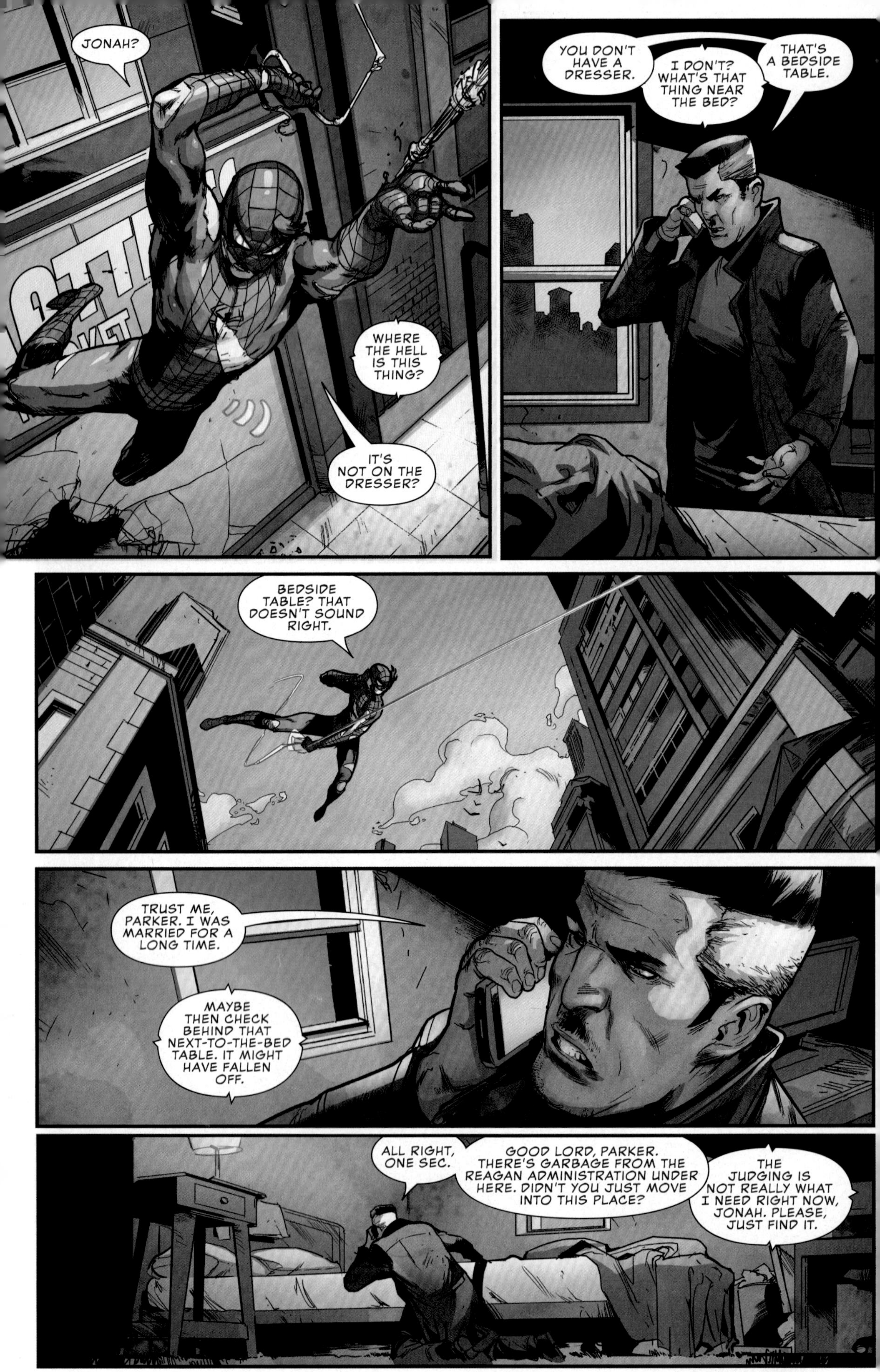
JONAH?
WHERE THE HELL IS THIS THING?
IT'S NOT ON THE DRESSER?
YOU DON'T HAVE A DRESSER.
I DON'T? WHAT'S THAT THING NEAR THE BED?
THAT'S A BEDSIDE TABLE.
BEDSIDE TABLE? THAT DOESN'T SOUND RIGHT.
TRUST ME, PARKER. I WAS MARRIED FOR A LONG TIME.
MAYBE THEN CHECK BEHIND THAT NEXT-TO-THE-BED TABLE. IT MIGHT HAVE FALLEN OFF.
ALL RIGHT, ONE SEC.
GOOD LORD, PARKER. THERE'S GARBAGE FROM THE REAGAN ADMINISTRATION UNDER HERE. DIDN'T YOU JUST MOVE INTO THIS PLACE?
THE JUDGING IS NOT REALLY WHAT I NEED RIGHT NOW, JONAH. PLEASE, JUST FIND IT.

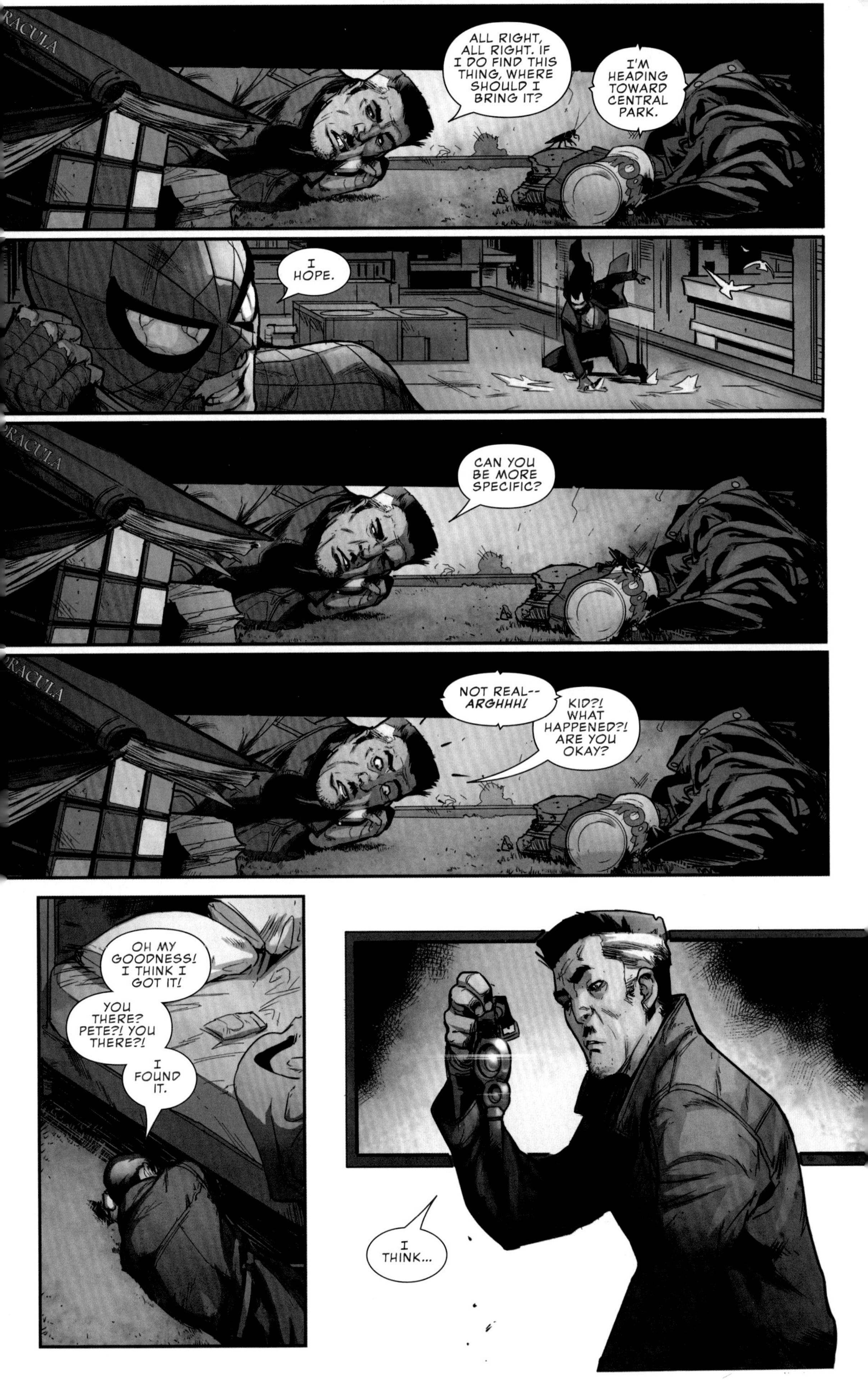

DRACULA
ALL RIGHT, ALL RIGHT. IF I DO FIND THIS THING, WHERE SHOULD I BRING IT?
I'M HEADING TOWARD CENTRAL PARK.
I HOPE.
DRACULA
CAN YOU BE MORE SPECIFIC?
DRACULA
NOT REAL-- ARGHHH!
KID?! WHAT HAPPENED?! ARE YOU OKAY?
OH MY GOODNESS! I THINK I GOT IT!
YOU THERE? PETE?! YOU THERE?!
I FOUND IT.
I THINK...

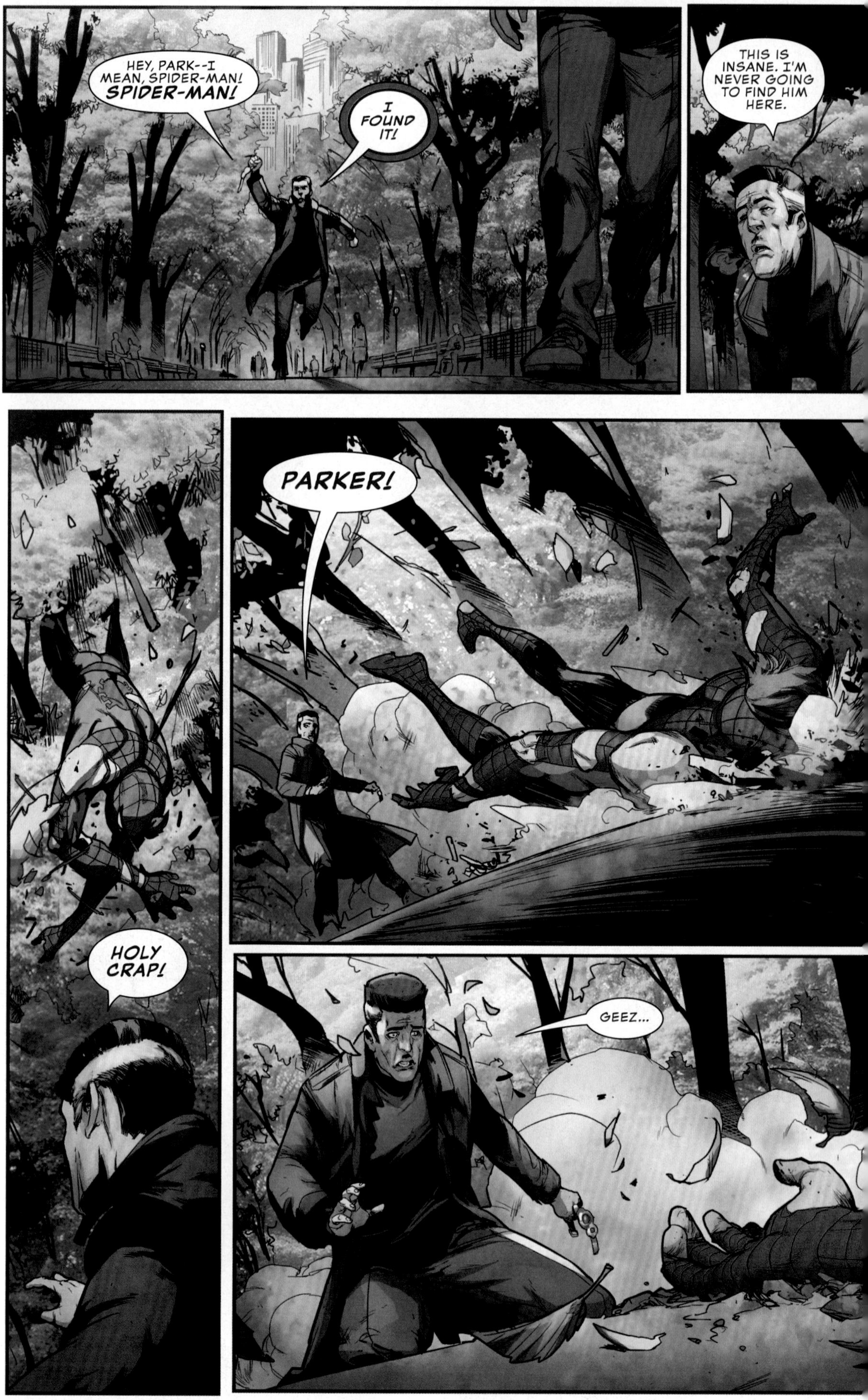
HEY, PARK--I MEAN, SPIDER-MAN! SPIDER-MAN!
I FOUND IT!
THIS IS INSANE. I'M NEVER GOING TO FIND HIM HERE.
PARKER!
HOLY CRAP!
GEEZ...

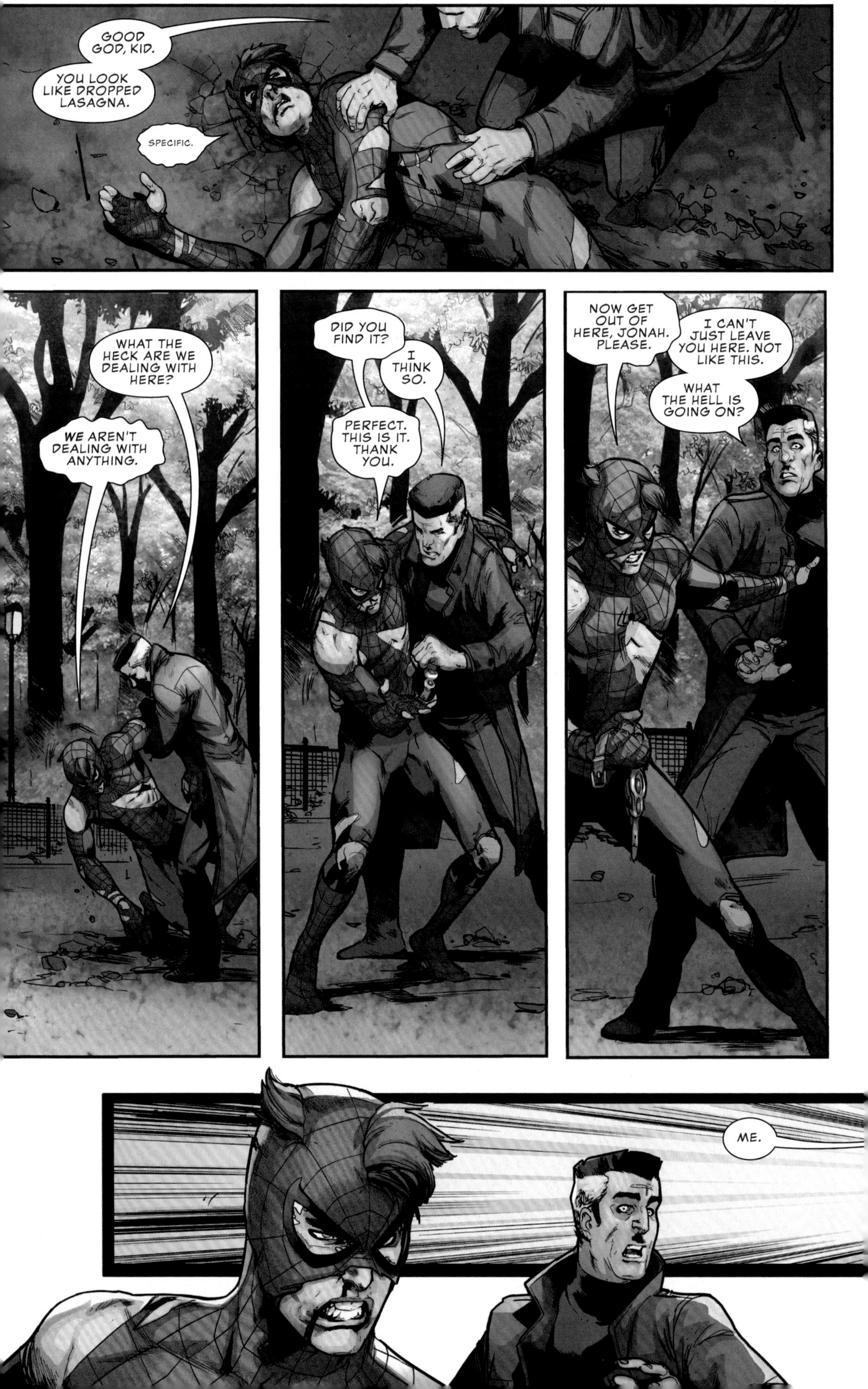
GOOD GOD, KID.
YOU LOOK LIKE DROPPED LASAGNA.
SPECIFIC.
WHAT THE HECK ARE WE DEALING WITH HERE?
WE AREN'T DEALING WITH ANYTHING.
DID YOU FIND IT?
I THINK SO.
PERFECT. THIS IS IT. THANK YOU.
NOW GET OUT OF HERE, JONAH. PLEASE.
I CAN'T JUST LEAVE YOU HERE. NOT LIKE THIS.
WHAT THE HELL IS GOING ON?
ME.

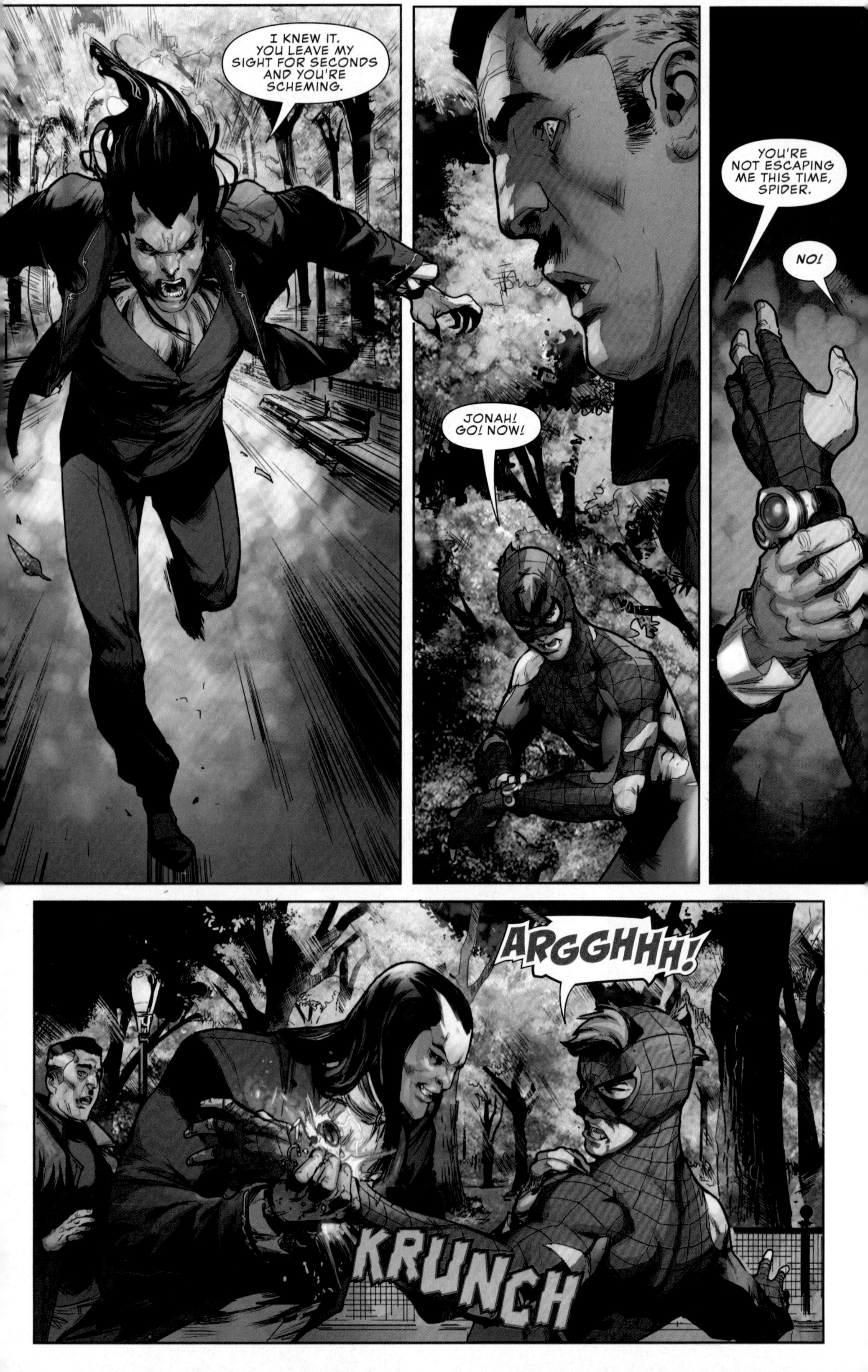
I KNEW IT. YOU LEAVE MY SIGHT FOR SECONDS AND YOU'RE SCHEMING.
JONAH! GO! NOW!
YOU'RE NOT ESCAPING ME THIS TIME, SPIDER.
NO!
ARGGHHH!
KRUNCH

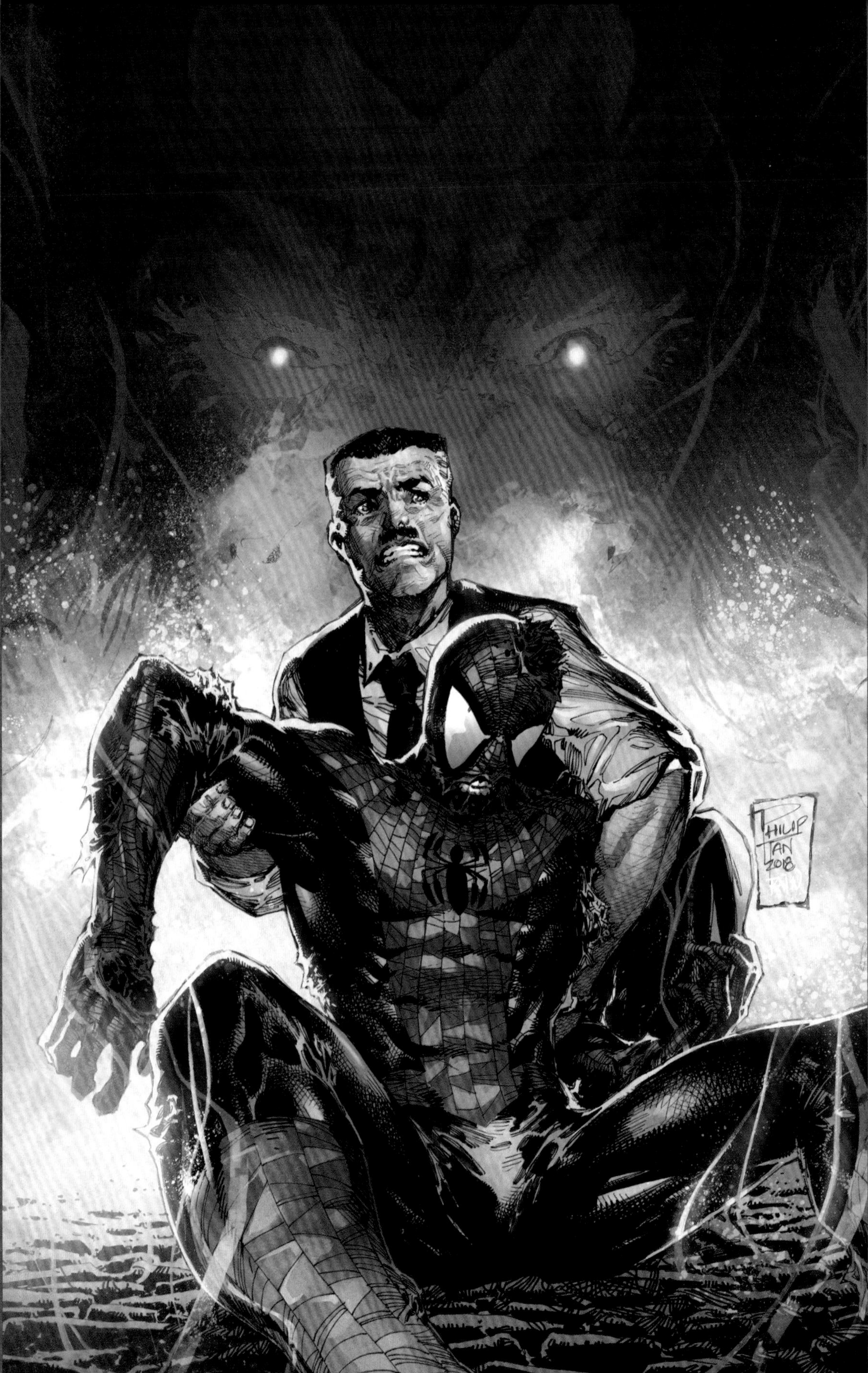
PHILIP TAN 2018

312

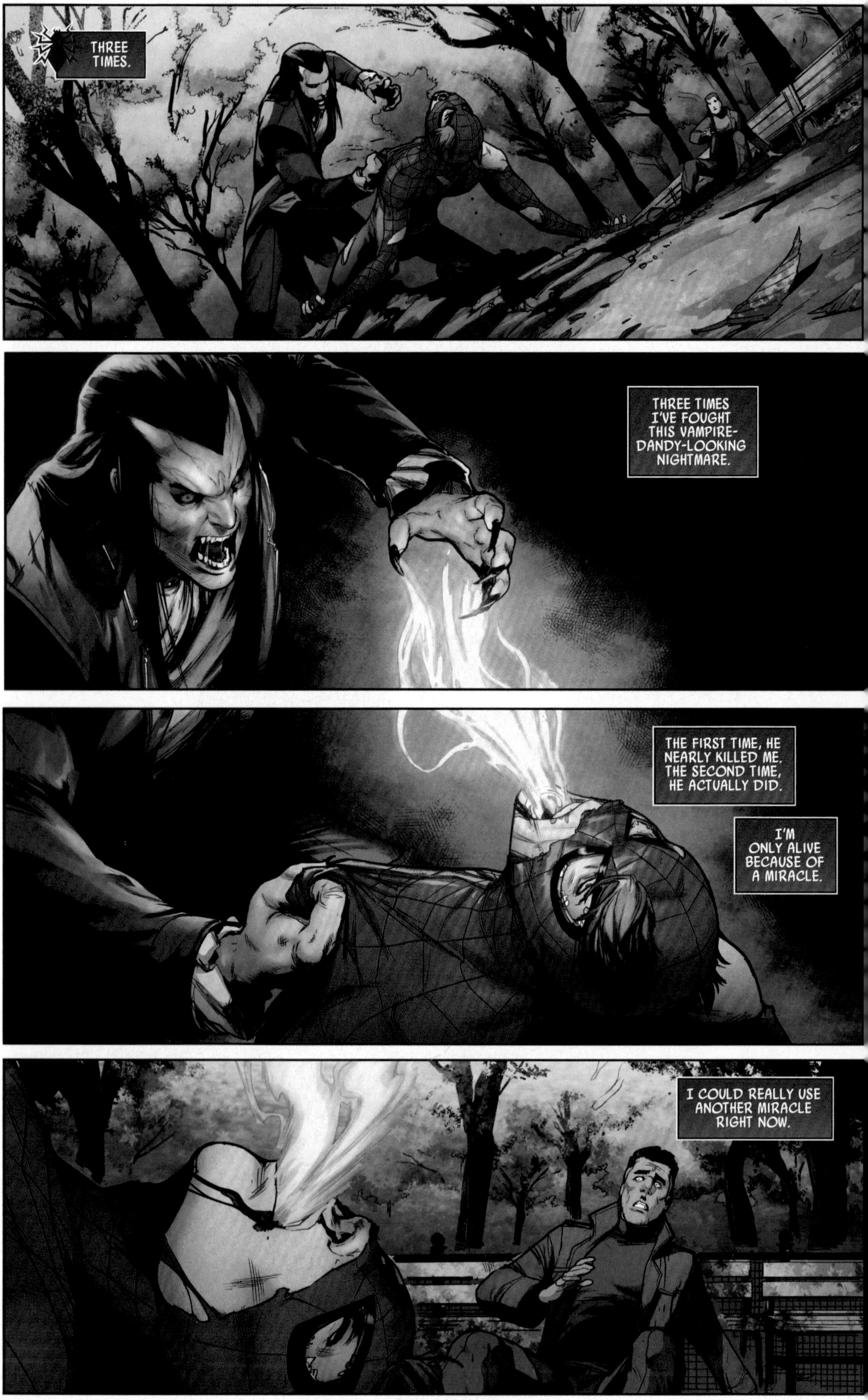
THREE TIMES.
THREE TIMES I'VE FOUGHT THIS VAMPIRE-DANDY-LOOKING NIGHTMARE.
THE FIRST TIME, HE NEARLY KILLED ME. THE SECOND TIME, HE ACTUALLY DID.
I'M ONLY ALIVE BECAUSE OF A MIRACLE.
I COULD REALLY USE ANOTHER MIRACLE RIGHT NOW.

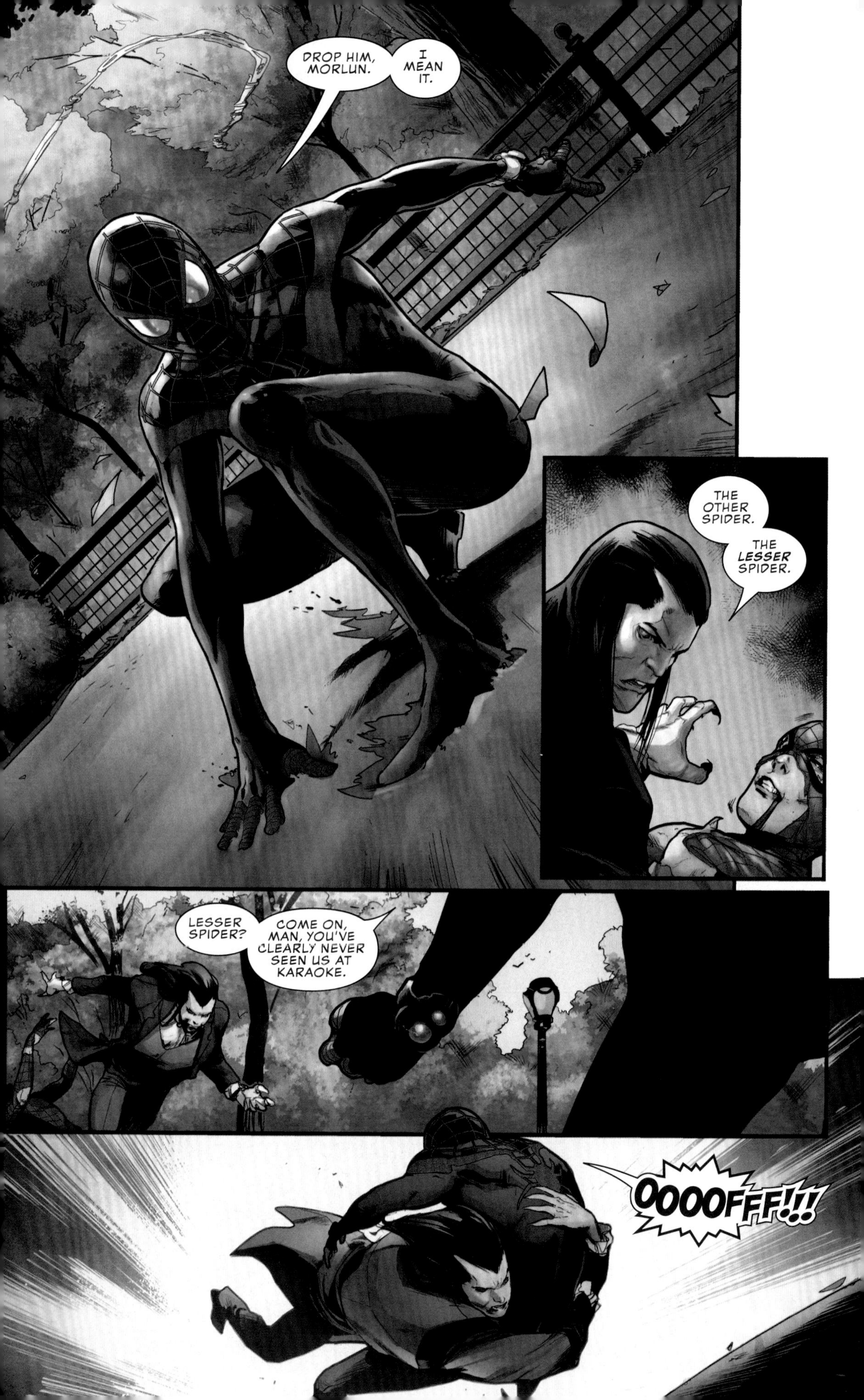
DROP HIM, MORLUN.
I MEAN IT.
THE OTHER SPIDER.
THE LESSER SPIDER.
LESSER SPIDER?
COME ON, MAN, YOU'VE CLEARLY NEVER SEEN US AT KARAOKE.
OOOOFFF!!!

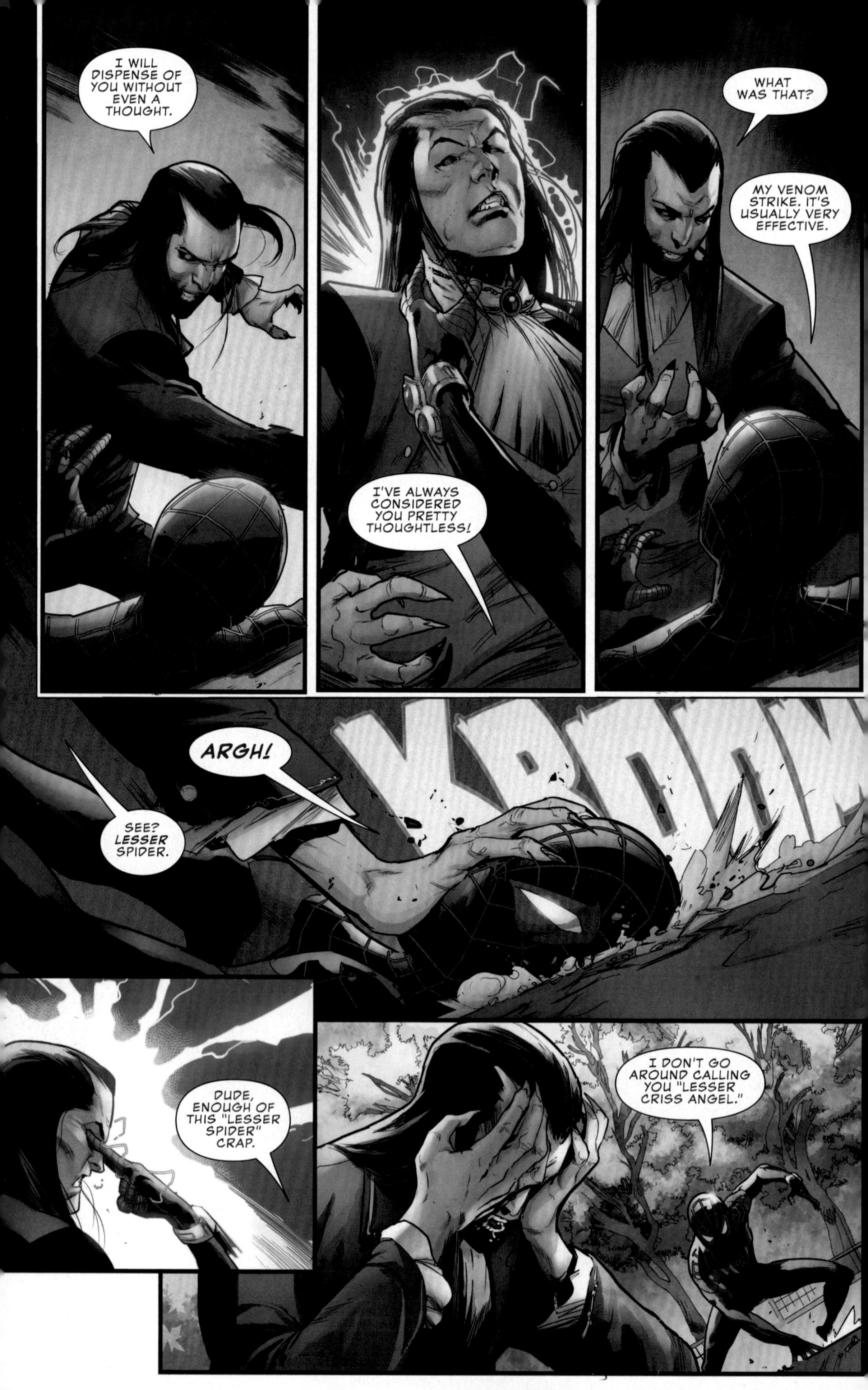
I WILL DISPENSE OF YOU WITHOUT EVEN A THOUGHT.
I'VE ALWAYS CONSIDERED YOU PRETTY THOUGHTLESS!
WHAT WAS THAT?
MY VENOM STRIKE. IT'S USUALLY VERY EFFECTIVE.
ARGH!
SEE? LESSER SPIDER.
DUDE, ENOUGH OF THIS "LESSER SPIDER" CRAP.
I DON'T GO AROUND CALLING YOU "LESSER CRISS ANGEL."

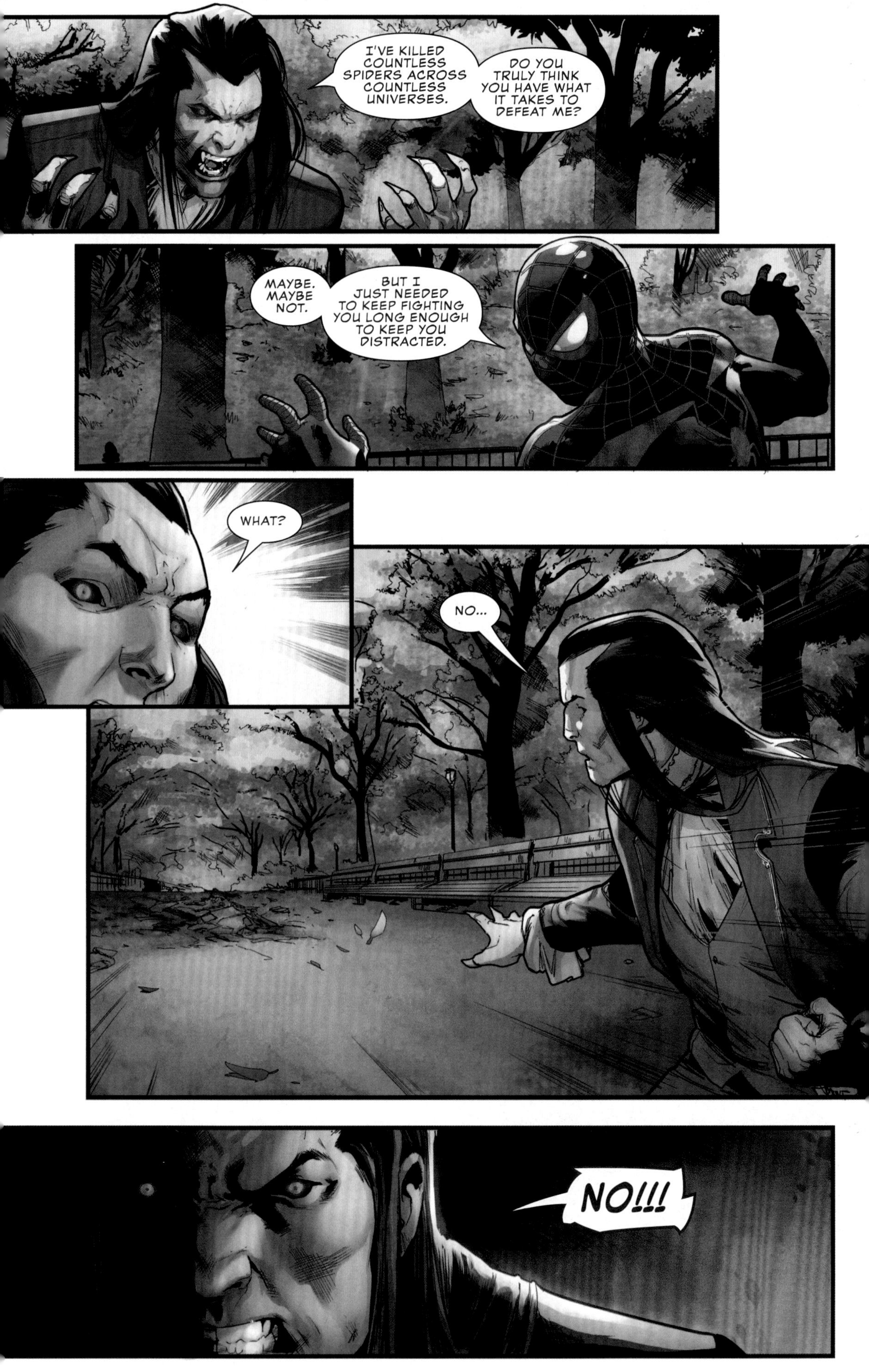
I'VE KILLED COUNTLESS SPIDERS ACROSS COUNTLESS UNIVERSES.
DO YOU TRULY THINK YOU HAVE WHAT IT TAKES TO DEFEAT ME?
MAYBE. MAYBE NOT.
BUT I JUST NEEDED TO KEEP FIGHTING YOU LONG ENOUGH TO KEEP YOU DISTRACTED.
WHAT?
NO...
NO!!!

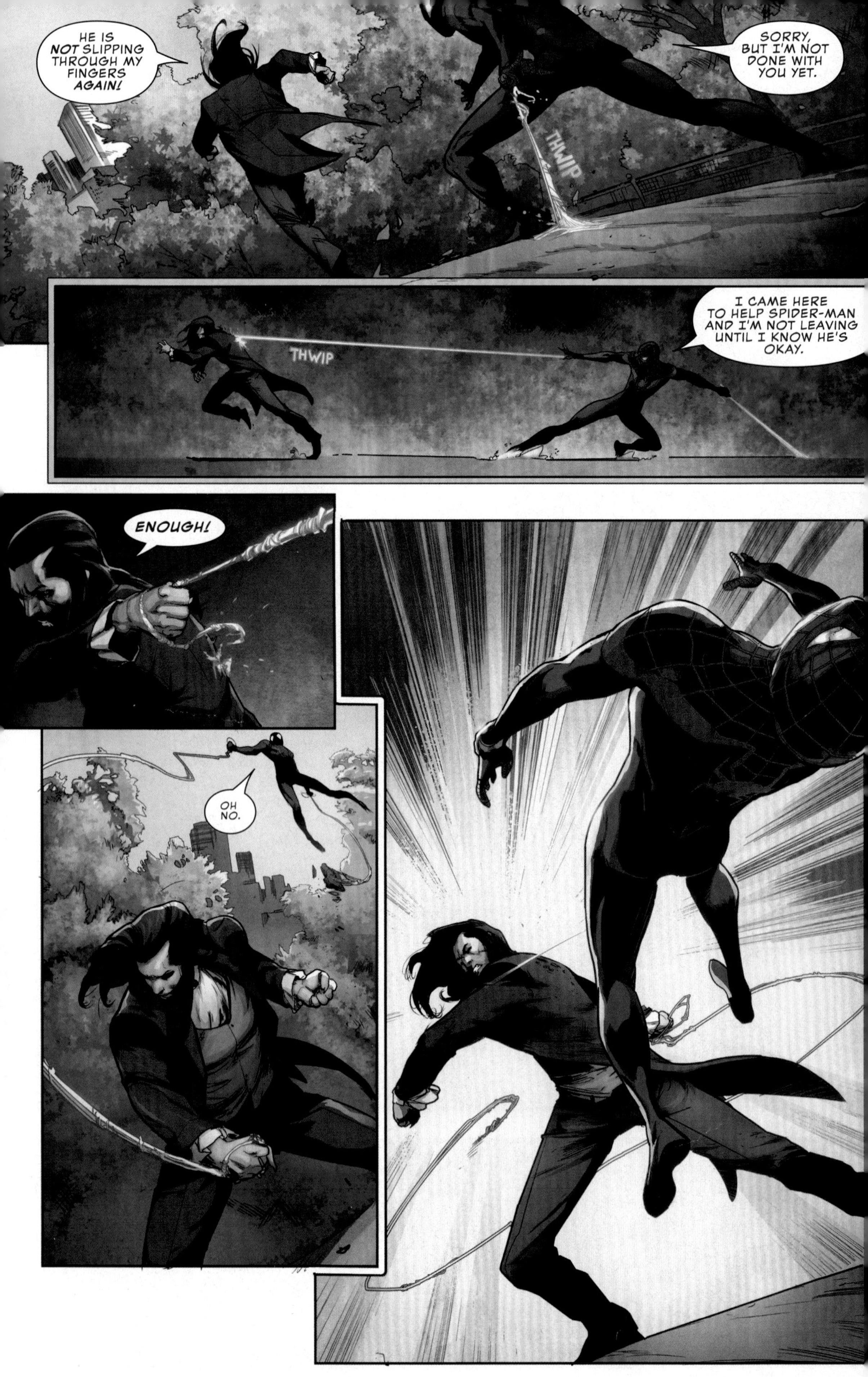
HE IS NOT SLIPPING THROUGH MY FINGERS AGAIN!
SORRY, BUT I'M NOT DONE WITH YOU YET.
THWIP
THWIP
I CAME HERE TO HELP SPIDER-MAN AND I'M NOT LEAVING UNTIL I KNOW HE'S OKAY.
ENOUGH!
OH NO.

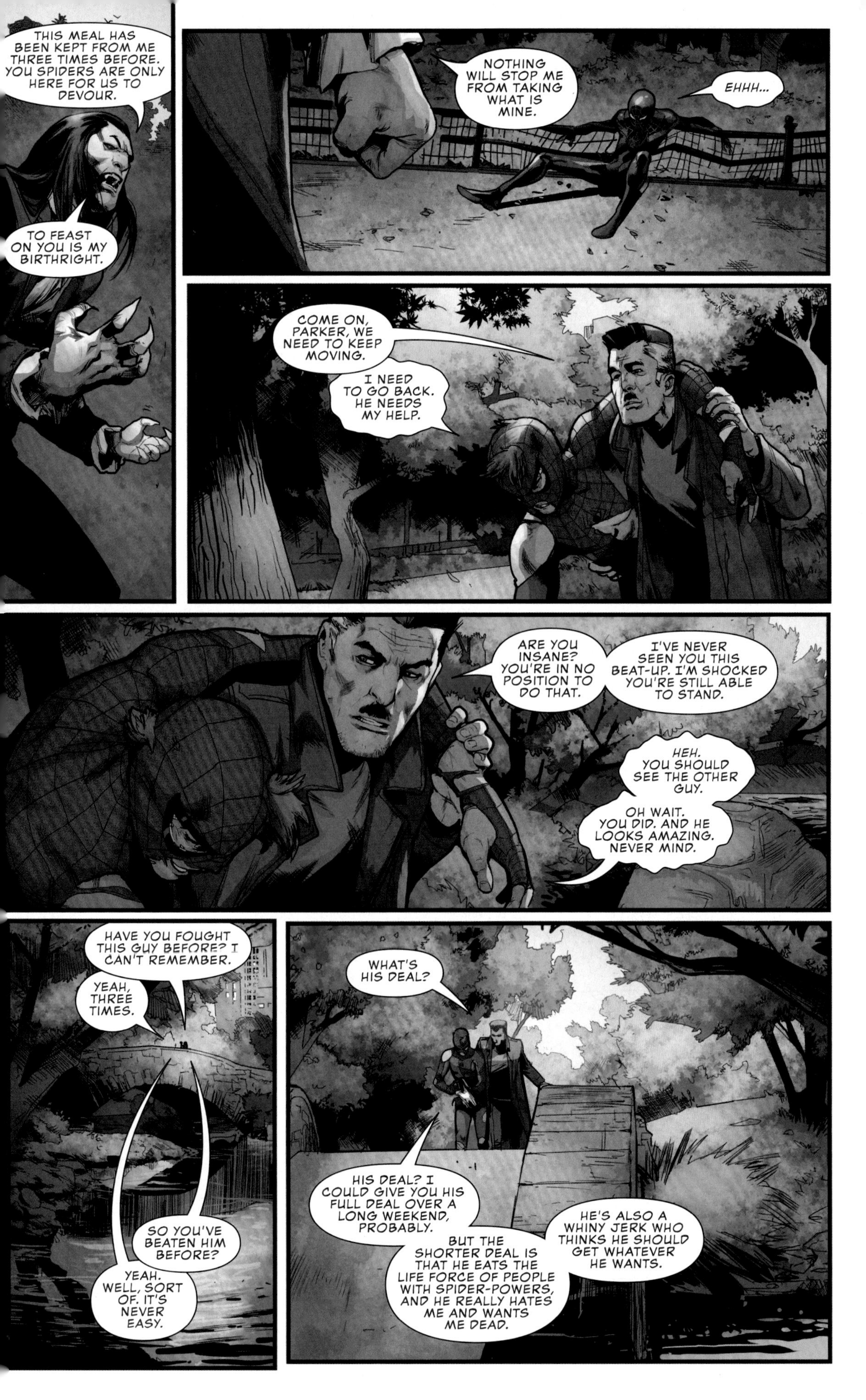
THIS MEAL HAS BEEN KEPT FROM ME THREE TIMES BEFORE. YOU SPIDERS ARE ONLY HERE FOR US TO DEVOUR.
TO FEAST ON YOU IS MY BIRTHRIGHT.
NOTHING WILL STOP ME FROM TAKING WHAT IS MINE.
EHHH...
COME ON, PARKER, WE NEED TO KEEP MOVING.
I NEED TO GO BACK. HE NEEDS MY HELP.
ARE YOU INSANE? YOU'RE IN NO POSITION TO DO THAT.
I'VE NEVER SEEN YOU THIS BEAT-UP. I'M SHOCKED YOU'RE STILL ABLE TO STAND.
HEH. YOU SHOULD SEE THE OTHER GUY.
OH WAIT. YOU DID. AND HE LOOKS AMAZING. NEVER MIND.
HAVE YOU FOUGHT THIS GUY BEFORE? I CAN'T REMEMBER.
YEAH, THREE TIMES.
SO YOU'VE BEATEN HIM BEFORE?
YEAH. WELL, SORT OF. IT'S NEVER EASY.
WHAT'S HIS DEAL?
HIS DEAL? I COULD GIVE YOU HIS FULL DEAL OVER A LONG WEEKEND, PROBABLY.
BUT THE SHORTER DEAL IS THAT HE EATS THE LIFE FORCE OF PEOPLE WITH SPIDER-POWERS, AND HE REALLY HATES ME AND WANTS ME DEAD.
HE'S ALSO A WHINY JERK WHO THINKS HE SHOULD GET WHATEVER HE WANTS.

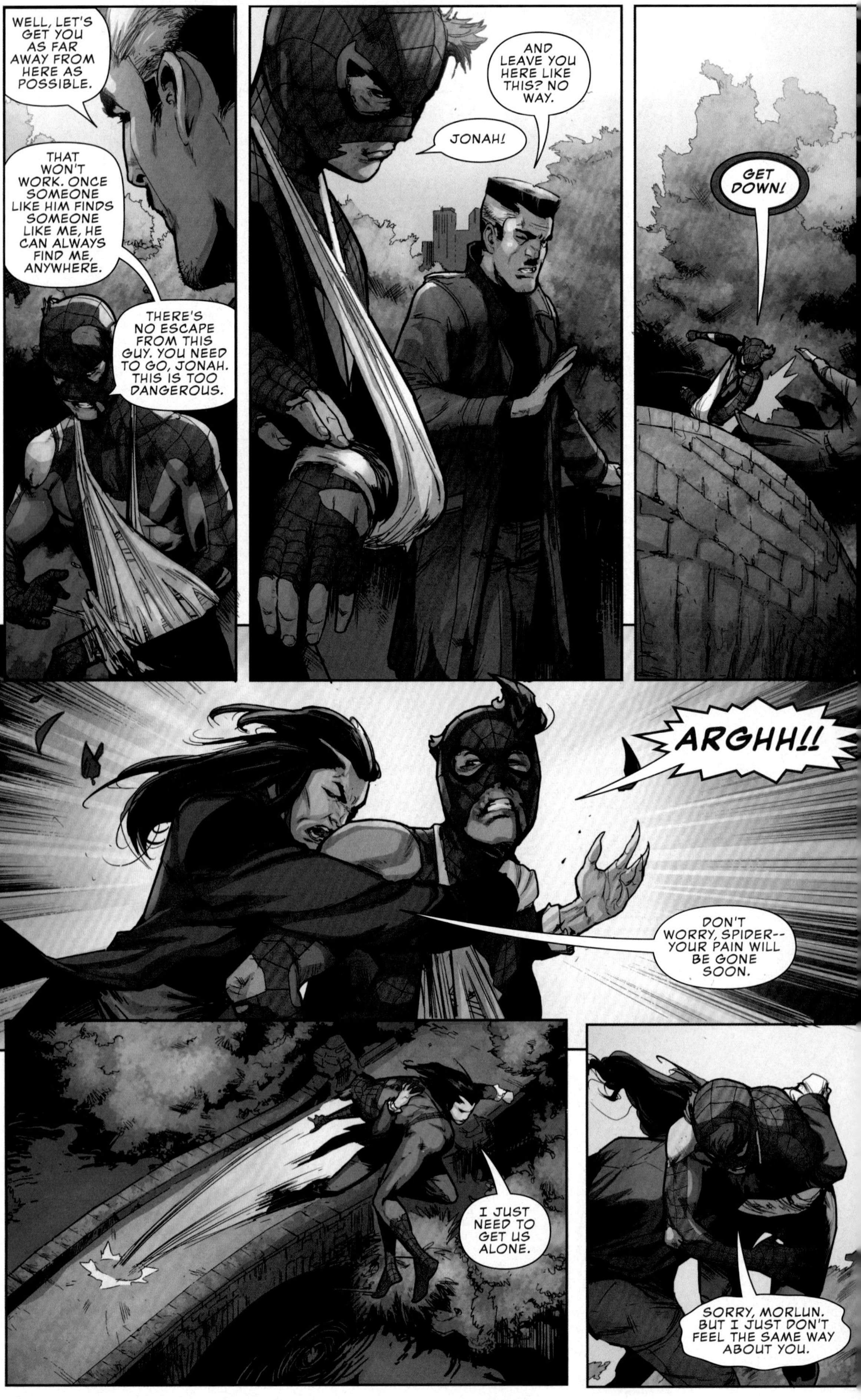
WELL, LET'S GET YOU AS FAR AWAY FROM HERE AS POSSIBLE.
THAT WON'T WORK. ONCE SOMEONE LIKE HIM FINDS SOMEONE LIKE ME, HE CAN ALWAYS FIND ME, ANYWHERE.
THERE'S NO ESCAPE FROM THIS GUY. YOU NEED TO GO, JONAH. THIS IS TOO DANGEROUS.
AND LEAVE YOU HERE LIKE THIS? NO WAY.
JONAH!
GET DOWN!
ARGHH!!
DON'T WORRY, SPIDER-- YOUR PAIN WILL BE GONE SOON.
I JUST NEED TO GET US ALONE.
SORRY, MORLUN. BUT I JUST DON'T FEEL THE SAME WAY ABOUT YOU.

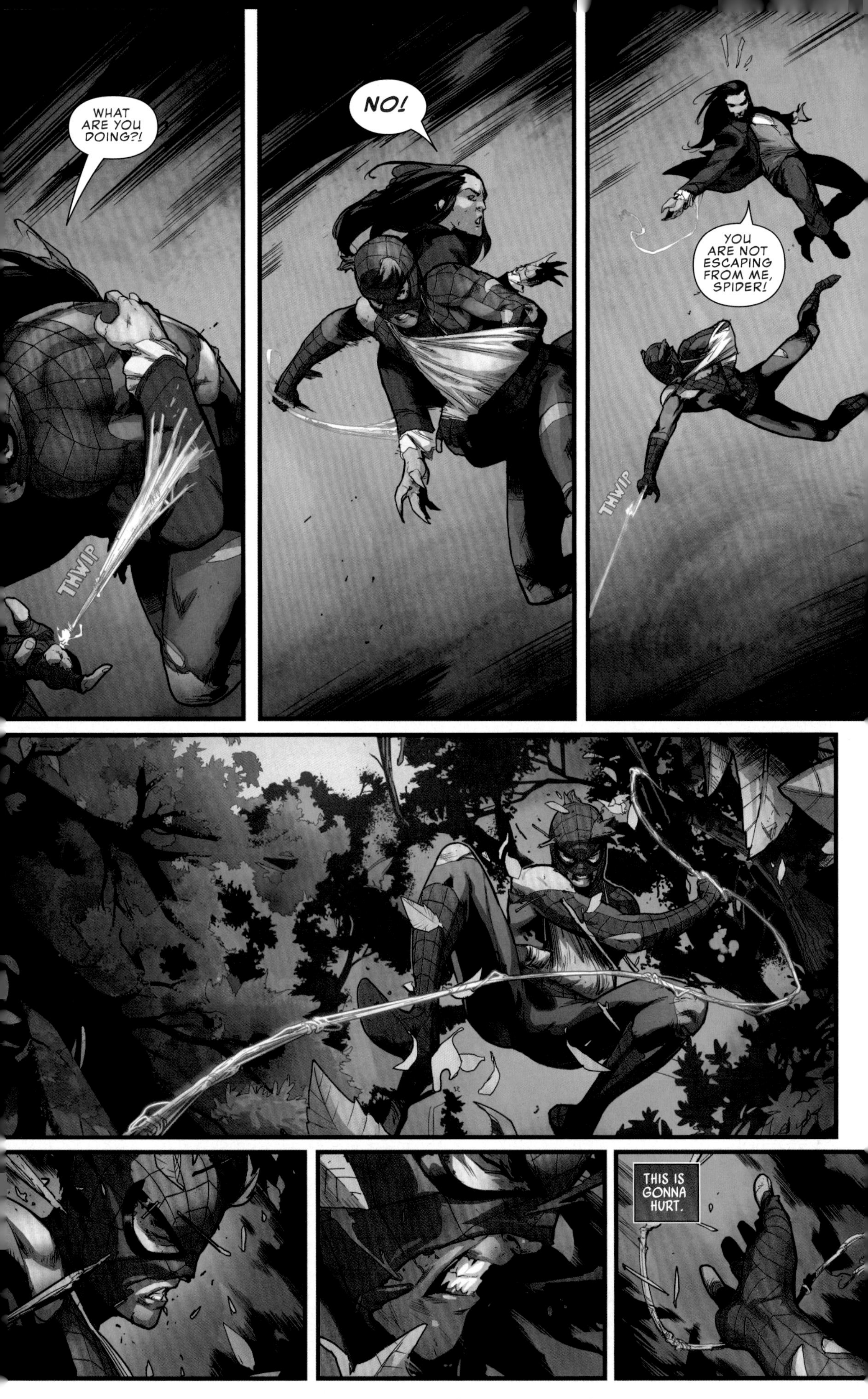
WHAT ARE YOU DOING?!
THWIP
NO!
YOU ARE NOT ESCAPING FROM ME, SPIDER!
THWIP
THIS IS GONNA HURT.

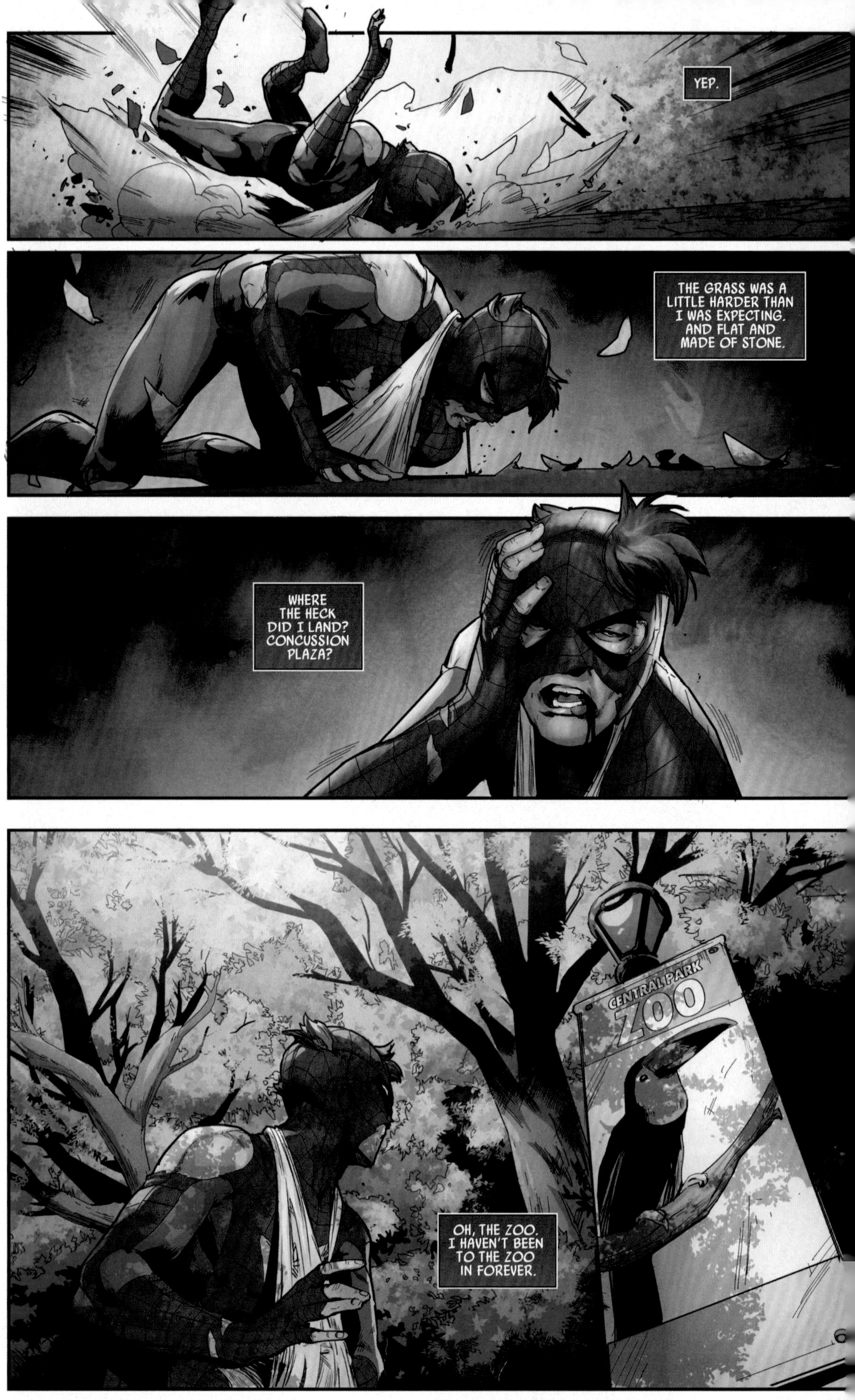
YEP.
THE GRASS WAS A LITTLE HARDER THAN I WAS EXPECTING. AND FLAT AND MADE OF STONE.
WHERE THE HECK DID I LAND? CONCUSSION PLAZA?
CENTRAL PARK ZOO
OH, THE ZOO. I HAVEN'T BEEN TO THE ZOO IN FOREVER.

MR. JAMESON! MR. JAMESON!

ARE YOU OKAY?

GOOD TO HEAR. WHERE'S THE OTHER SPIDER-MAN? WHAT HAPPENED?

THAT MONSTER GRABBED HIM AND JUMPED THAT WAY.

I'M FINE. I'M FINE.

DO YOU KNOW WHAT HAPPENED TO THIS?

THAT KOOK CRUSHED IT ON PETE--I MEAN, SPIDER-MAN'S WRIST.

CRAP. HE NEEDS THIS.

I'LL HOLD ON TO IT, BUT GETTING IT FIXED NEEDS TO TAKE A BACK SEAT RIGHT NOW.

SIR, I NEED YOU TO STAY HERE, OR PROBABLY EVEN BETTER, GET AS FAR AWAY FROM HERE AS POSSIBLE.

MORLUN IS NO JOKE.

I CAN'T JUST RUN AWAY. THERE'S GOT TO BE A WAY I CAN HELP.

YOU CAN HELP BY STAYING CLEAR. WE'RE GONNA HAVE OUR HANDS FULL ENOUGH WITHOUT NEEDING TO WORRY ABOUT YOU TOO.

THANKS. NOW I NEED TO GO FIND HIM AND MAKE SURE HE'S STILL ALIVE.

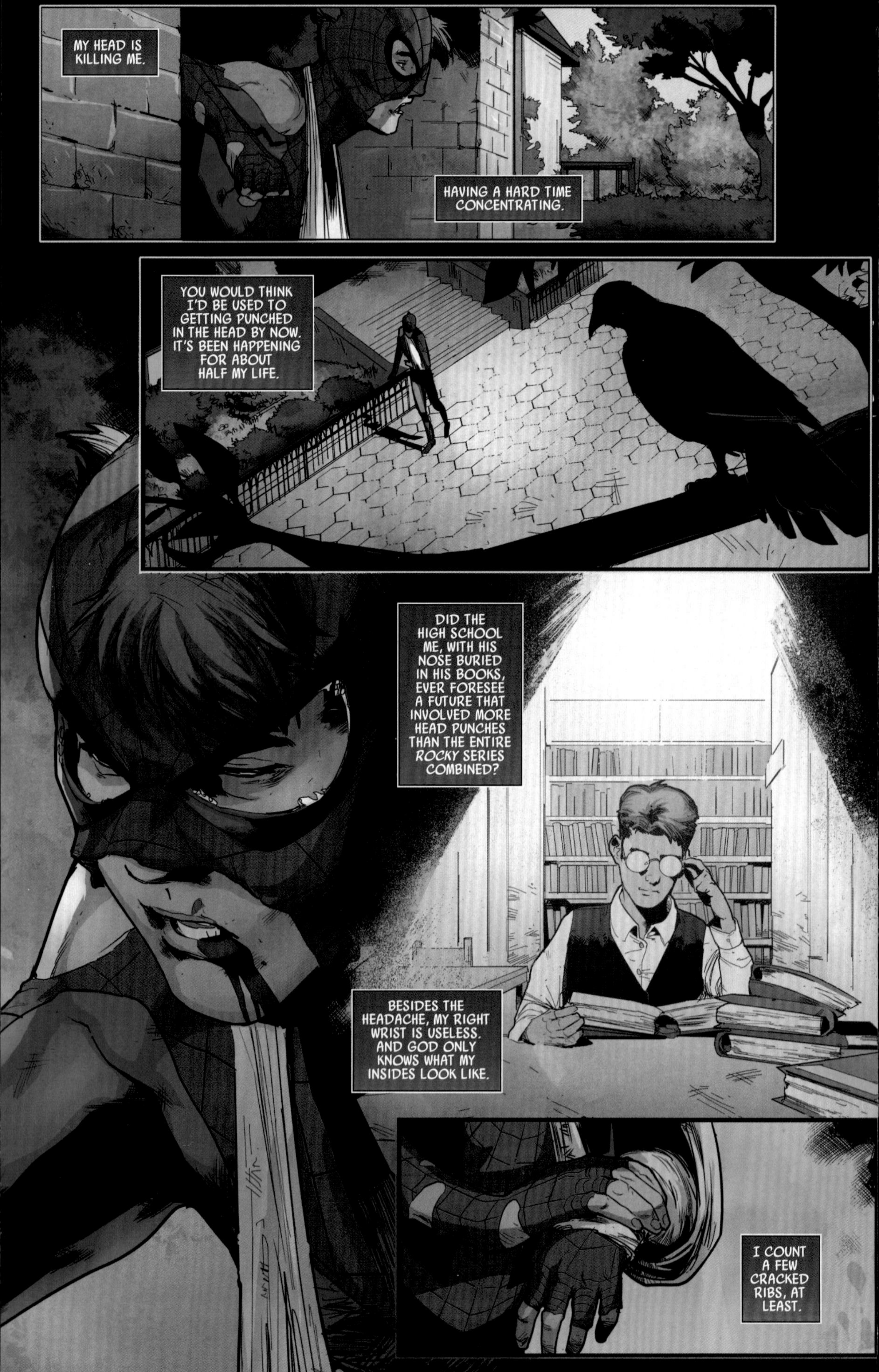
MY HEAD IS KILLING ME.
HAVING A HARD TIME CONCENTRATING.
YOU WOULD THINK I'D BE USED TO GETTING PUNCHED IN THE HEAD BY NOW. IT'S BEEN HAPPENING FOR ABOUT HALF MY LIFE.
DID THE HIGH SCHOOL ME, WITH HIS NOSE BURIED IN HIS BOOKS, EVER FORESEE A FUTURE THAT INVOLVED MORE HEAD PUNCHES THAN THE ENTIRE *ROCKY* SERIES COMBINED?
BESIDES THE HEADACHE, MY RIGHT WRIST IS USELESS. AND GOD ONLY KNOWS WHAT MY INSIDES LOOK LIKE.
I COUNT A FEW CRACKED RIBS, AT LEAST.

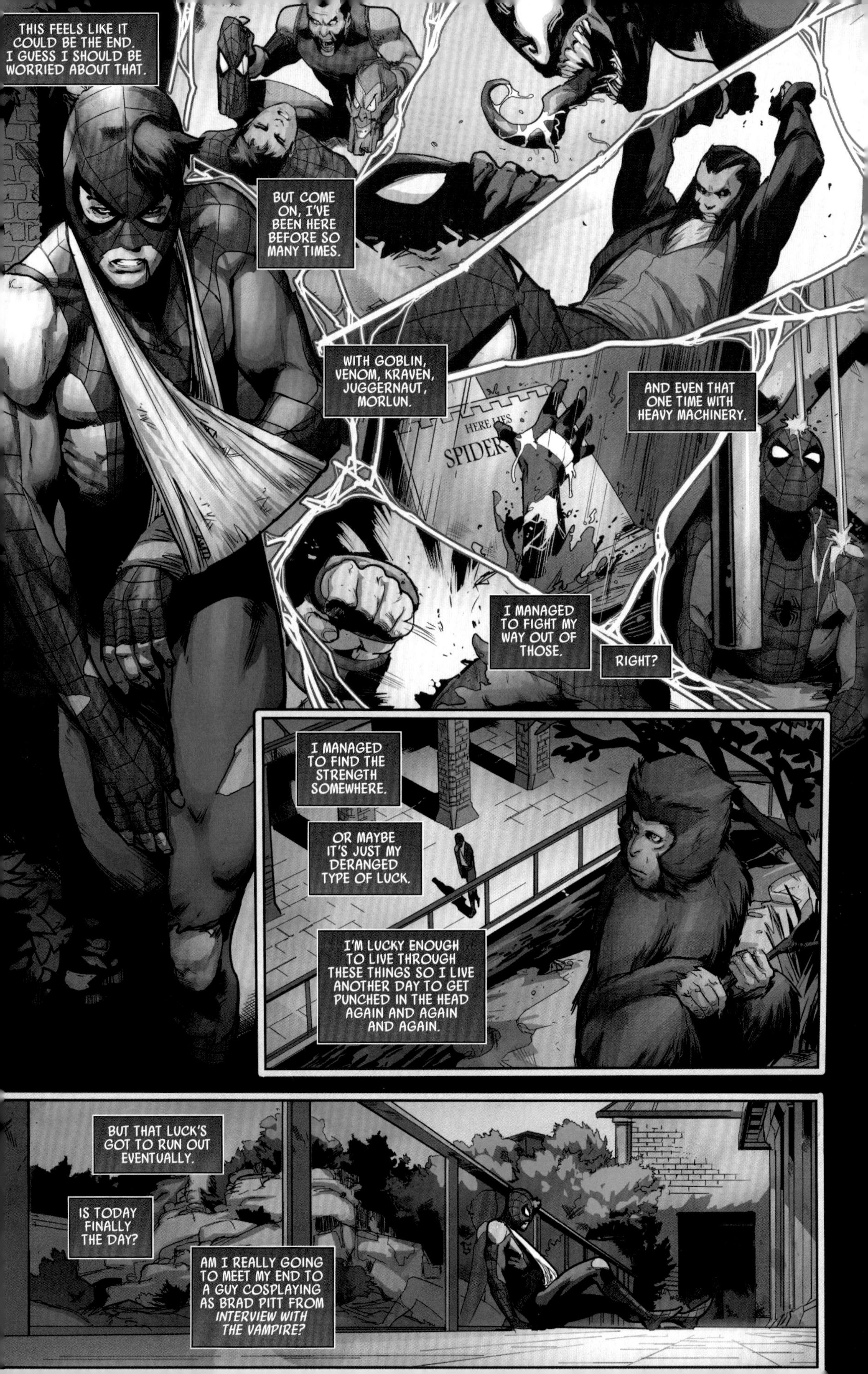
THIS FEELS LIKE IT COULD BE THE END. I GUESS I SHOULD BE WORRIED ABOUT THAT.
BUT COME ON, I'VE BEEN HERE BEFORE SO MANY TIMES.
WITH GOBLIN, VENOM, KRAVEN, JUGGERNAUT, MORLUN.
HERE LIES SPIDER-
AND EVEN THAT ONE TIME WITH HEAVY MACHINERY.
I MANAGED TO FIGHT MY WAY OUT OF THOSE.
RIGHT?
I MANAGED TO FIND THE STRENGTH SOMEWHERE.
OR MAYBE IT'S JUST MY DERANGED TYPE OF LUCK.
I'M LUCKY ENOUGH TO LIVE THROUGH THESE THINGS SO I LIVE ANOTHER DAY TO GET PUNCHED IN THE HEAD AGAIN AND AGAIN AND AGAIN.
BUT THAT LUCK'S GOT TO RUN OUT EVENTUALLY.
IS TODAY FINALLY THE DAY?
AM I REALLY GOING TO MEET MY END TO A GUY COSPLAYING AS BRAD PITT FROM *INTERVIEW WITH THE VAMPIRE?*

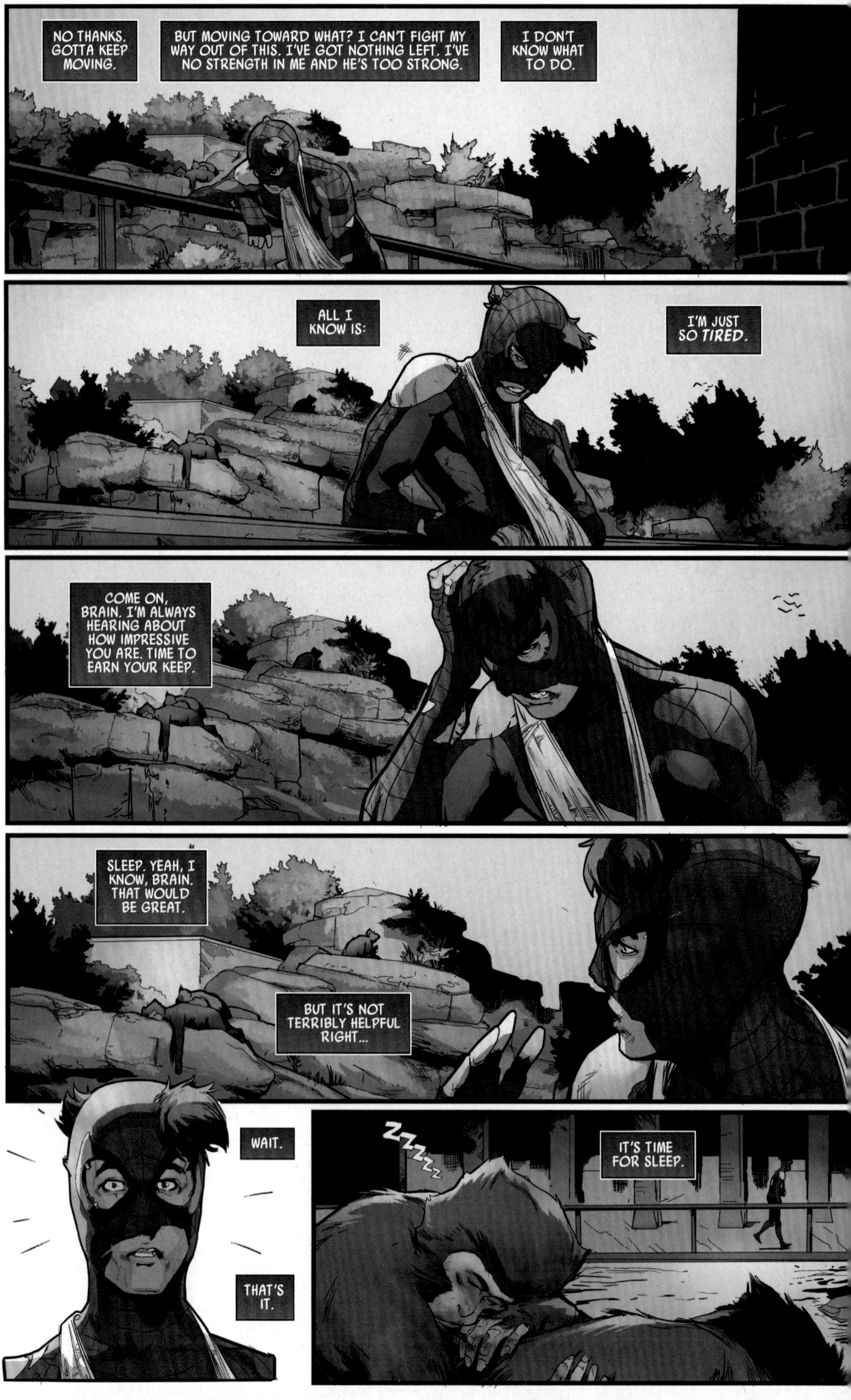
NO THANKS. GOTTA KEEP MOVING.
BUT MOVING TOWARD WHAT? I CAN'T FIGHT MY WAY OUT OF THIS. I'VE GOT NOTHING LEFT. I'VE NO STRENGTH IN ME AND HE'S TOO STRONG.
I DON'T KNOW WHAT TO DO.
ALL I KNOW IS:
I'M JUST SO *TIRED*.
COME ON, BRAIN. I'M ALWAYS HEARING ABOUT HOW IMPRESSIVE YOU ARE. TIME TO EARN YOUR KEEP.
SLEEP. YEAH, I KNOW, BRAIN. THAT WOULD BE GREAT.
BUT IT'S NOT TERRIBLY HELPFUL RIGHT...
WAIT.
THAT'S IT.
ZZZZZ
IT'S TIME FOR SLEEP.

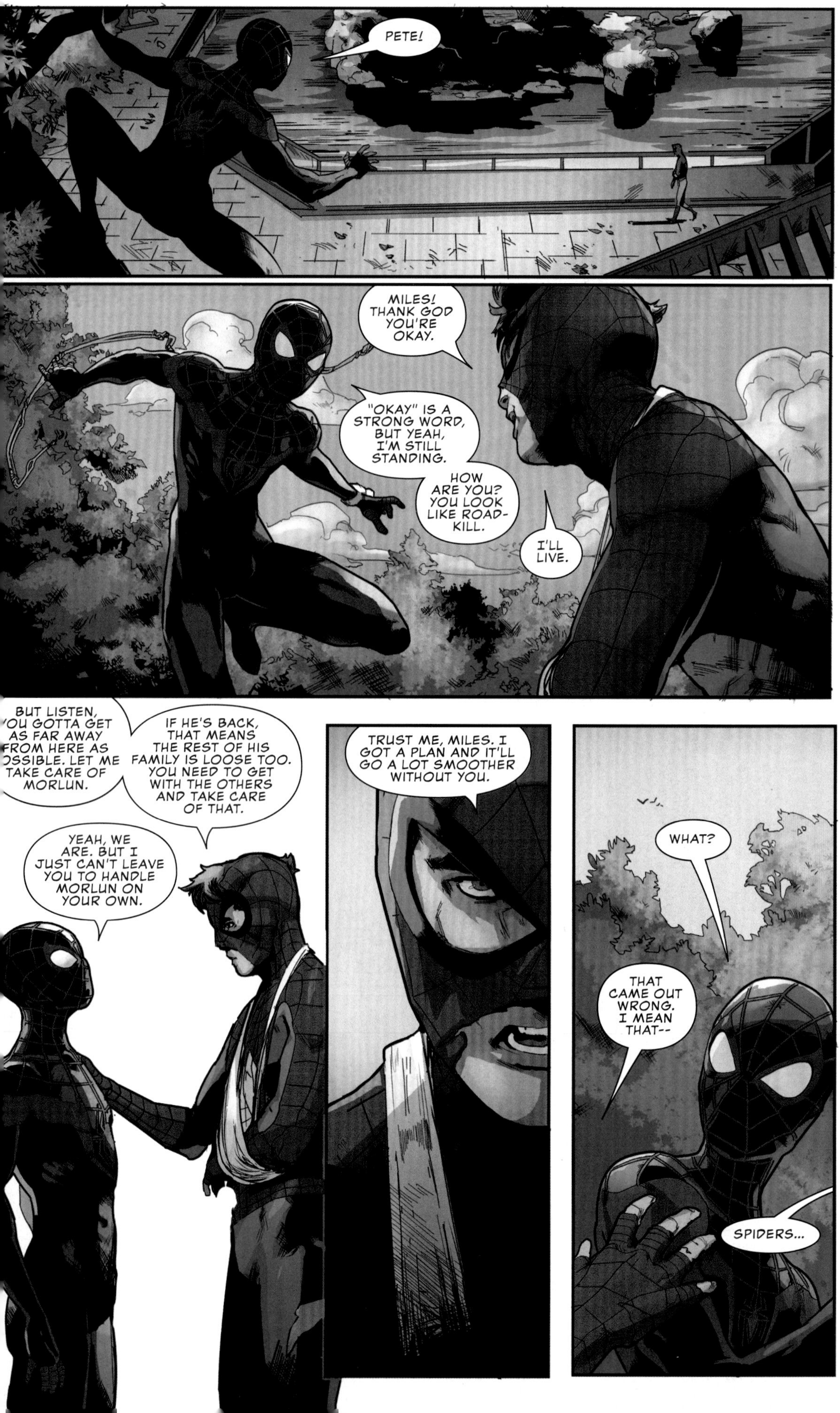
PETE!
MILES! THANK GOD YOU'RE OKAY.
"OKAY" IS A STRONG WORD, BUT YEAH, I'M STILL STANDING.
HOW ARE YOU? YOU LOOK LIKE ROAD-KILL.
I'LL LIVE.
BUT LISTEN, YOU GOTTA GET AS FAR AWAY FROM HERE AS POSSIBLE. LET ME TAKE CARE OF MORLUN.
IF HE'S BACK, THAT MEANS THE REST OF HIS FAMILY IS LOOSE TOO. YOU NEED TO GET WITH THE OTHERS AND TAKE CARE OF THAT.
YEAH, WE ARE. BUT I JUST CAN'T LEAVE YOU TO HANDLE MORLUN ON YOUR OWN.
TRUST ME, MILES. I GOT A PLAN AND IT'LL GO A LOT SMOOTHER WITHOUT YOU.
WHAT?
THAT CAME OUT WRONG. I MEAN THAT--
SPIDERS...

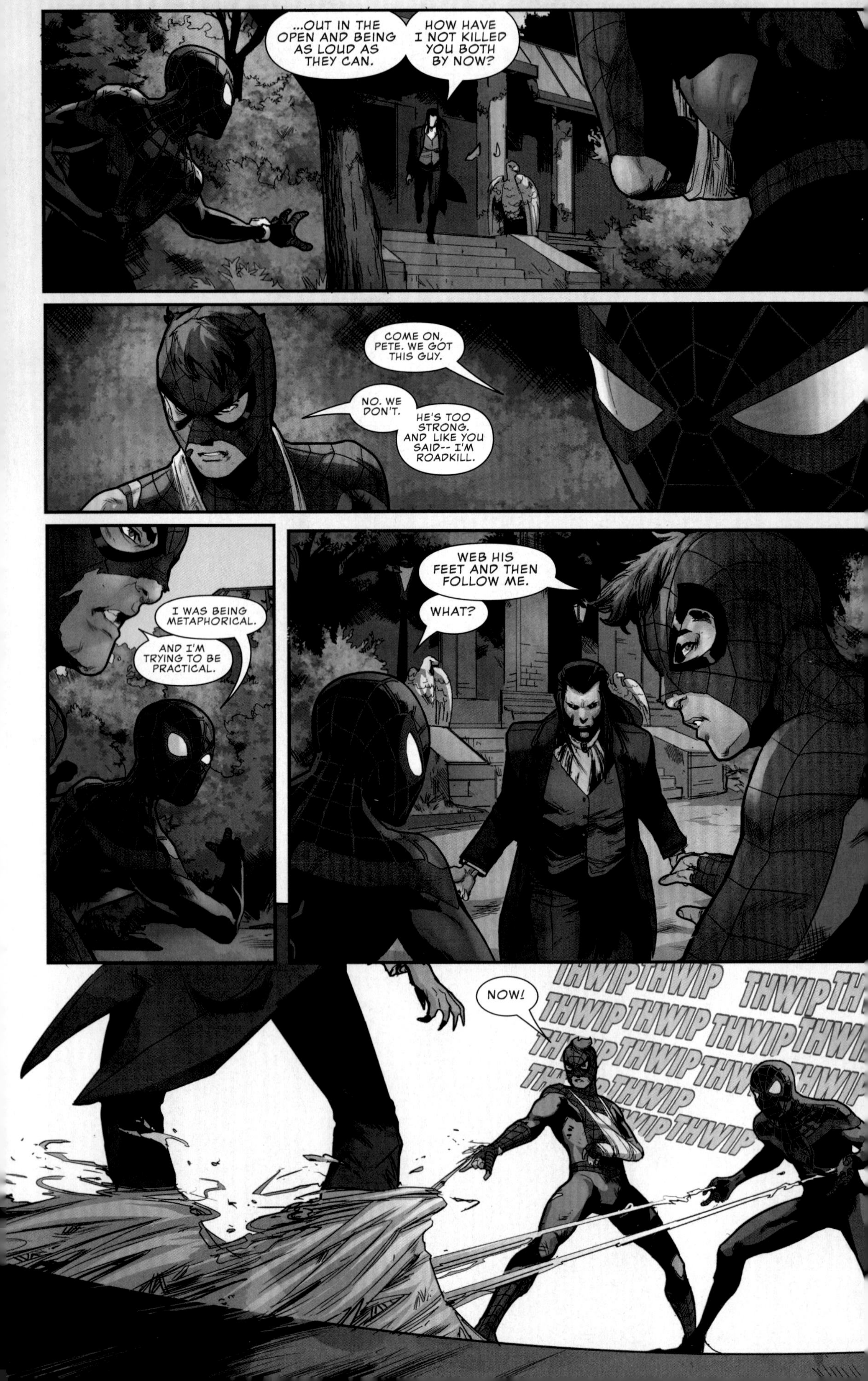
...OUT IN THE OPEN AND BEING AS LOUD AS THEY CAN.
HOW HAVE I NOT KILLED YOU BOTH BY NOW?
COME ON, PETE. WE GOT THIS GUY.
NO. WE DON'T.
HE'S TOO STRONG. AND LIKE YOU SAID-- I'M ROADKILL.
I WAS BEING METAPHORICAL.
AND I'M TRYING TO BE PRACTICAL.
WEB HIS FEET AND THEN FOLLOW ME.
WHAT?
NOW!
THWIP THWIP THWIP THWIP THWIP THWIP THWIP THWIP THWIP THWIP THWIP

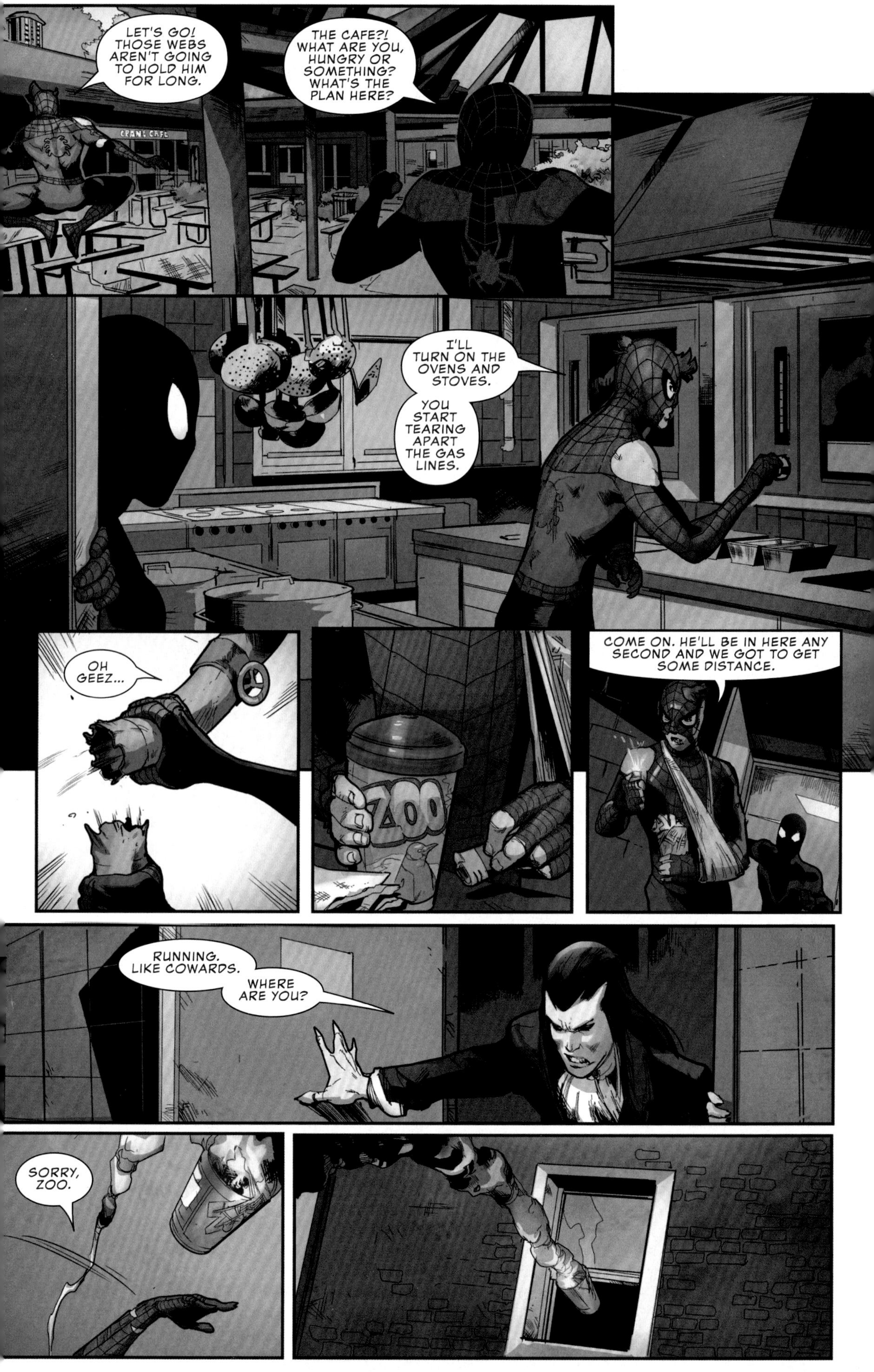
LET'S GO! THOSE WEBS AREN'T GOING TO HOLD HIM FOR LONG.
THE CAFE?! WHAT ARE YOU, HUNGRY OR SOMETHING? WHAT'S THE PLAN HERE?
I'LL TURN ON THE OVENS AND STOVES.
YOU START TEARING APART THE GAS LINES.
OH GEEZ...
ZOO
COME ON. HE'LL BE IN HERE ANY SECOND AND WE GOT TO GET SOME DISTANCE.
RUNNING. LIKE COWARDS.
WHERE ARE YOU?
SORRY, ZOO.

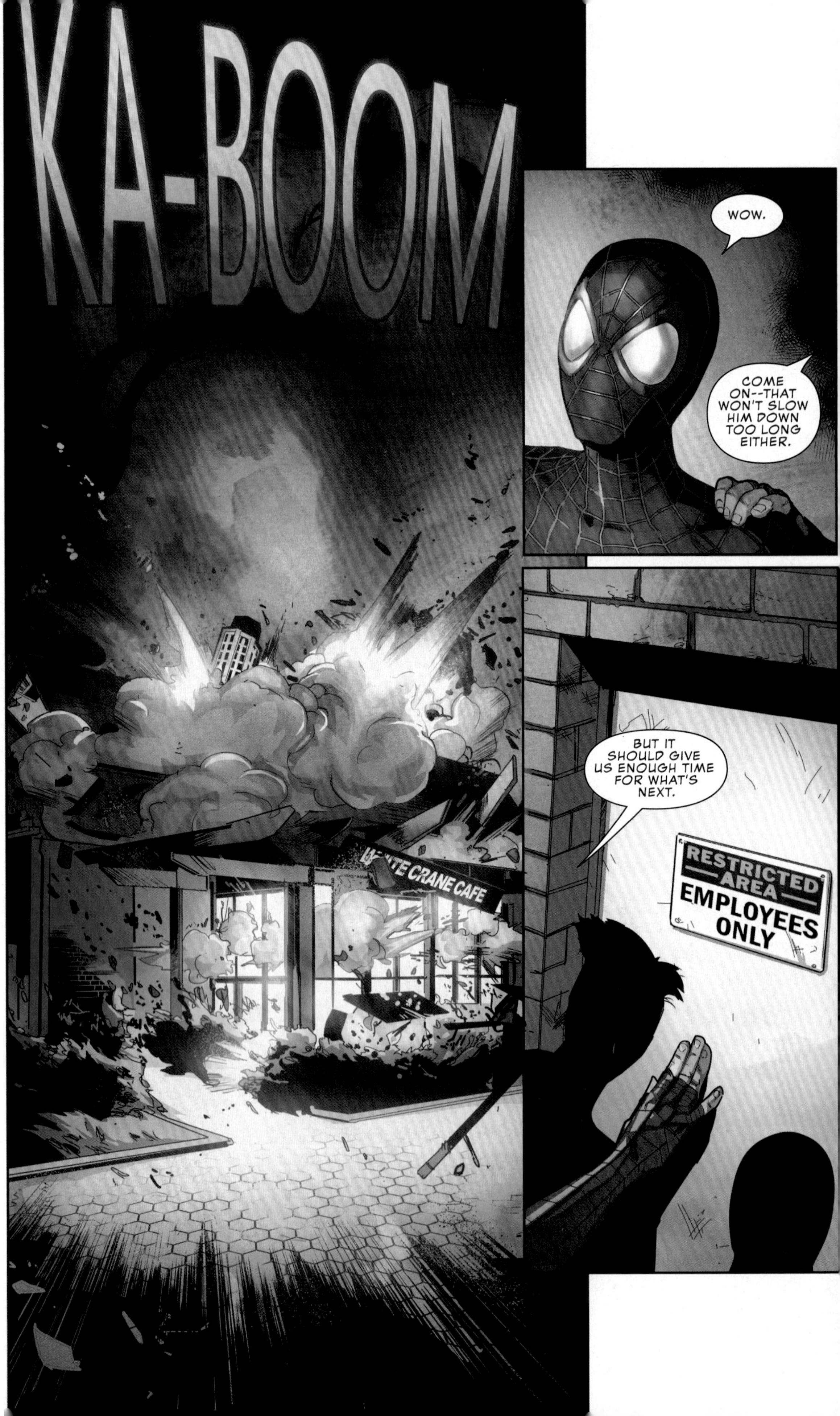
KA-BOOM
CRANE CAFE
WOW.
COME ON--THAT WON'T SLOW HIM DOWN TOO LONG EITHER.
BUT IT SHOULD GIVE US ENOUGH TIME FOR WHAT'S NEXT.
RESTRICTED AREA
EMPLOYEES ONLY

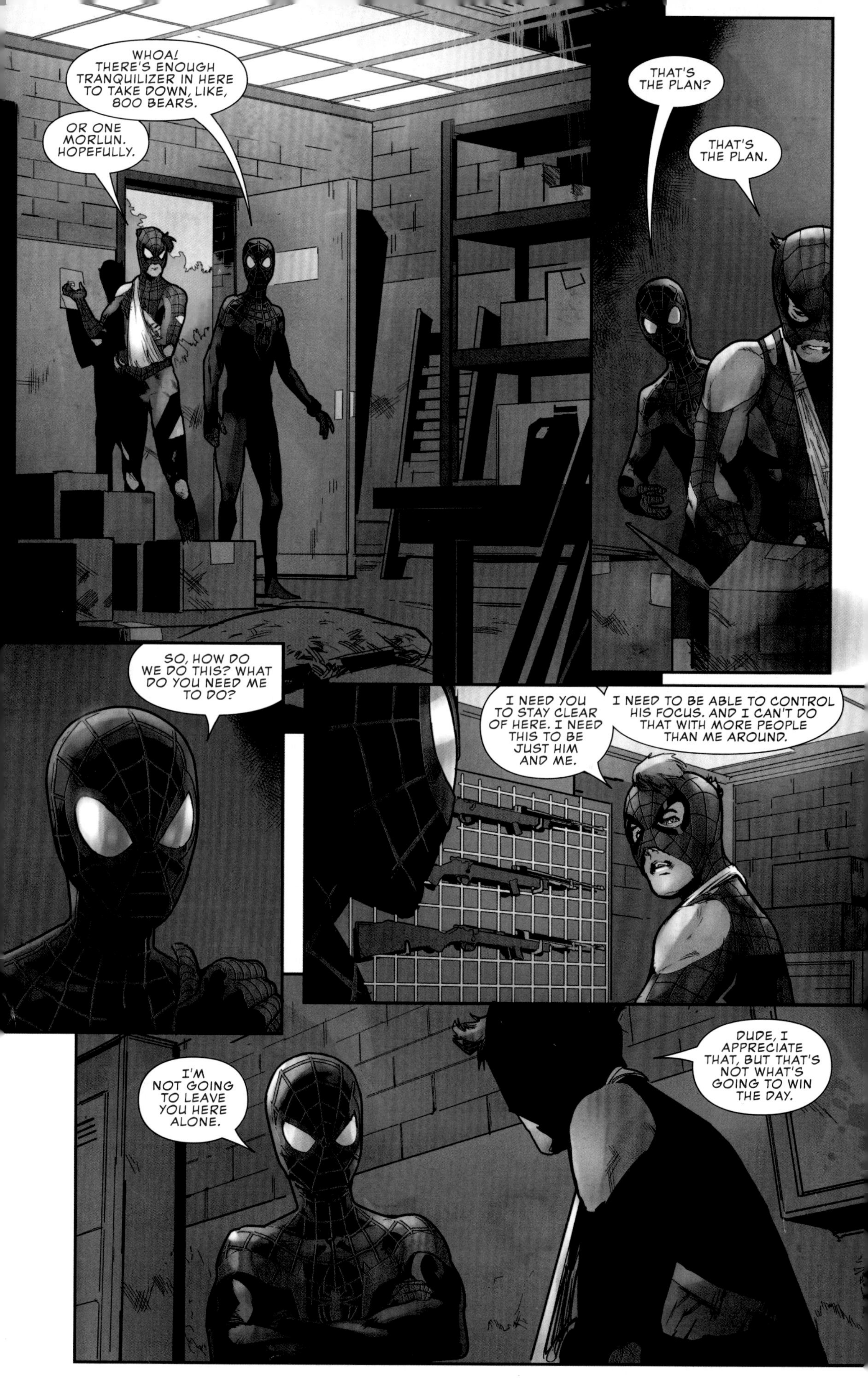
WHOA! THERE'S ENOUGH TRANQUILIZER IN HERE TO TAKE DOWN, LIKE, 800 BEARS.
OR ONE MORLUN. HOPEFULLY.
THAT'S THE PLAN?
THAT'S THE PLAN.
SO, HOW DO WE DO THIS? WHAT DO YOU NEED ME TO DO?
I NEED YOU TO STAY CLEAR OF HERE. I NEED THIS TO BE JUST HIM AND ME.
I NEED TO BE ABLE TO CONTROL HIS FOCUS. AND I CAN'T DO THAT WITH MORE PEOPLE THAN ME AROUND.
I'M NOT GOING TO LEAVE YOU HERE ALONE.
DUDE, I APPRECIATE THAT, BUT THAT'S NOT WHAT'S GOING TO WIN THE DAY.

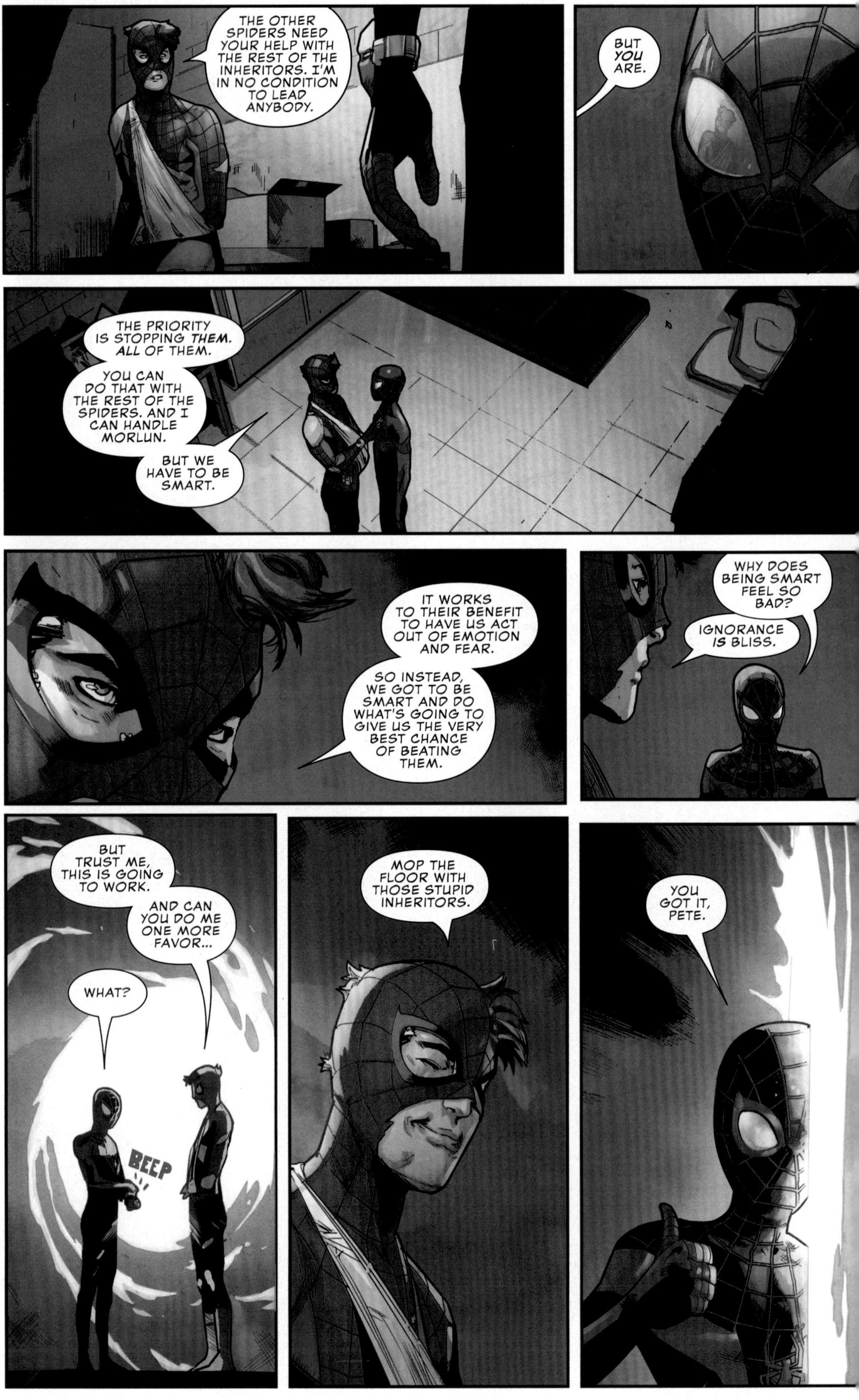
THE OTHER SPIDERS NEED YOUR HELP WITH THE REST OF THE INHERITORS. I'M IN NO CONDITION TO LEAD ANYBODY.
BUT *YOU* ARE.
THE PRIORITY IS STOPPING *THEM. ALL* OF THEM.
YOU CAN DO THAT WITH THE REST OF THE SPIDERS. AND I CAN HANDLE MORLUN.
BUT WE HAVE TO BE SMART.
IT WORKS TO THEIR BENEFIT TO HAVE US ACT OUT OF EMOTION AND FEAR.
SO INSTEAD, WE GOT TO BE SMART AND DO WHAT'S GOING TO GIVE US THE VERY BEST CHANCE OF BEATING THEM.
WHY DOES BEING SMART FEEL SO BAD?
IGNORANCE *IS* BLISS.
BUT TRUST ME, THIS IS GOING TO WORK.
AND CAN YOU DO ME ONE MORE FAVOR...
WHAT?
BEEP
MOP THE FLOOR WITH THOSE STUPID INHERITORS.
YOU GOT IT, PETE.

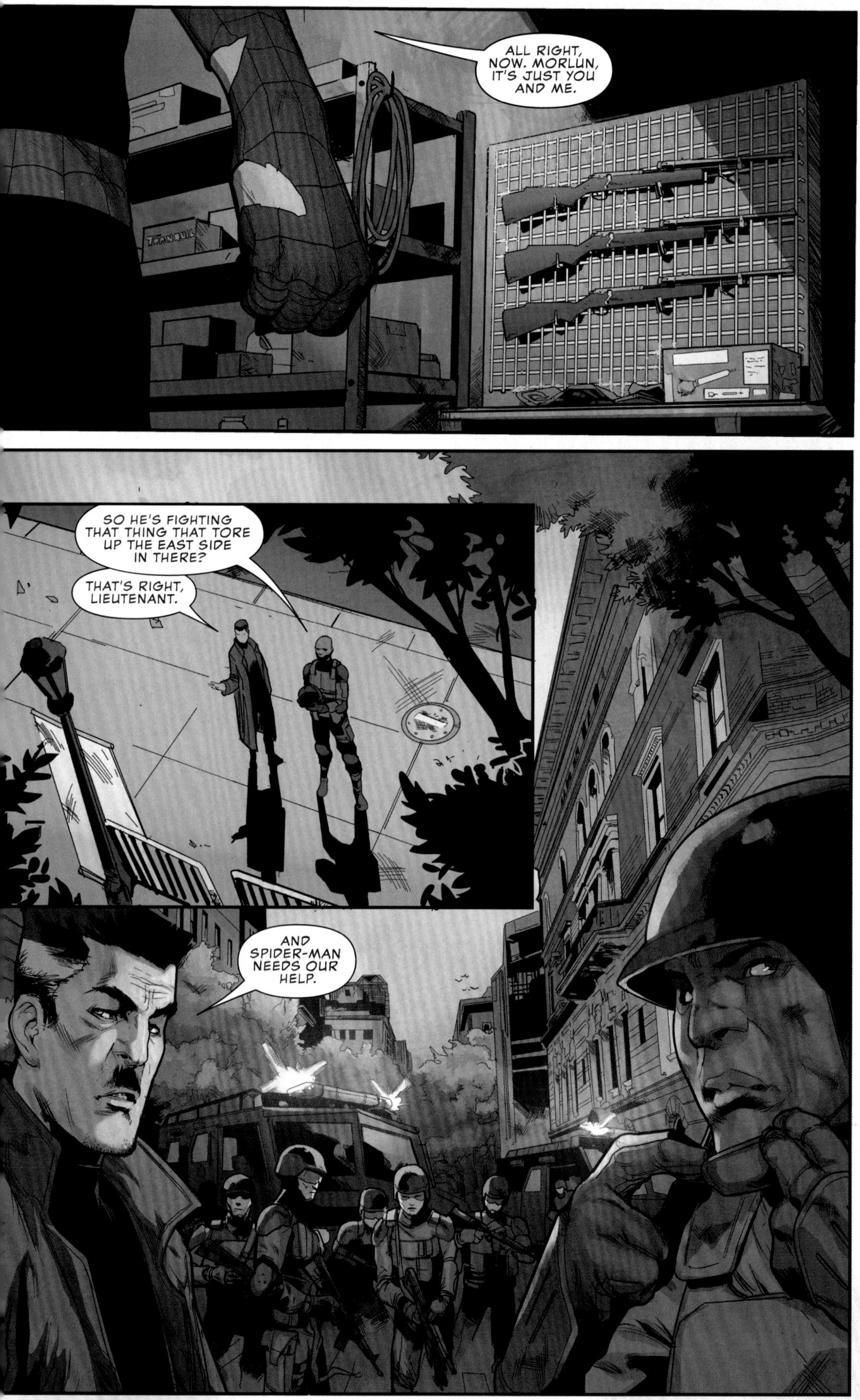
ALL RIGHT, NOW. MORLUN, IT'S JUST YOU AND ME.
SO HE'S FIGHTING THAT THING THAT TORE UP THE EAST SIDE IN THERE?
THAT'S RIGHT, LIEUTENANT.
AND SPIDER-MAN NEEDS OUR HELP.

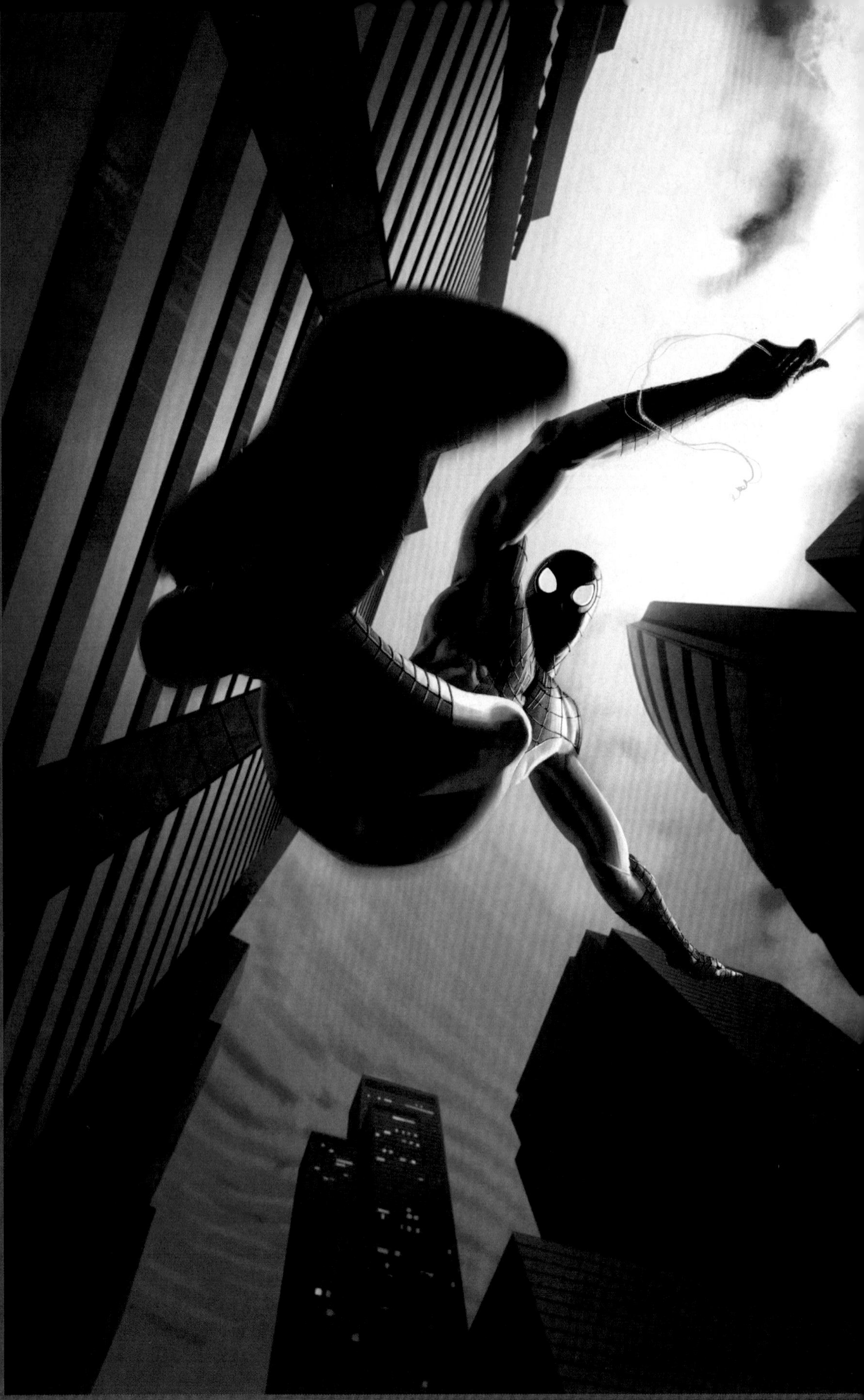

THREE TIMES.

THREE TIMES.

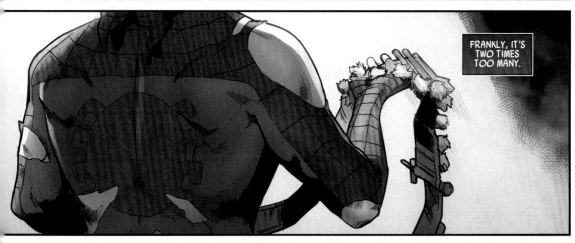

FRANKLY, IT'S TWO TIMES TOO MANY.

I SHOULD HAVE CONSUMED THIS SPIDER THE VERY FIRST TIME I ENCOUNTERED HIM.

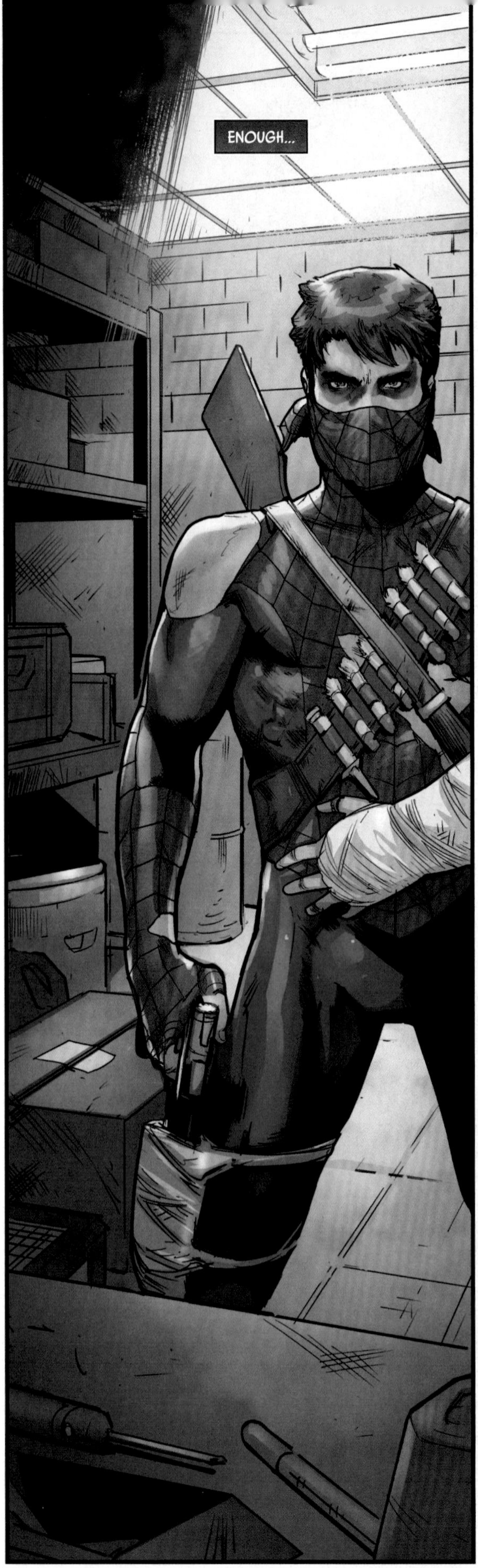
ENOUGH...

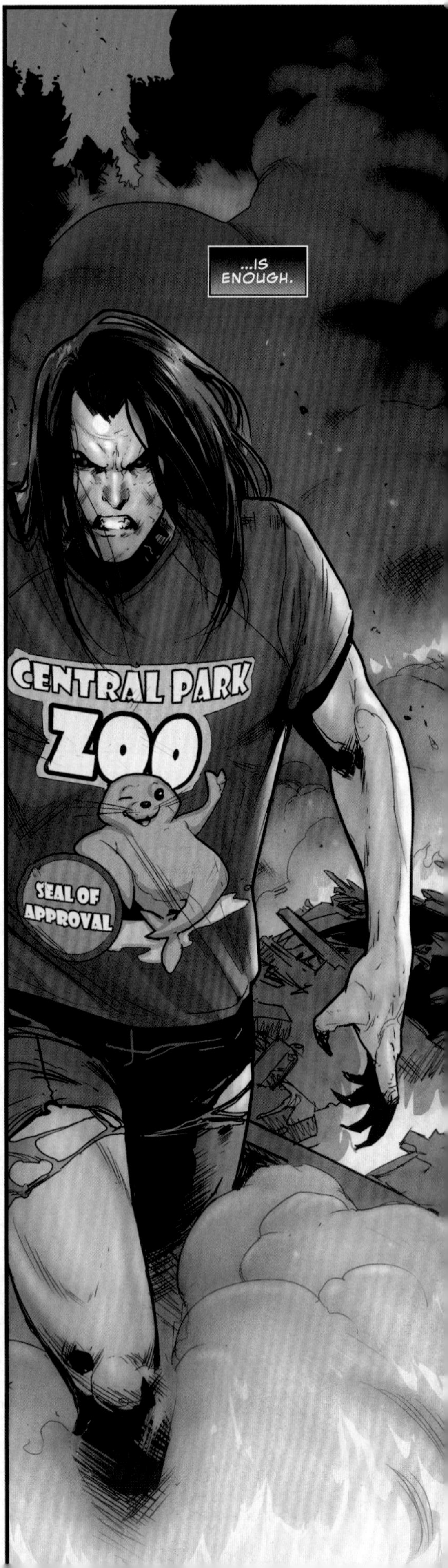
...IS ENOUGH.
CENTRAL PARK
ZOO
SEAL OF APPROVAL

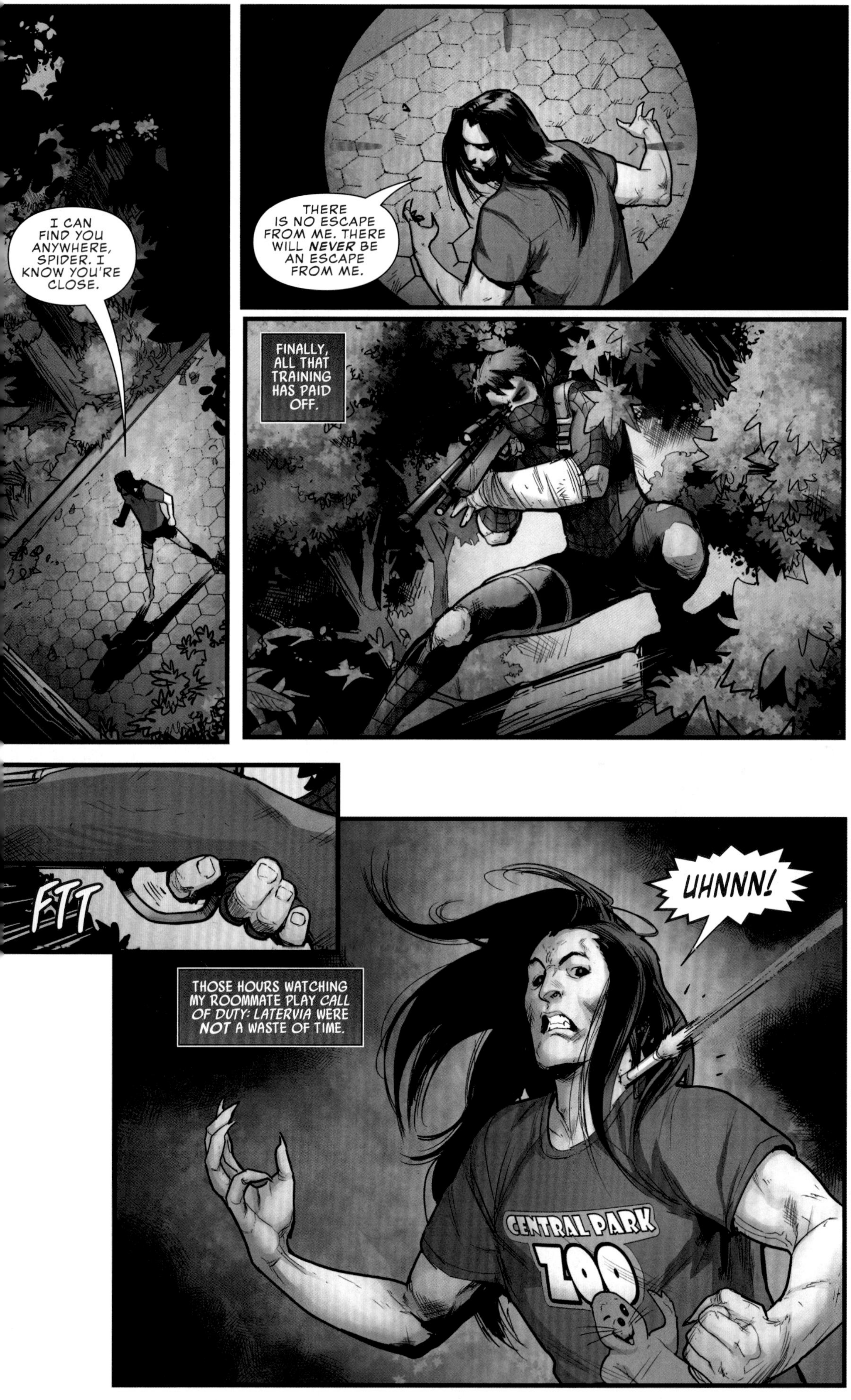
I CAN FIND YOU ANYWHERE, SPIDER. I KNOW YOU'RE CLOSE.
THERE IS NO ESCAPE FROM ME. THERE WILL NEVER BE AN ESCAPE FROM ME.
FINALLY, ALL THAT TRAINING HAS PAID OFF.
FTT
THOSE HOURS WATCHING MY ROOMMATE PLAY CALL OF DUTY: LATERVIA WERE NOT A WASTE OF TIME.
UHNNN!
CENTRAL PARK ZOO

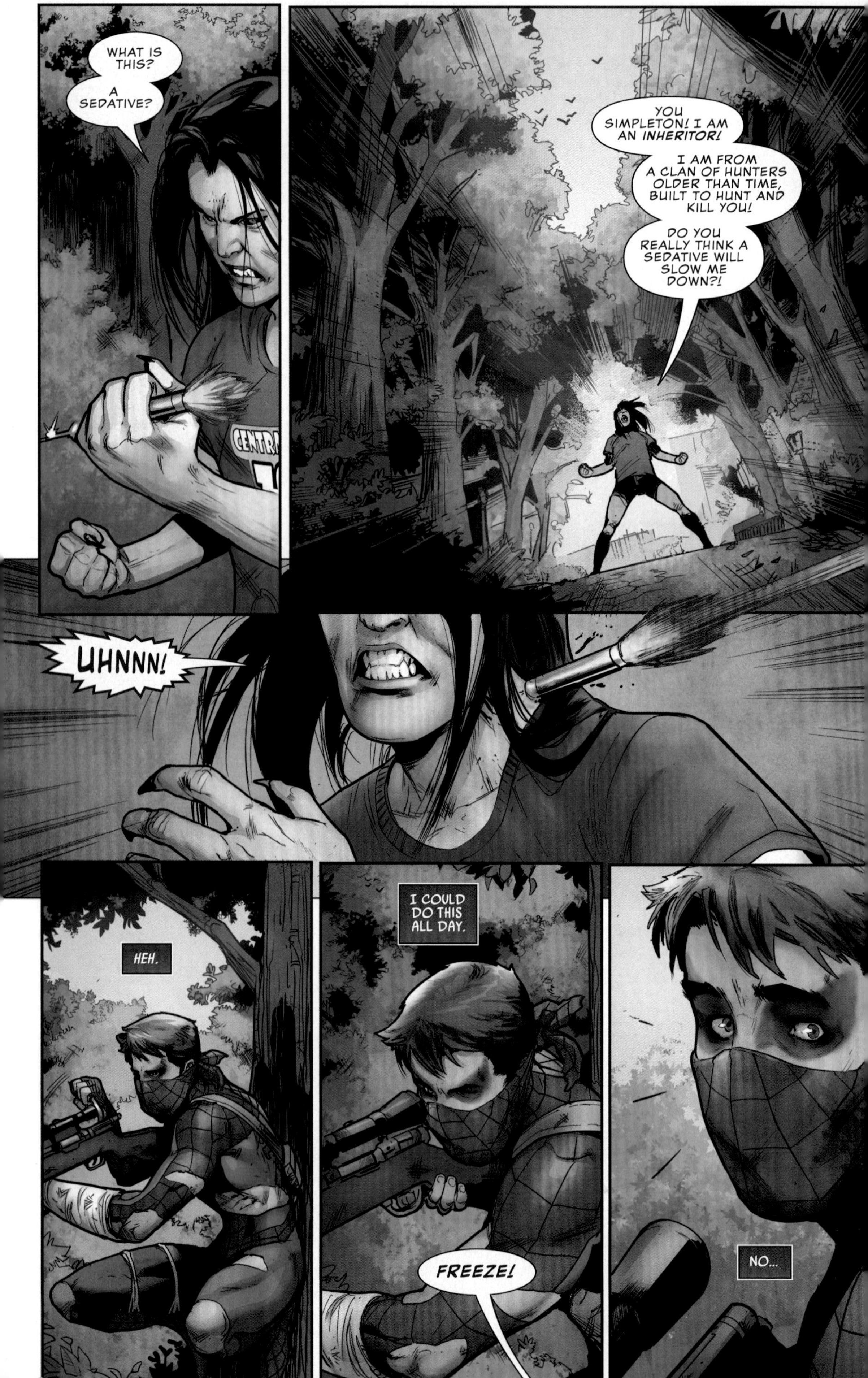
WHAT IS THIS?
A SEDATIVE?
YOU SIMPLETON! I AM AN INHERITOR!
I AM FROM A CLAN OF HUNTERS OLDER THAN TIME, BUILT TO HUNT AND KILL YOU!
DO YOU REALLY THINK A SEDATIVE WILL SLOW ME DOWN?!
UHNNN!
HEH.
I COULD DO THIS ALL DAY.
FREEZE!
NO...

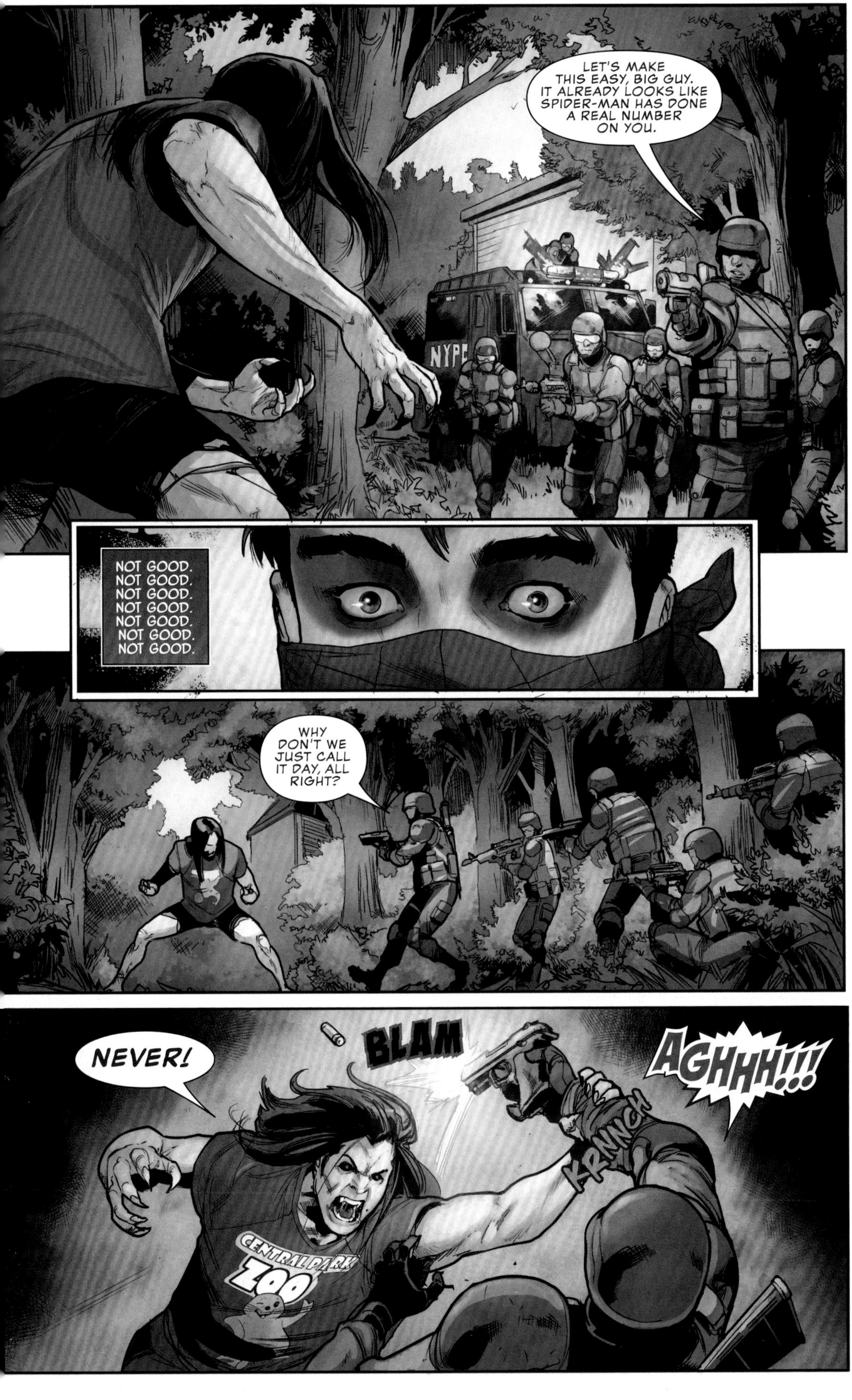
LET'S MAKE THIS EASY, BIG GUY. IT ALREADY LOOKS LIKE SPIDER-MAN HAS DONE A REAL NUMBER ON YOU.
NYPD
NOT GOOD. NOT GOOD. NOT GOOD. NOT GOOD. NOT GOOD. NOT GOOD. NOT GOOD.
WHY DON'T WE JUST CALL IT DAY, ALL RIGHT?
NEVER!
BLAM
AGHHH!!!
KRNNCH
CENTRAL PARK ZOO

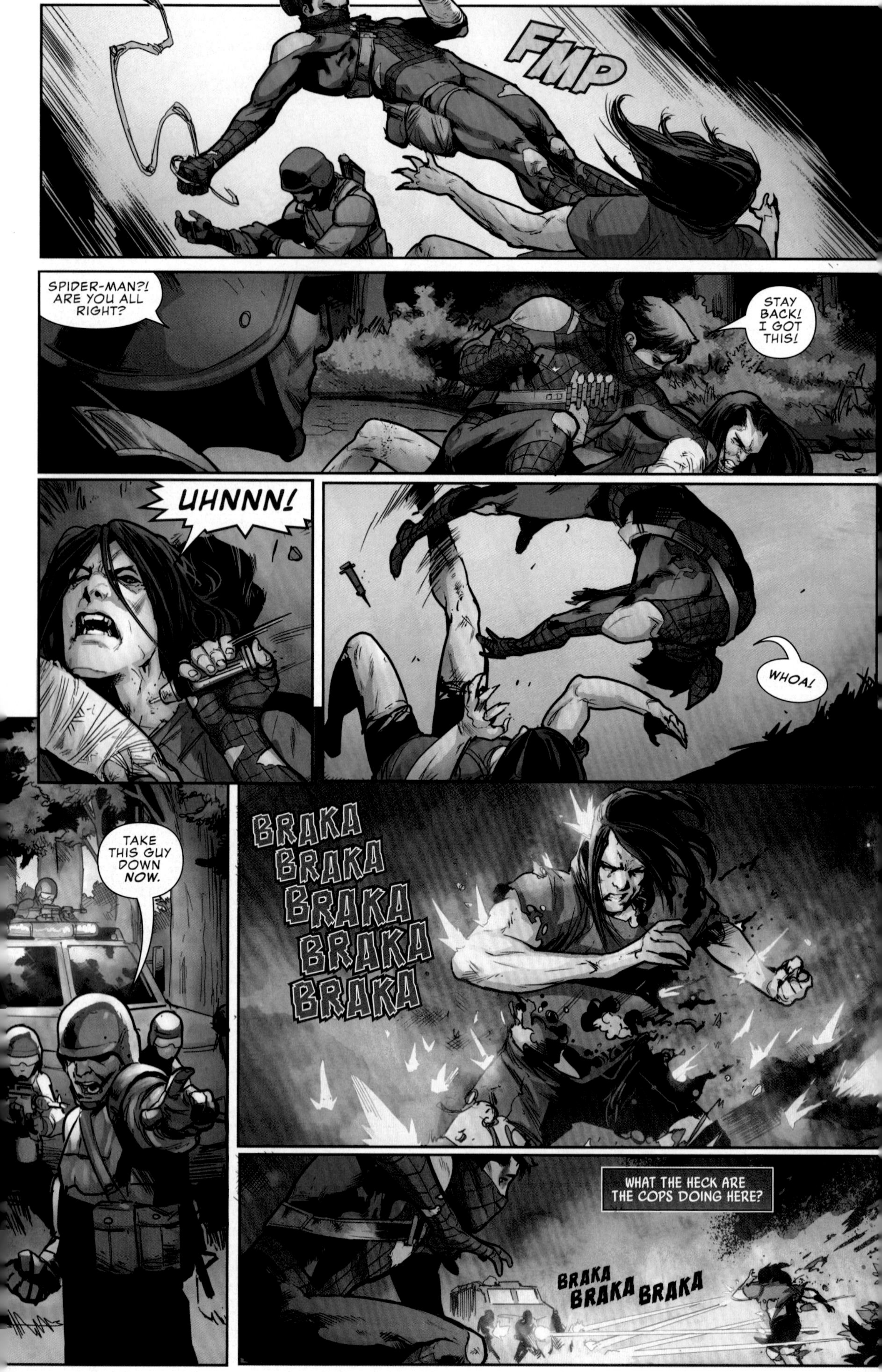
FMP
SPIDER-MAN?! ARE YOU ALL RIGHT?
STAY BACK! I GOT THIS!
UHNNN!
WHOA!
TAKE THIS GUY DOWN NOW.
BRAKA BRAKA BRAKA BRAKA BRAKA
WHAT THE HECK ARE THE COPS DOING HERE?
BRAKA BRAKA BRAKA

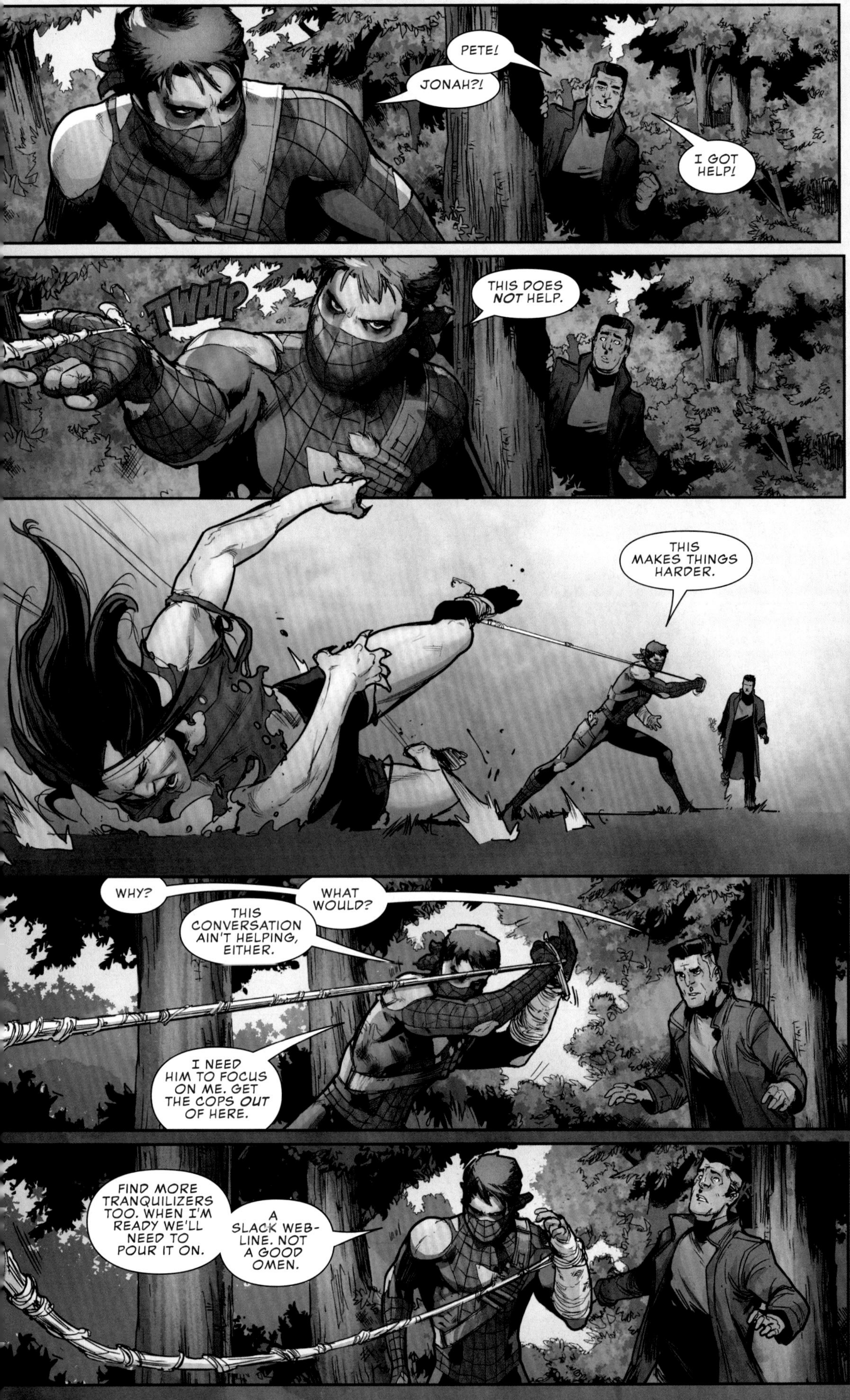
PETE!
JONAH?!
I GOT HELP!
TWHIP
THIS DOES NOT HELP.
THIS MAKES THINGS HARDER.
WHY?
WHAT WOULD?
THIS CONVERSATION AIN'T HELPING, EITHER.
I NEED HIM TO FOCUS ON ME. GET THE COPS OUT OF HERE.
FIND MORE TRANQUILIZERS TOO. WHEN I'M READY WE'LL NEED TO POUR IT ON.
A SLACK WEB-LINE. NOT A GOOD OMEN.

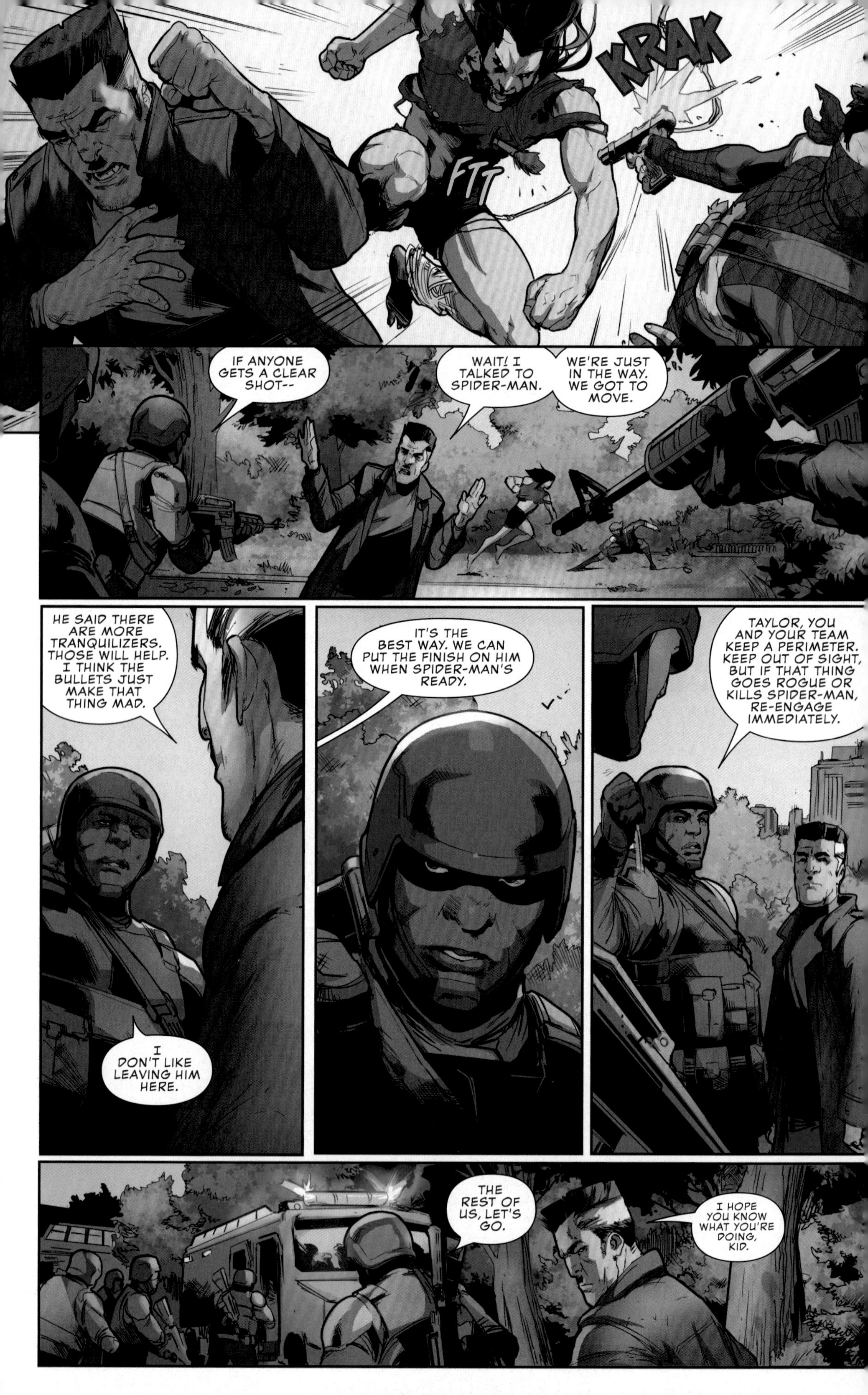
KRAK
FTT
IF ANYONE GETS A CLEAR SHOT--
WAIT! I TALKED TO SPIDER-MAN.
WE'RE JUST IN THE WAY. WE GOT TO MOVE.
HE SAID THERE ARE MORE TRANQUILIZERS. THOSE WILL HELP. I THINK THE BULLETS JUST MAKE THAT THING MAD.
I DON'T LIKE LEAVING HIM HERE.
IT'S THE BEST WAY. WE CAN PUT THE FINISH ON HIM WHEN SPIDER-MAN'S READY.
TAYLOR, YOU AND YOUR TEAM KEEP A PERIMETER. KEEP OUT OF SIGHT, BUT IF THAT THING GOES ROGUE OR KILLS SPIDER-MAN, RE-ENGAGE IMMEDIATELY.
THE REST OF US, LET'S GO.
I HOPE YOU KNOW WHAT YOU'RE DOING, KID.

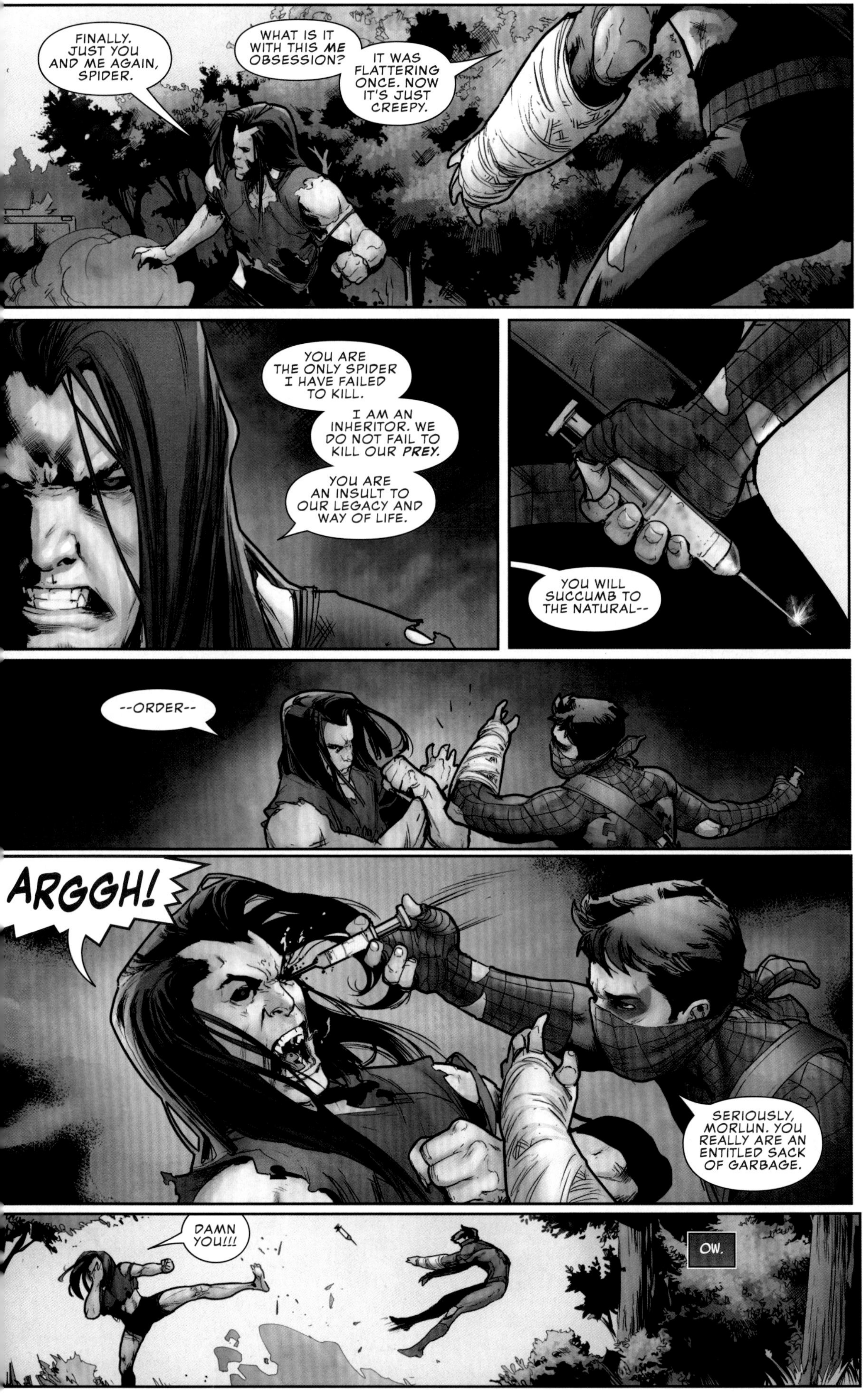
FINALLY. JUST YOU AND ME AGAIN, SPIDER.
WHAT IS IT WITH THIS ME OBSESSION?
IT WAS FLATTERING ONCE. NOW IT'S JUST CREEPY.
YOU ARE THE ONLY SPIDER I HAVE FAILED TO KILL.
I AM AN INHERITOR. WE DO NOT FAIL TO KILL OUR PREY.
YOU ARE AN INSULT TO OUR LEGACY AND WAY OF LIFE.
YOU WILL SUCCUMB TO THE NATURAL--
--ORDER--
ARGGH!
SERIOUSLY, MORLUN. YOU REALLY ARE AN ENTITLED SACK OF GARBAGE.
DAMN YOU!!!
OW.

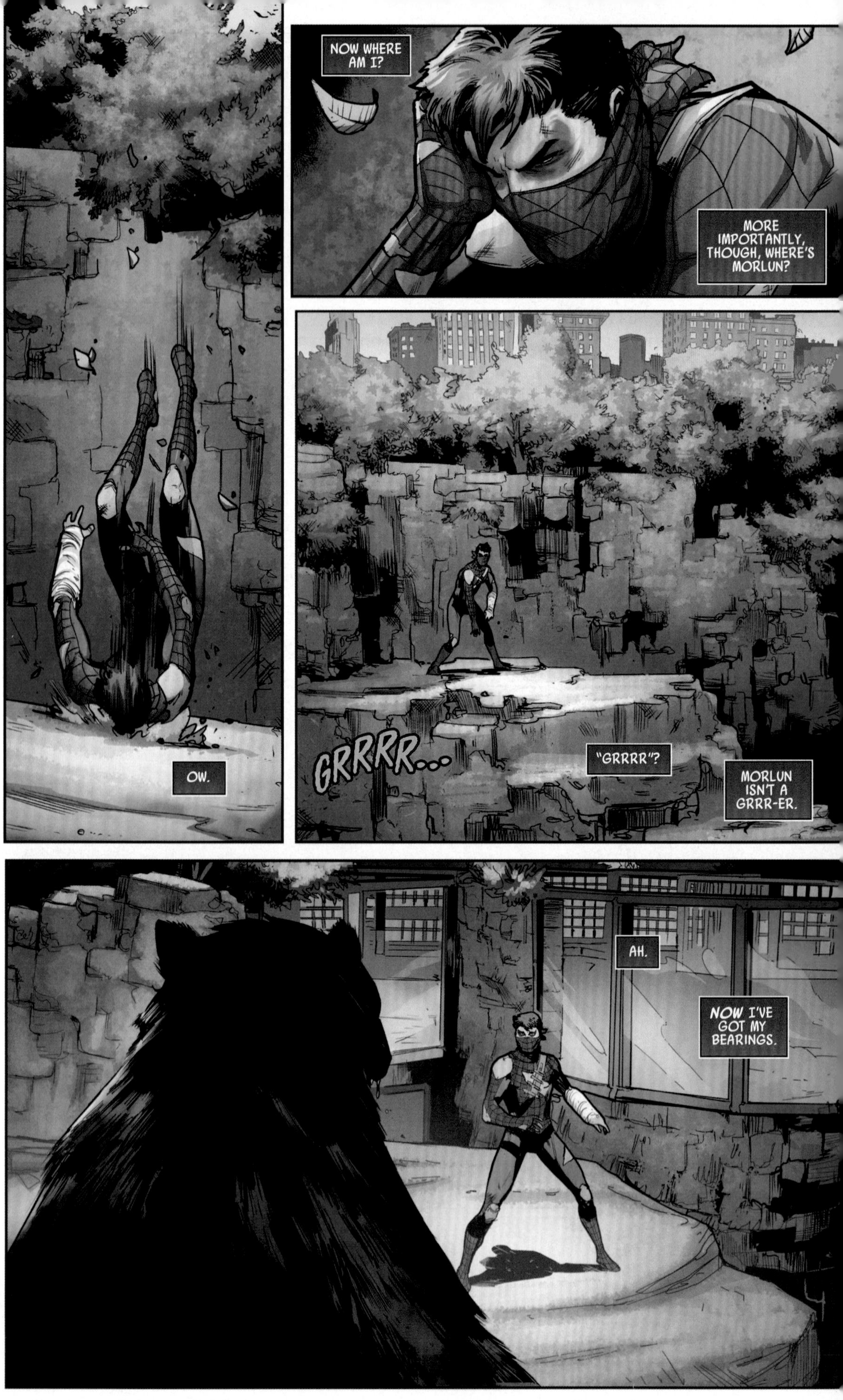
OW.
NOW WHERE AM I?
MORE IMPORTANTLY, THOUGH, WHERE'S MORLUN?
GRRRR...
"GRRRR"?
MORLUN ISN'T A GRRR-ER.
AH.
NOW I'VE GOT MY BEARINGS.

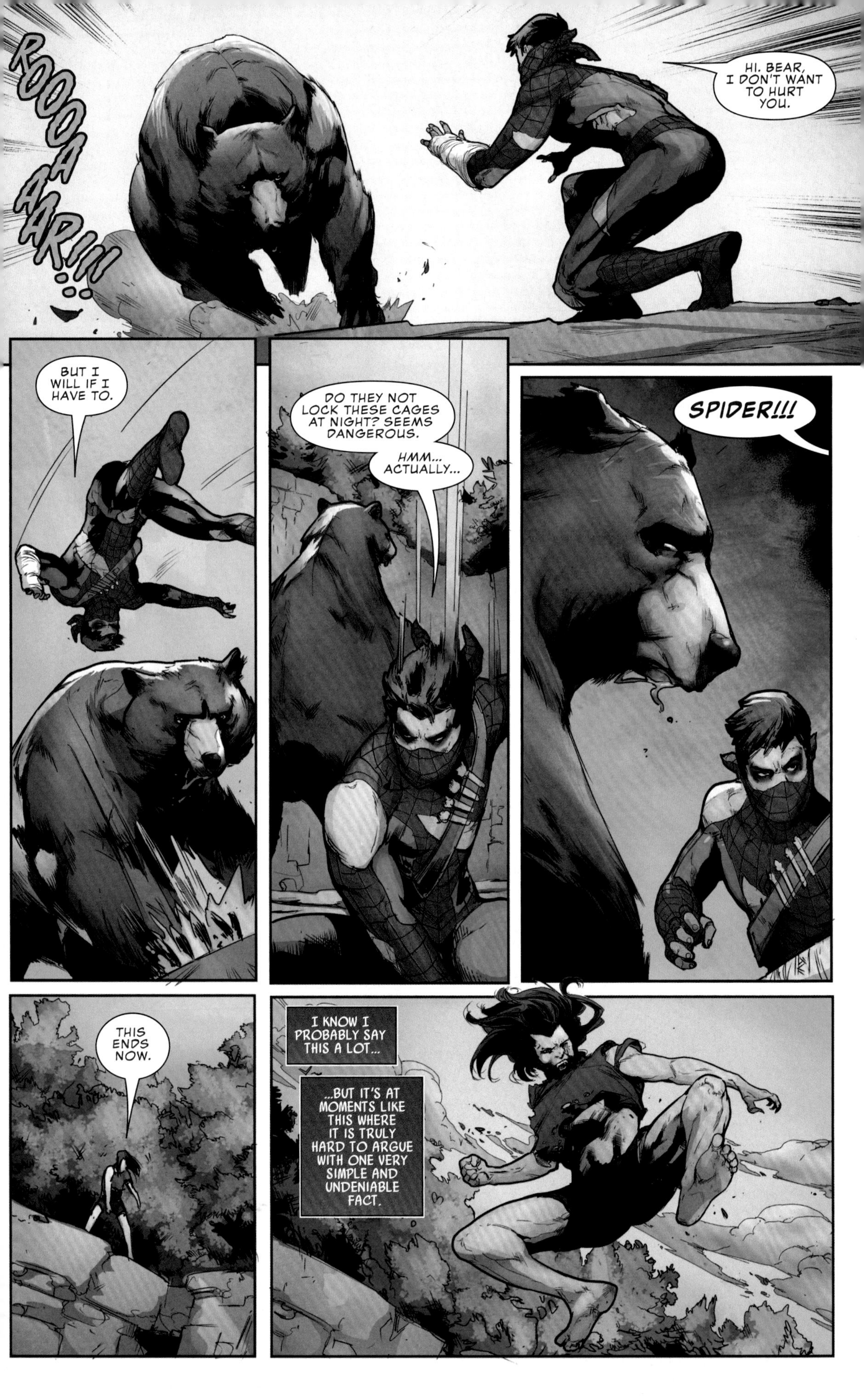
ROOOAAAR!!!
HI. BEAR, I DON'T WANT TO HURT YOU.
BUT I WILL IF I HAVE TO.
DO THEY NOT LOCK THESE CAGES AT NIGHT? SEEMS DANGEROUS.
HMM... ACTUALLY...
SPIDER!!!
THIS ENDS NOW.
I KNOW I PROBABLY SAY THIS A LOT...
...BUT IT'S AT MOMENTS LIKE THIS WHERE IT IS TRULY HARD TO ARGUE WITH ONE VERY SIMPLE AND UNDENIABLE FACT.

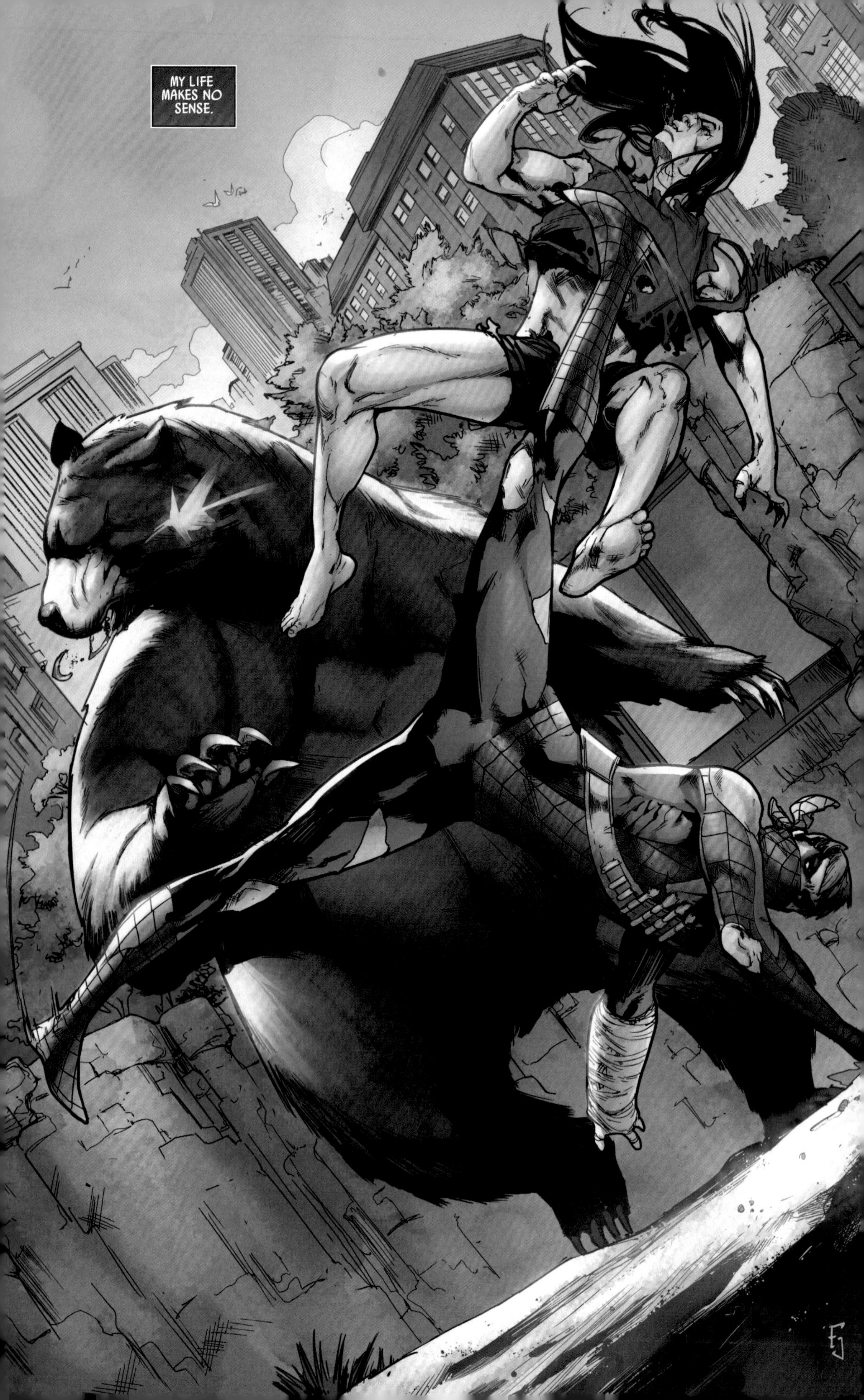
MY LIFE MAKES NO SENSE.

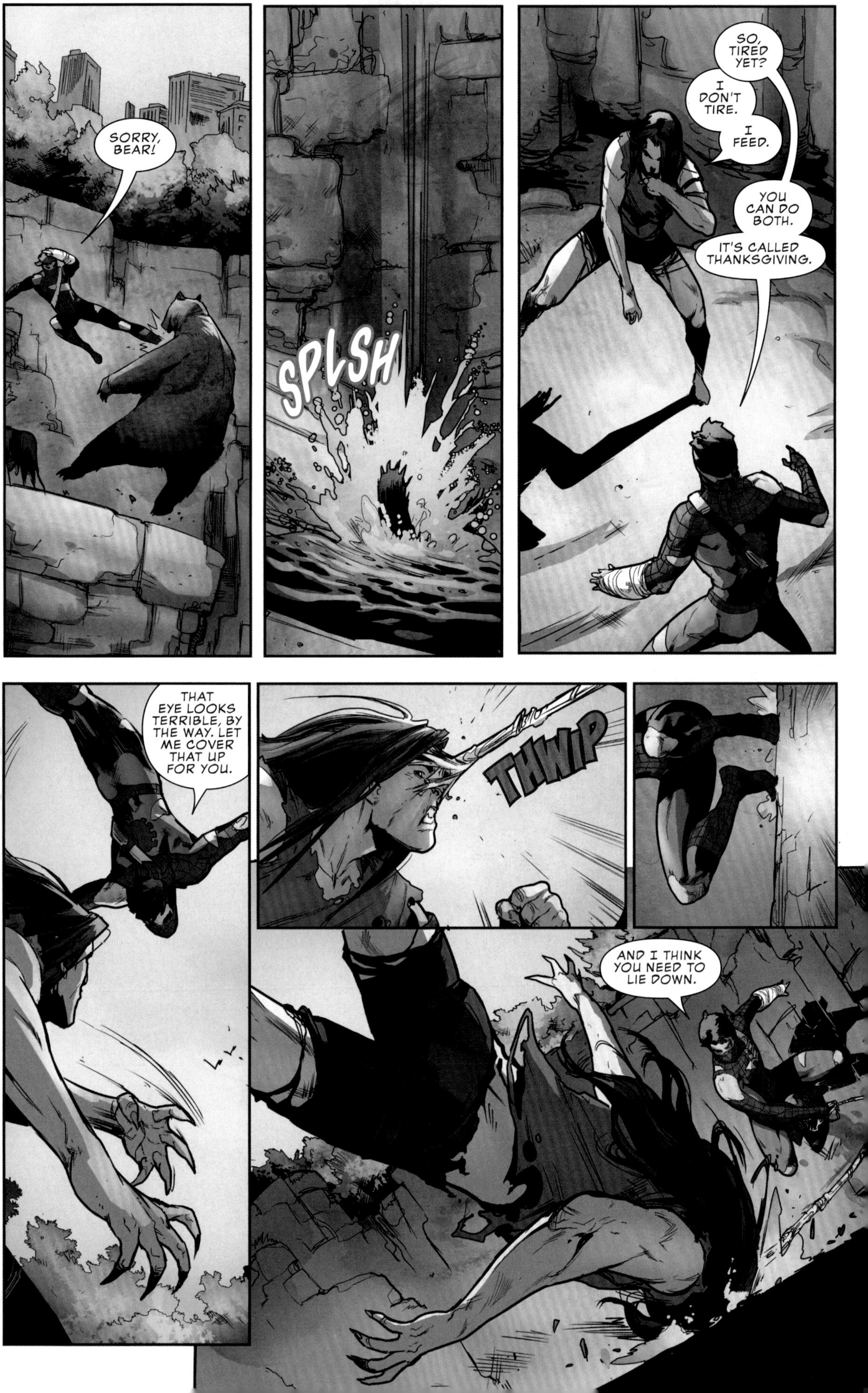
SORRY, BEAR!
SPLSH
SO, TIRED YET?
I DON'T TIRE.
I FEED.
YOU CAN DO BOTH.
IT'S CALLED THANKSGIVING.
THAT EYE LOOKS TERRIBLE, BY THE WAY. LET ME COVER THAT UP FOR YOU.
THWIP
AND I THINK YOU NEED TO LIE DOWN.

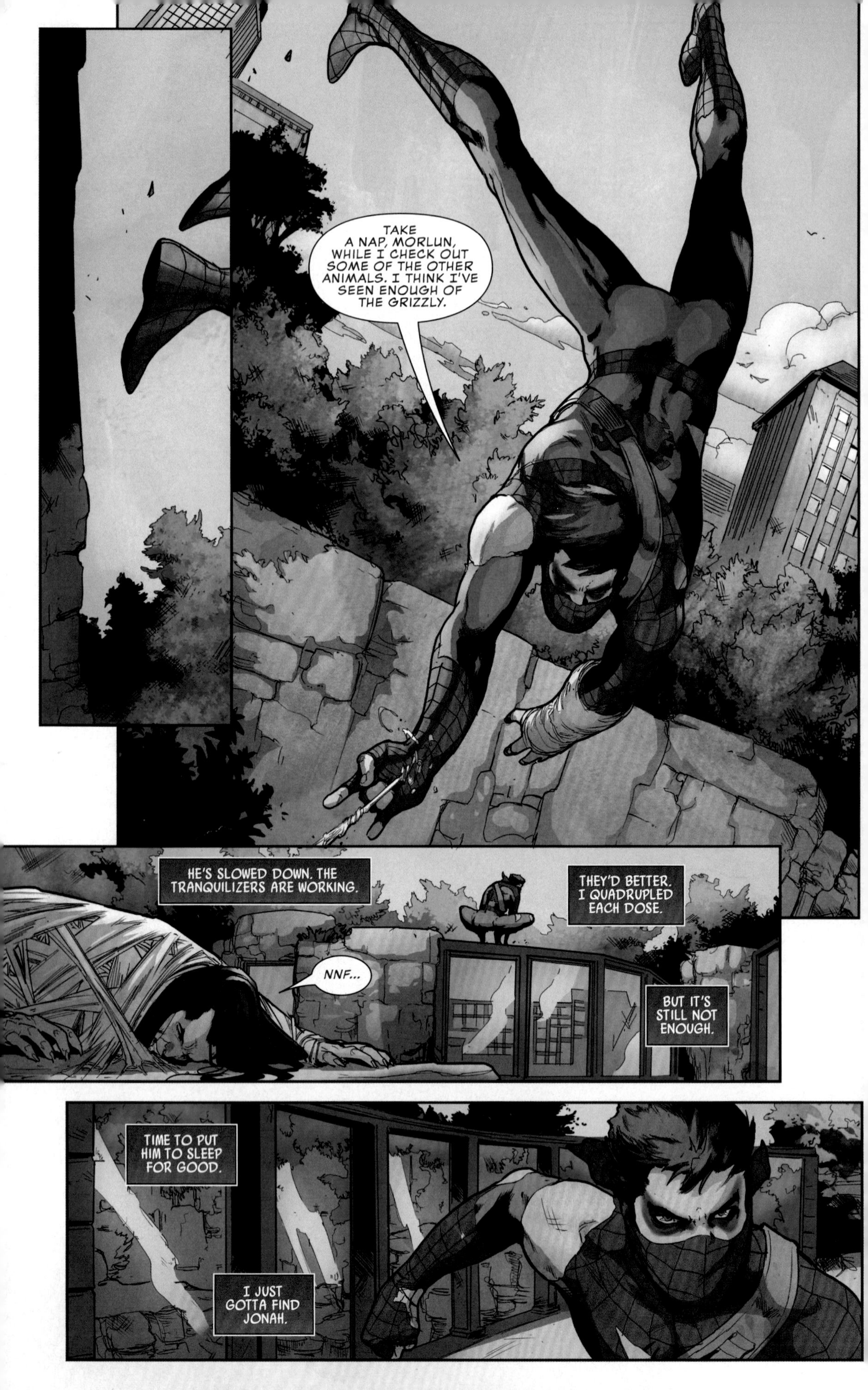
TAKE A NAP, MORLUN, WHILE I CHECK OUT SOME OF THE OTHER ANIMALS. I THINK I'VE SEEN ENOUGH OF THE GRIZZLY.
HE'S SLOWED DOWN. THE TRANQUILIZERS ARE WORKING.
NNF...
THEY'D BETTER. I QUADRUPLED EACH DOSE.
BUT IT'S STILL NOT ENOUGH.
TIME TO PUT HIM TO SLEEP FOR GOOD.
I JUST GOTTA FIND JONAH.

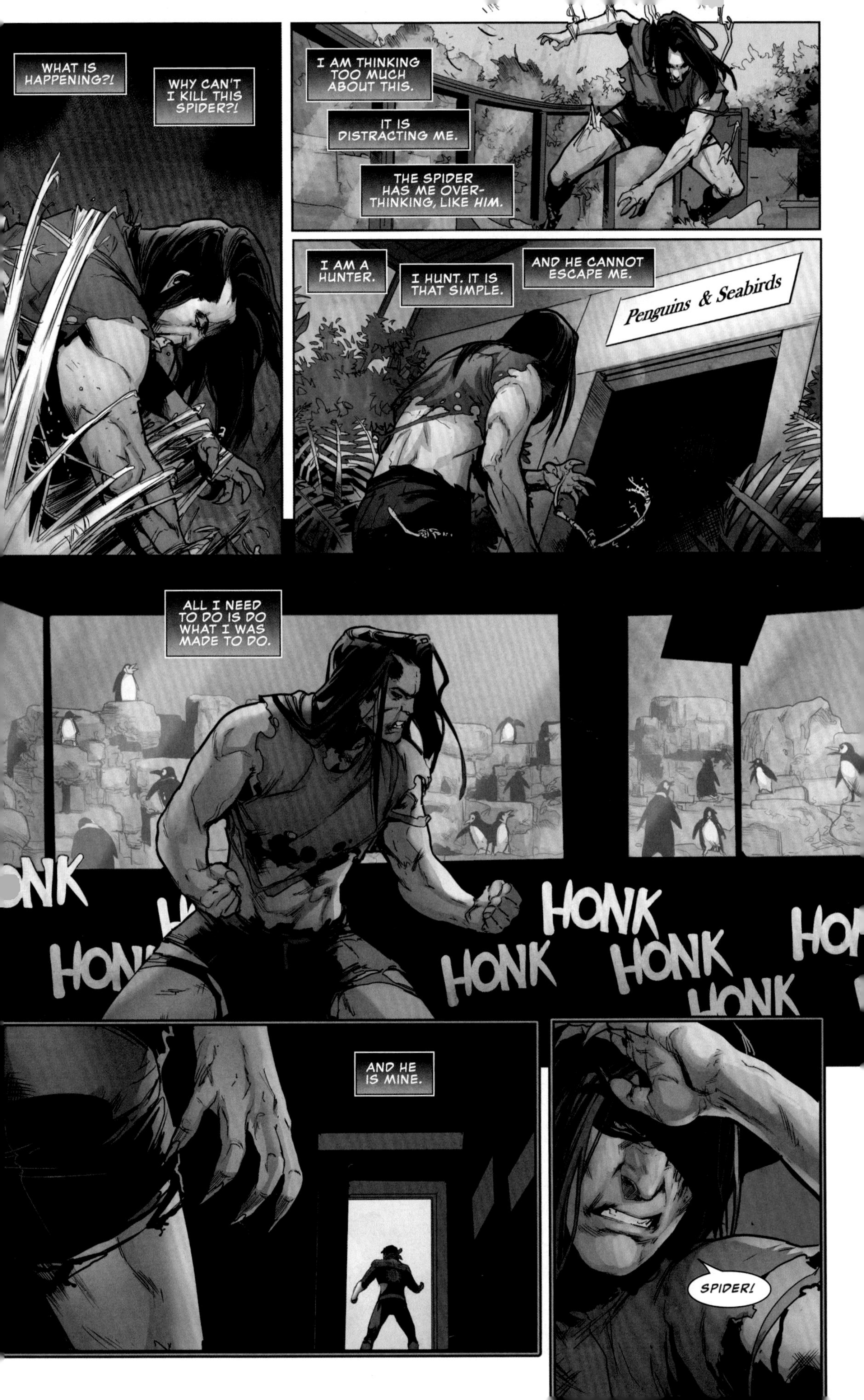

WHAT IS HAPPENING?!
WHY CAN'T I KILL THIS SPIDER?!
I AM THINKING TOO MUCH ABOUT THIS.
IT IS DISTRACTING ME.
THE SPIDER HAS ME OVER-THINKING, LIKE HIM.
I AM A HUNTER.
I HUNT. IT IS THAT SIMPLE.
AND HE CANNOT ESCAPE ME.
Penguins & Seabirds
ALL I NEED TO DO IS DO WHAT I WAS MADE TO DO.
HONK
HONK
HONK
HONK
HONK
AND HE IS MINE.
SPIDER!

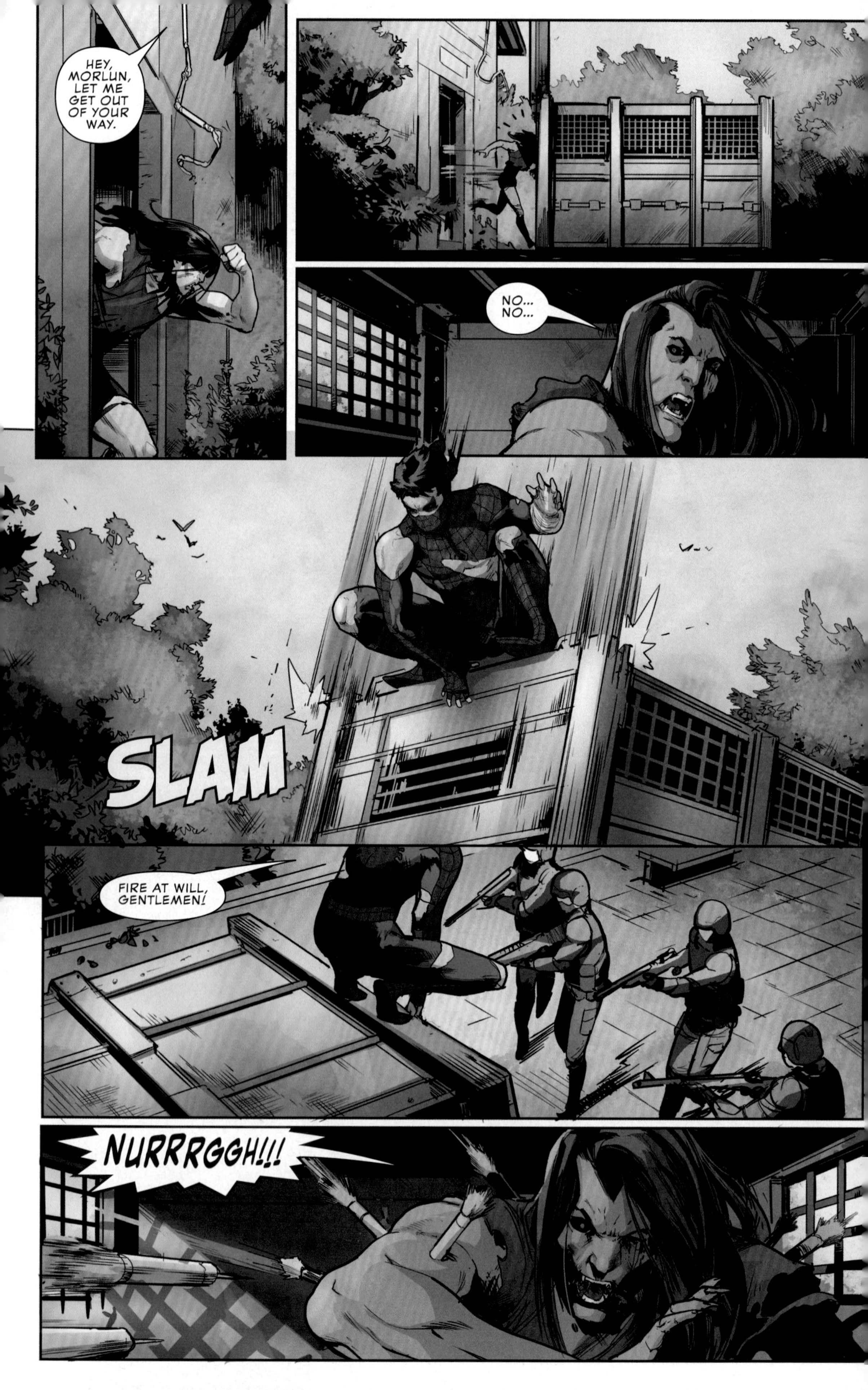
HEY, MORLUN, LET ME GET OUT OF YOUR WAY.
NO... NO...
SLAM
FIRE AT WILL, GENTLEMEN!
NURRRGGH!!!

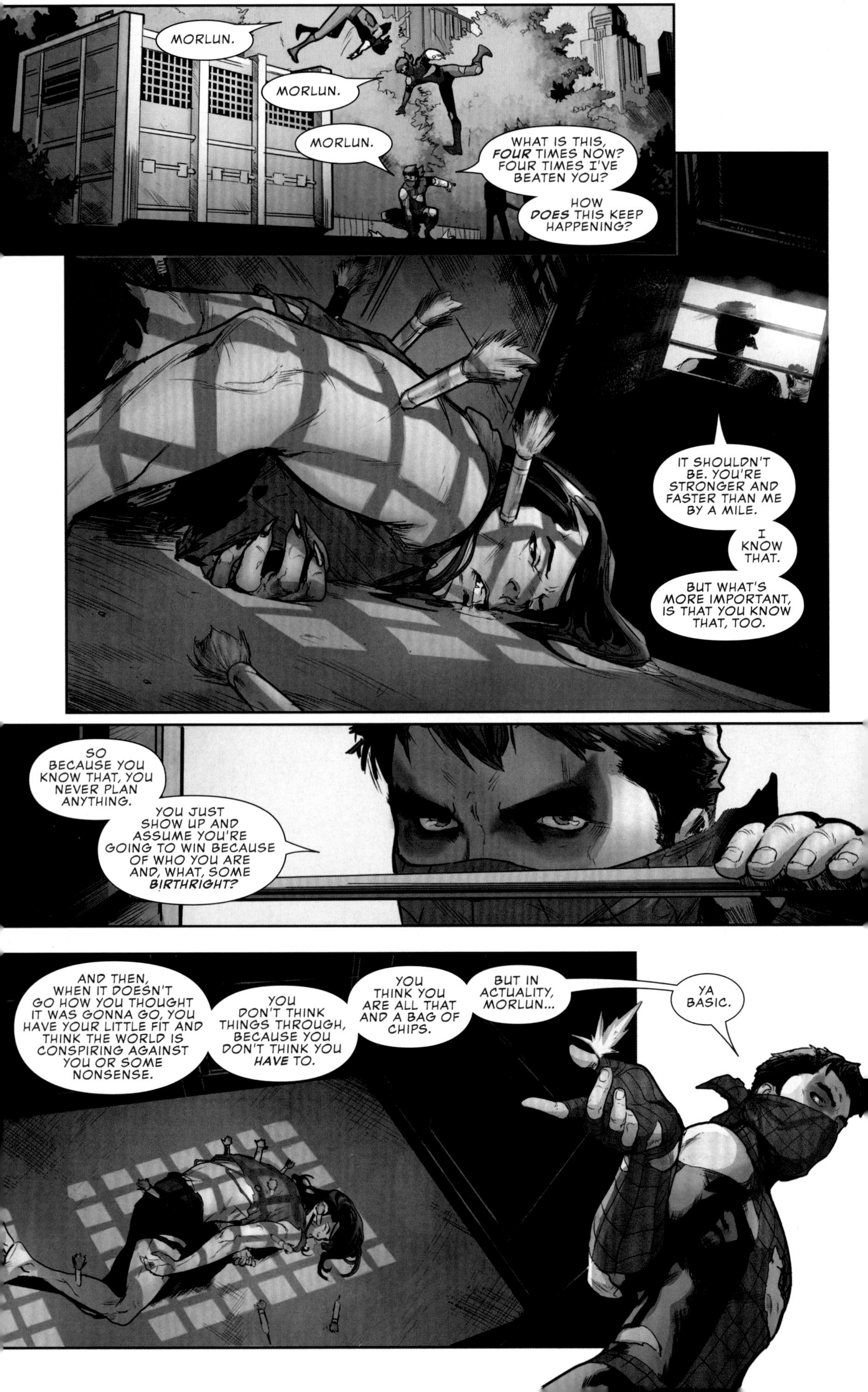
MORLUN.
MORLUN.
MORLUN.
WHAT IS THIS, FOUR TIMES NOW? FOUR TIMES I'VE BEATEN YOU?
HOW DOES THIS KEEP HAPPENING?
IT SHOULDN'T BE. YOU'RE STRONGER AND FASTER THAN ME BY A MILE.
I KNOW THAT.
BUT WHAT'S MORE IMPORTANT, IS THAT YOU KNOW THAT, TOO.
SO BECAUSE YOU KNOW THAT, YOU NEVER PLAN ANYTHING.
YOU JUST SHOW UP AND ASSUME YOU'RE GOING TO WIN BECAUSE OF WHO YOU ARE AND, WHAT, SOME BIRTHRIGHT?
AND THEN, WHEN IT DOESN'T GO HOW YOU THOUGHT IT WAS GONNA GO, YOU HAVE YOUR LITTLE FIT AND THINK THE WORLD IS CONSPIRING AGAINST YOU OR SOME NONSENSE.
YOU DON'T THINK THINGS THROUGH, BECAUSE YOU DON'T THINK YOU HAVE TO.
YOU THINK YOU ARE ALL THAT AND A BAG OF CHIPS.
BUT IN ACTUALITY, MORLUN...
YA BASIC.

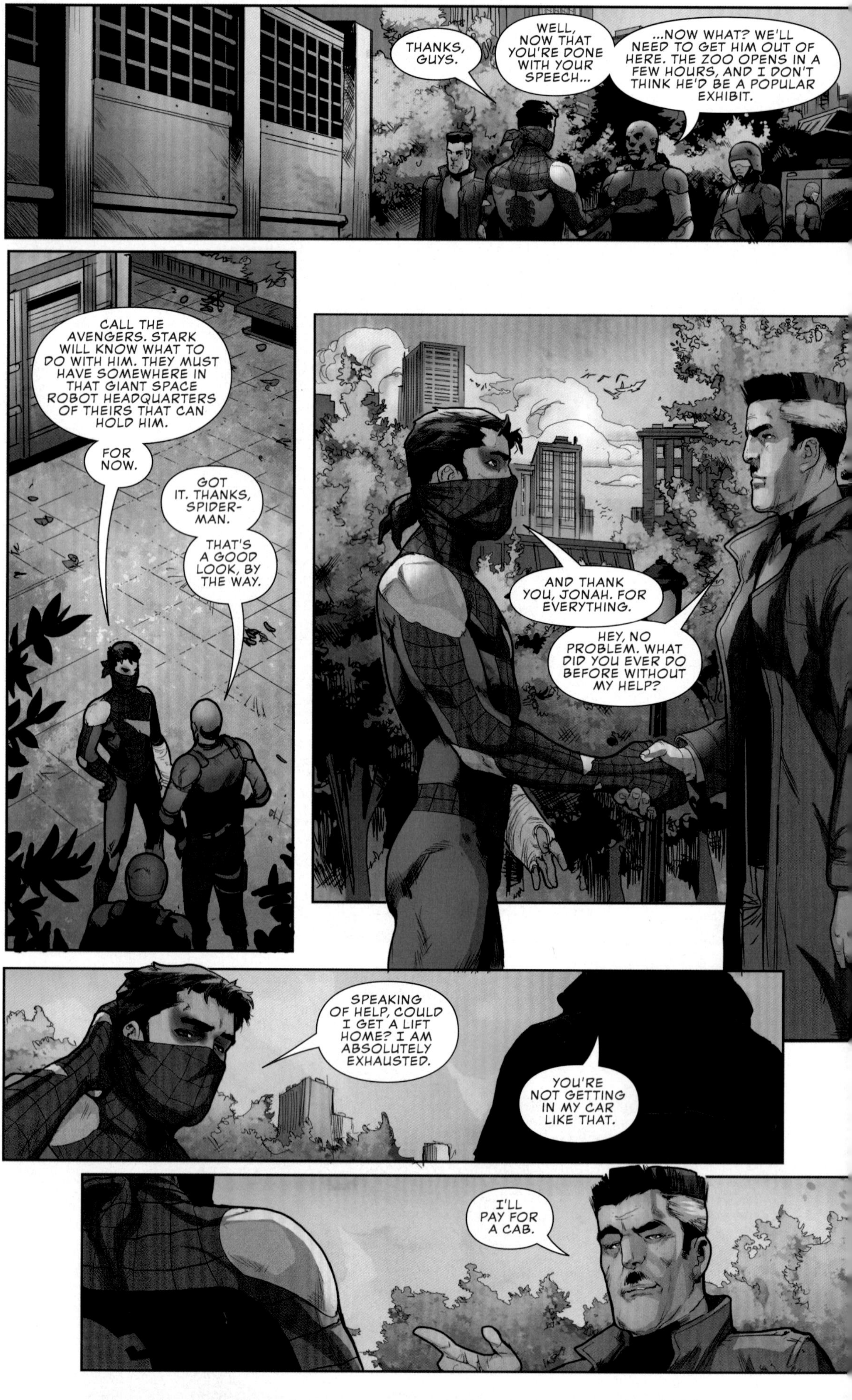
THANKS, GUYS.
WELL, NOW THAT YOU'RE DONE WITH YOUR SPEECH...
...NOW WHAT? WE'LL NEED TO GET HIM OUT OF HERE. THE ZOO OPENS IN A FEW HOURS, AND I DON'T THINK HE'D BE A POPULAR EXHIBIT.
CALL THE AVENGERS. STARK WILL KNOW WHAT TO DO WITH HIM. THEY MUST HAVE SOMEWHERE IN THAT GIANT SPACE ROBOT HEADQUARTERS OF THEIRS THAT CAN HOLD HIM.
FOR NOW.
GOT IT. THANKS, SPIDER-MAN.
THAT'S A GOOD LOOK, BY THE WAY.
AND THANK YOU, JONAH. FOR EVERYTHING.
HEY, NO PROBLEM. WHAT DID YOU EVER DO BEFORE WITHOUT MY HELP?
SPEAKING OF HELP, COULD I GET A LIFT HOME? I AM ABSOLUTELY EXHAUSTED.
YOU'RE NOT GETTING IN MY CAR LIKE THAT.
I'LL PAY FOR A CAB.

HEAVENLY RECTANGLE.

BOX OF SPRINGS UNDERNEATH A MATTRESS OF DREAMS.

I FALL INTO YOUR EMBRACE.

AND YOU WELCOME ME WITHOUT QUESTION.

I FEEL YOUR WARMTH BEFORE WE EVEN TOUCH.

AND INSTANTLY, MY PAIN, MY AGONY, MY WOE ALL WASH AWAY.

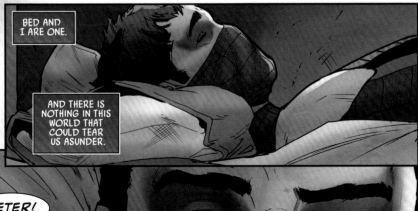

BED AND I ARE ONE.

AND THERE IS NOTHING IN THIS WORLD THAT COULD TEAR US ASUNDER.

PETER!

SON OF A BUCKET.

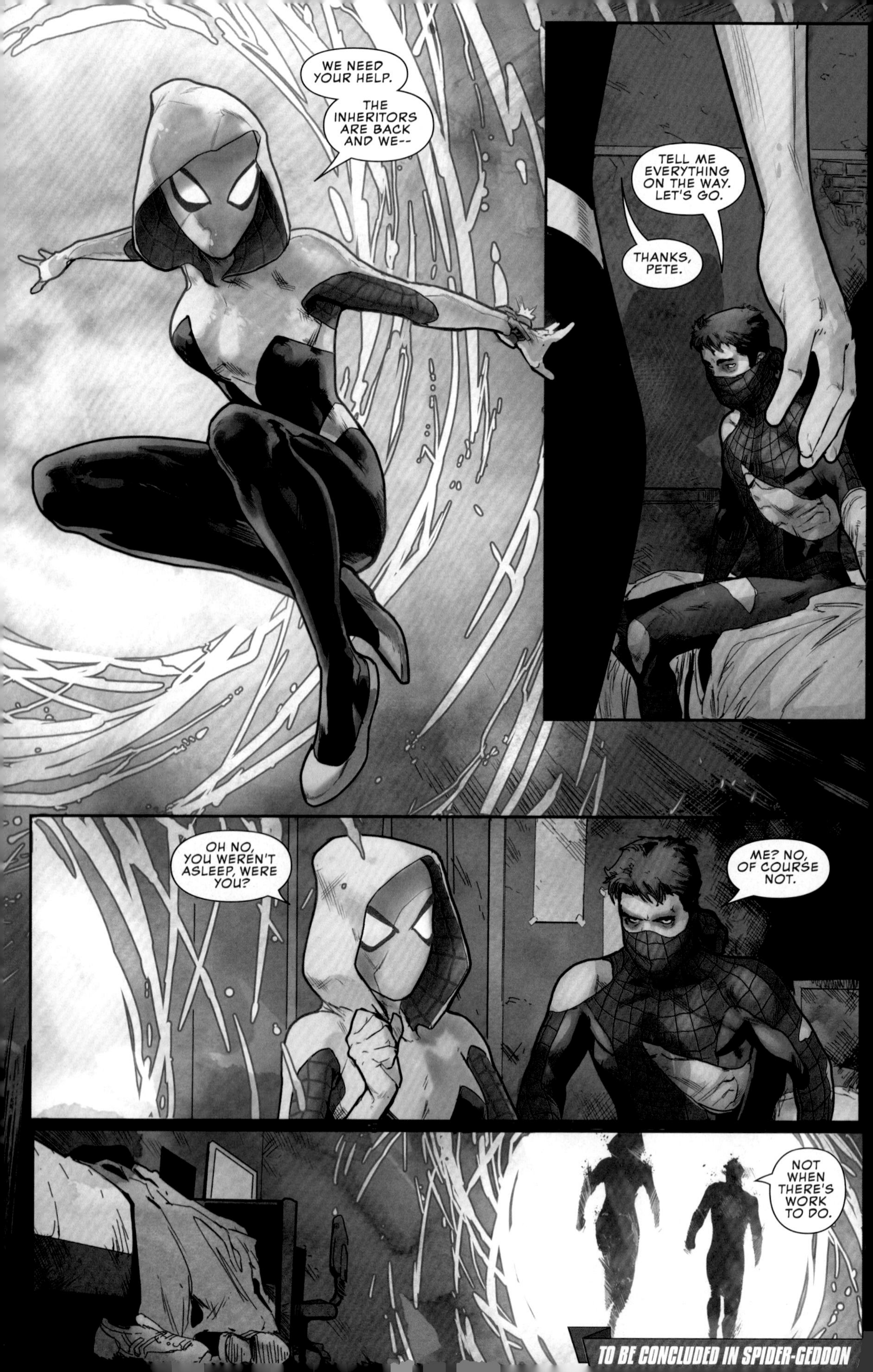
WE NEED YOUR HELP.
THE INHERITORS ARE BACK AND WE--
TELL ME EVERYTHING ON THE WAY. LET'S GO.
THANKS, PETE.
OH NO, YOU WEREN'T ASLEEP, WERE YOU?
ME? NO, OF COURSE NOT.
NOT WHEN THERE'S WORK TO DO.
TO BE CONCLUDED IN SPIDER-GEDDON

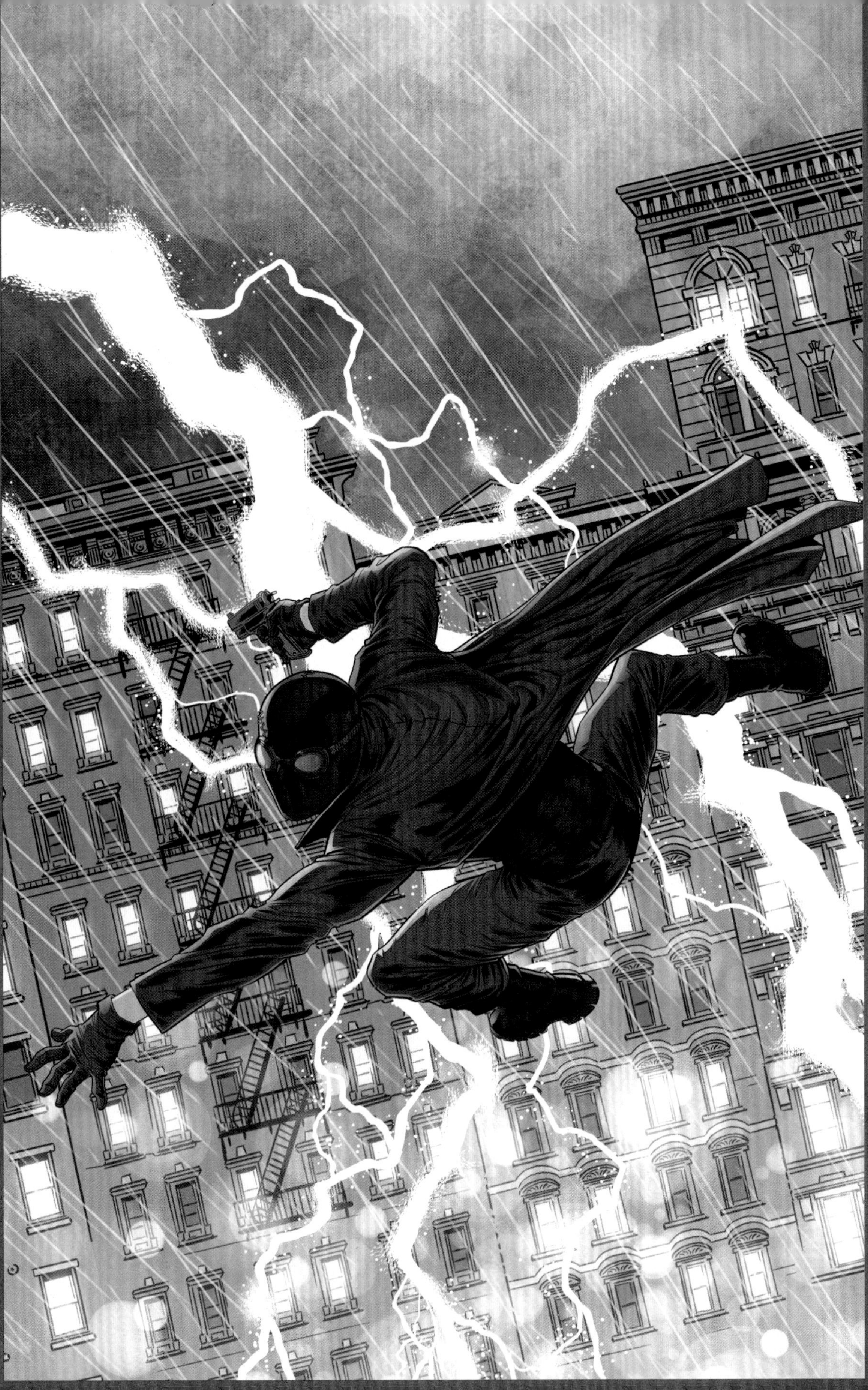

SPIDER-GEDDON: NOIR VIDEO COMIC

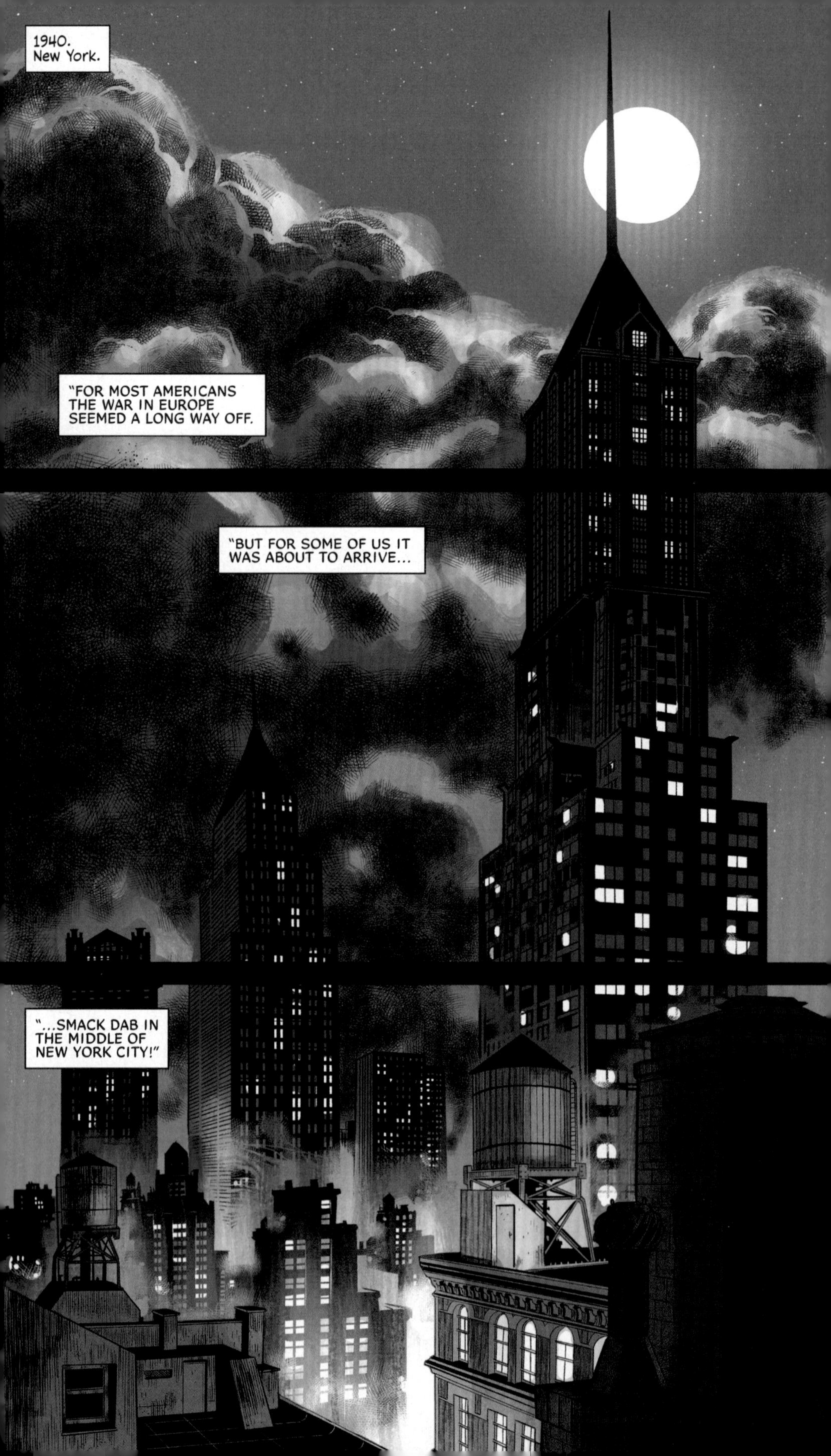
1940.
New York.
"FOR MOST AMERICANS THE WAR IN EUROPE SEEMED A LONG WAY OFF.
"BUT FOR SOME OF US IT WAS ABOUT TO ARRIVE...
"...SMACK DAB IN THE MIDDLE OF NEW YORK CITY!"

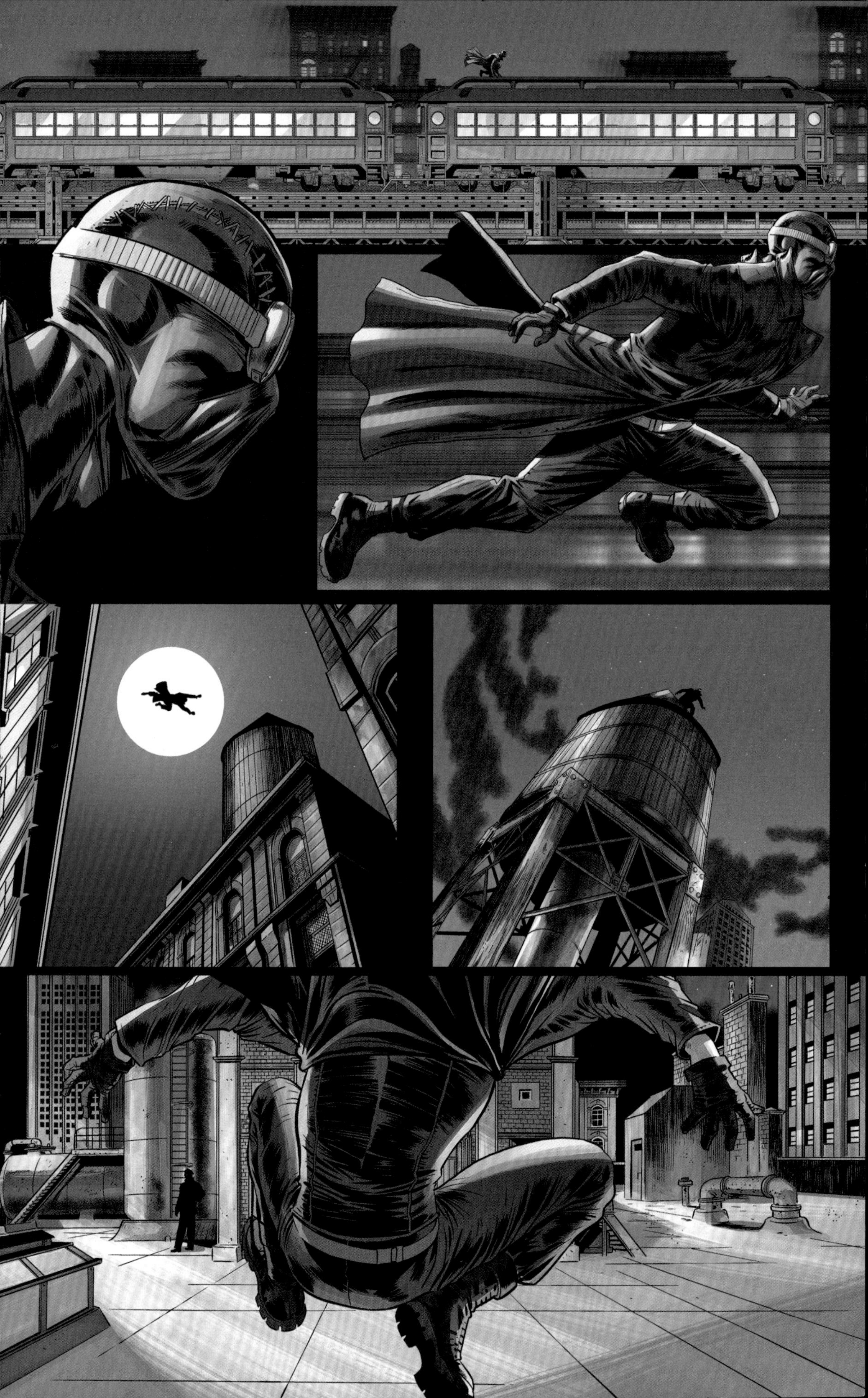

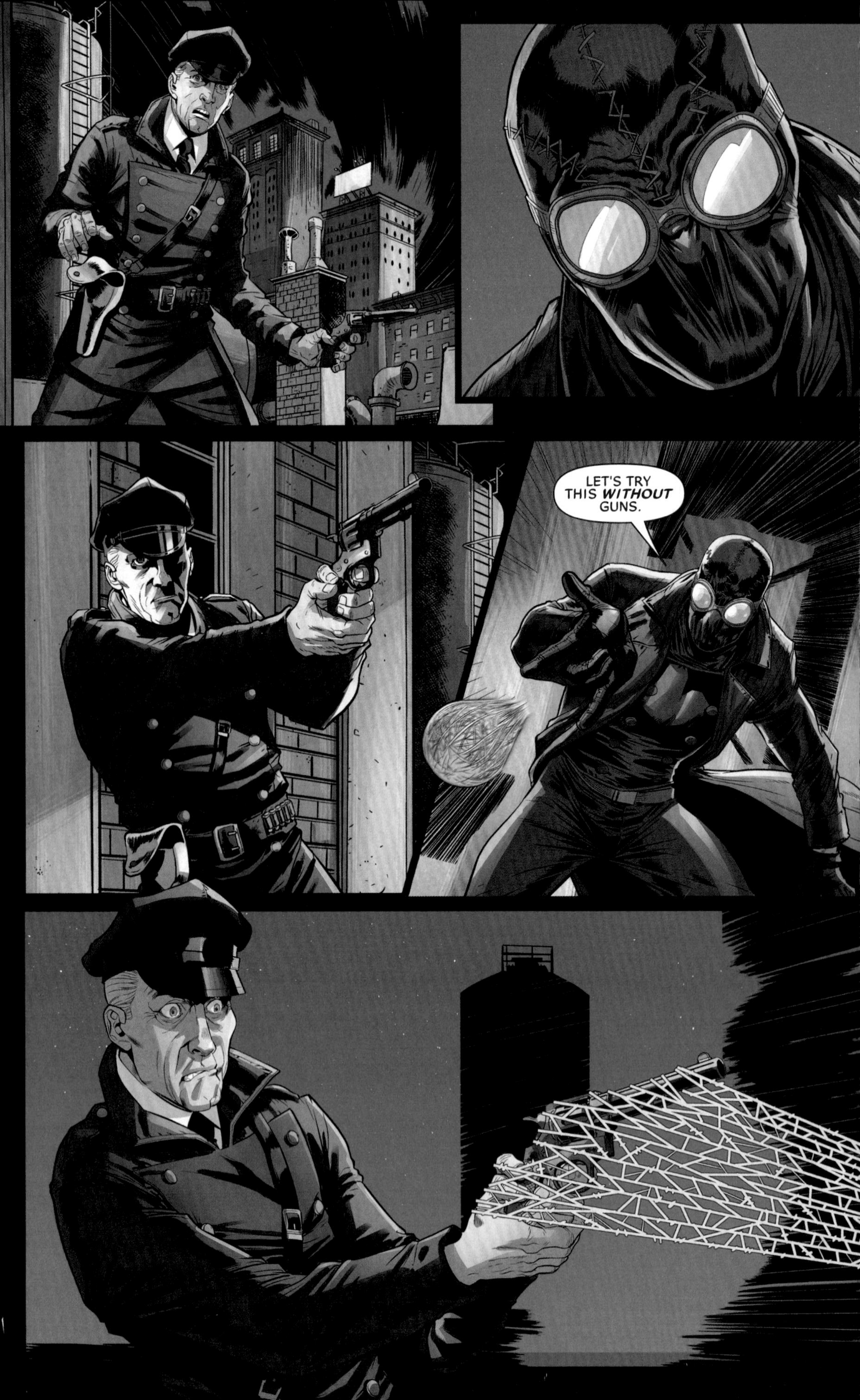
LET'S TRY THIS *WITHOUT* GUNS.

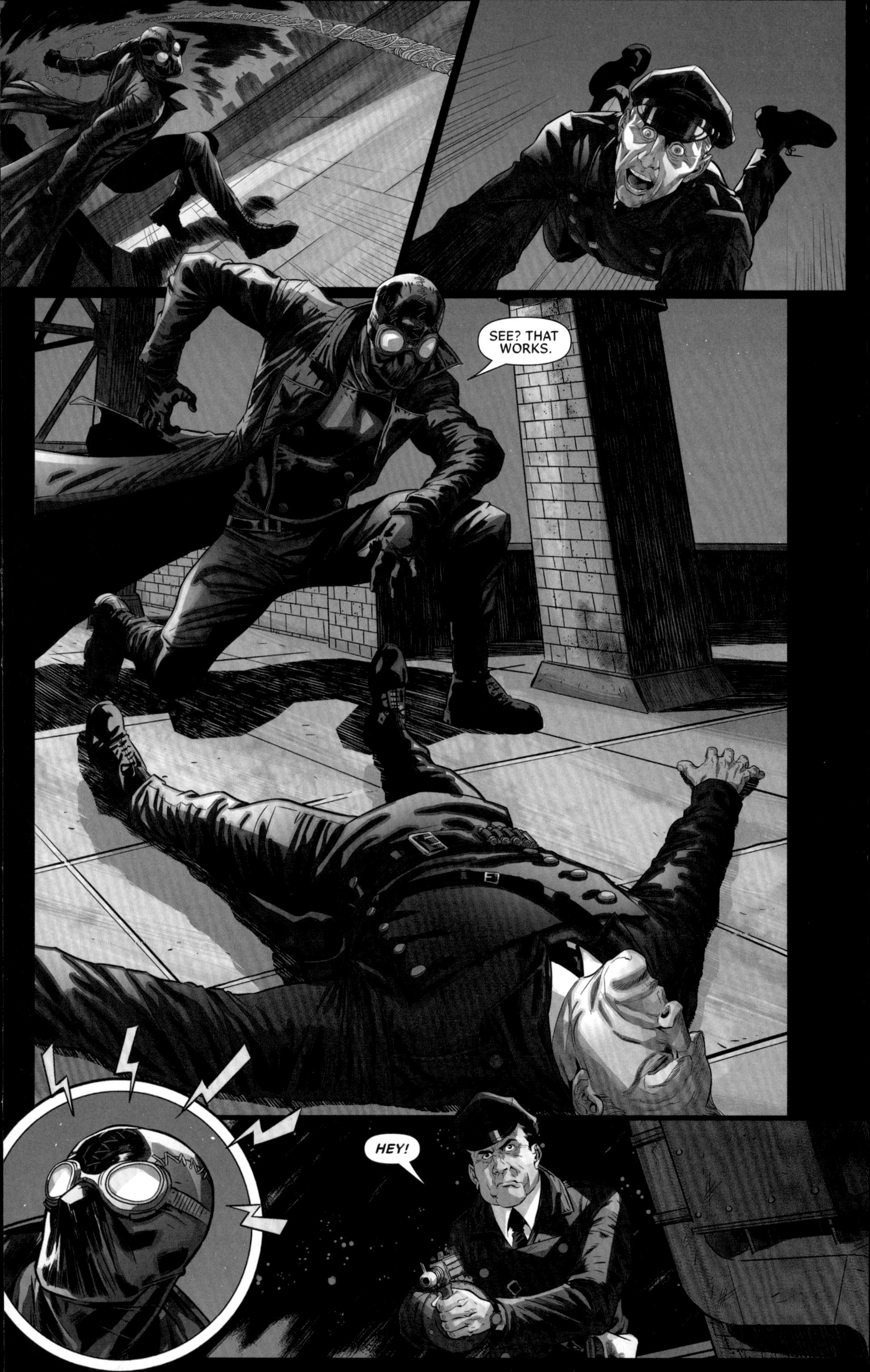

SEE? THAT WORKS.
HEY!

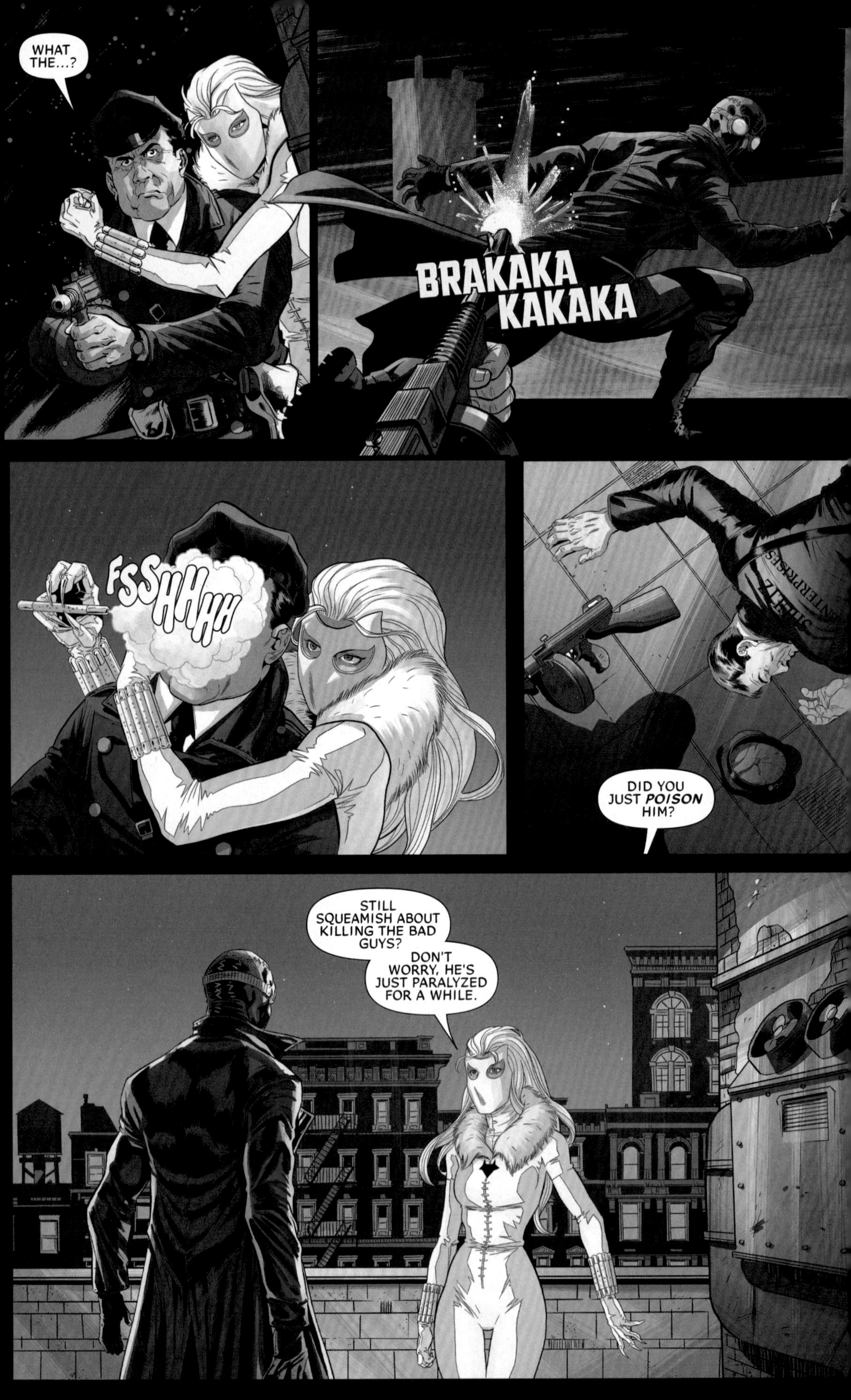

WHAT THE...?
BRAKAKA KAKAKA
FSSHHHH
DID YOU JUST *POISON* HIM?
STILL SQUEAMISH ABOUT KILLING THE BAD GUYS?
DON'T WORRY, HE'S JUST PARALYZED FOR A WHILE.

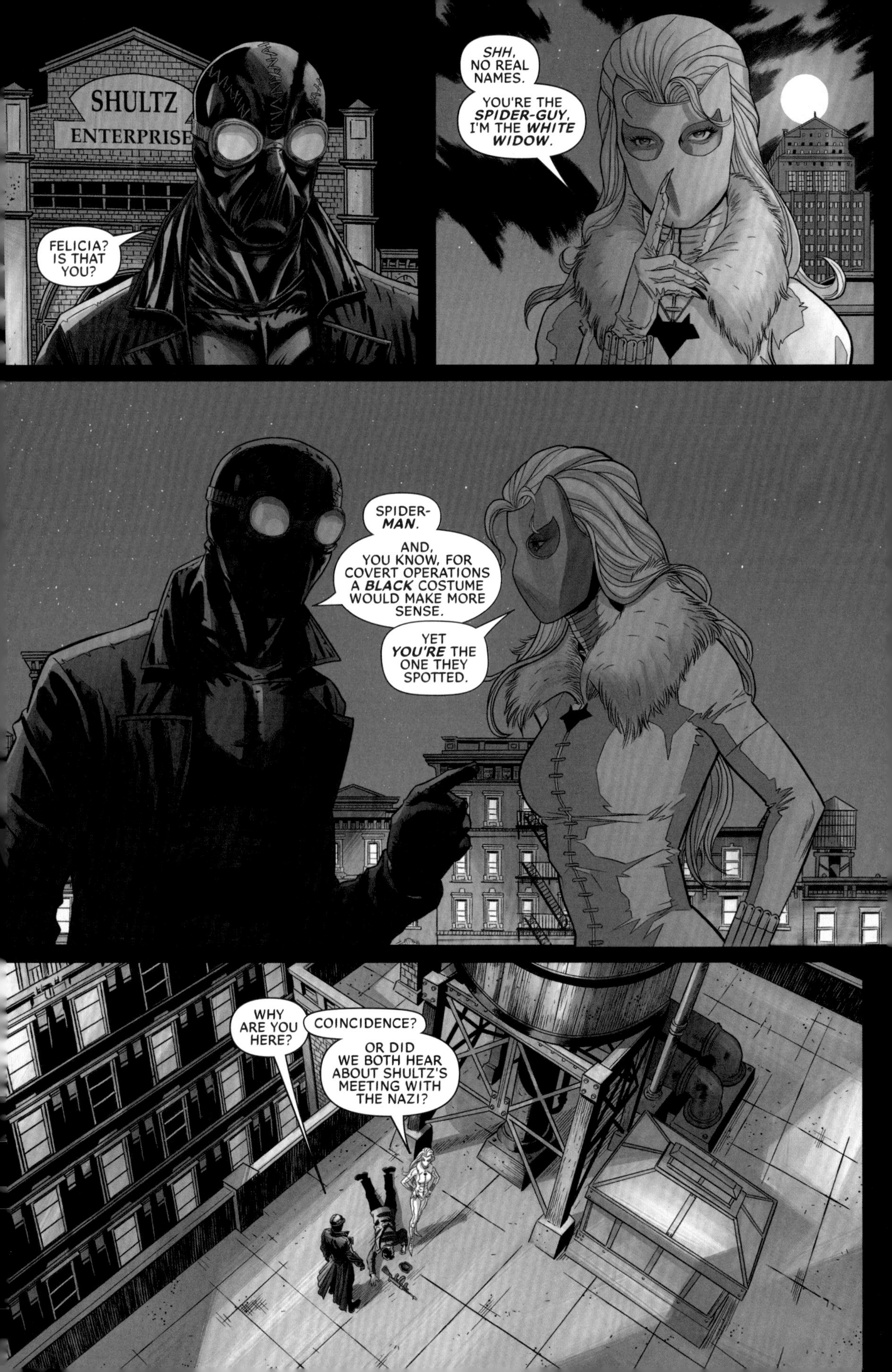
SHULTZ
ENTERPRISE
FELICIA? IS THAT YOU?
SHH, NO REAL NAMES.
YOU'RE THE SPIDER-GUY, I'M THE WHITE WIDOW.
SPIDER-MAN.
AND, YOU KNOW, FOR COVERT OPERATIONS A BLACK COSTUME WOULD MAKE MORE SENSE.
YET YOU'RE THE ONE THEY SPOTTED.
WHY ARE YOU HERE?
COINCIDENCE?
OR DID WE BOTH HEAR ABOUT SHULTZ'S MEETING WITH THE NAZI?

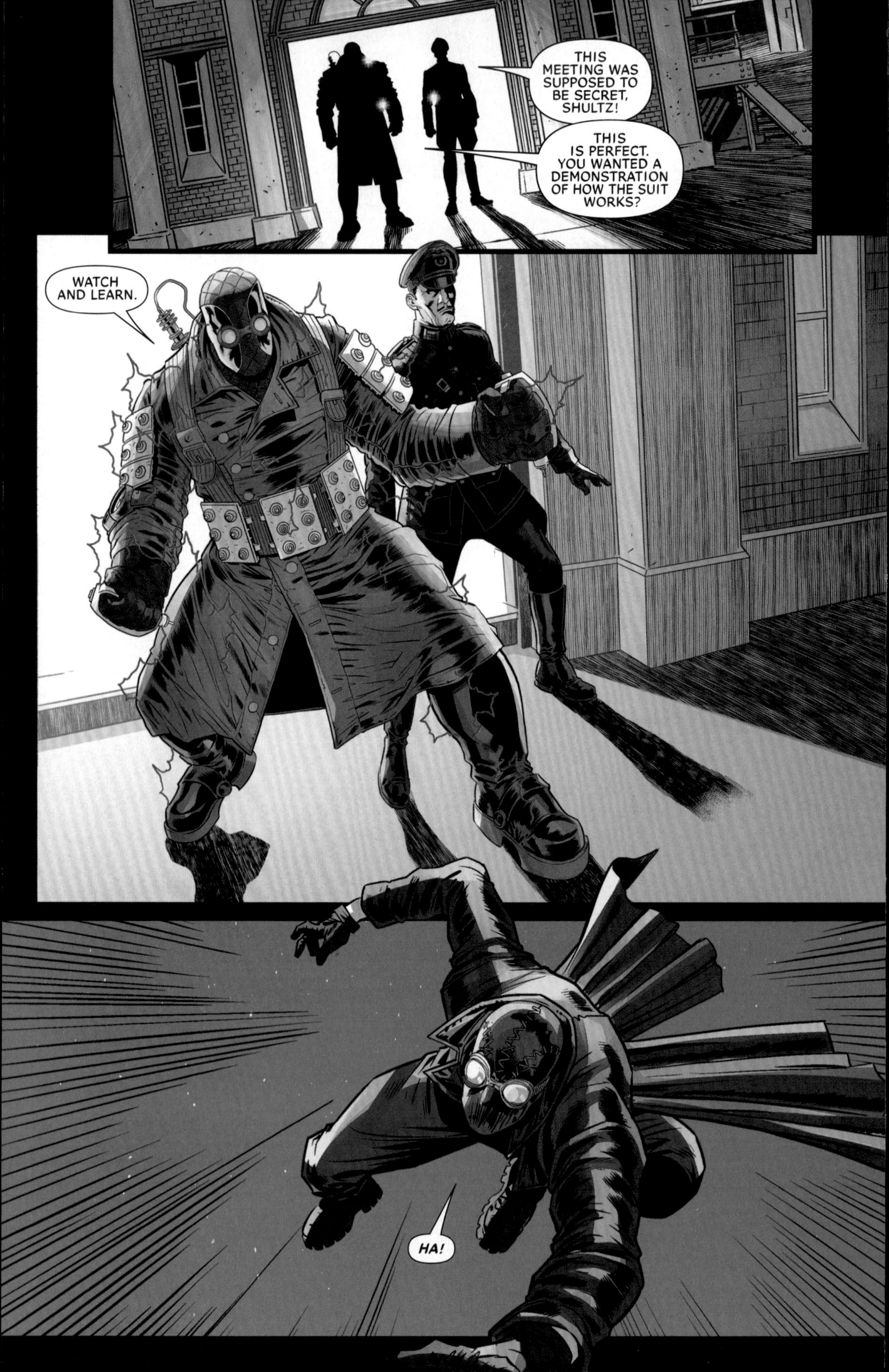
THIS MEETING WAS SUPPOSED TO BE SECRET, SHULTZ!
THIS IS PERFECT. YOU WANTED A DEMONSTRATION OF HOW THE SUIT WORKS?
WATCH AND LEARN.
HA!

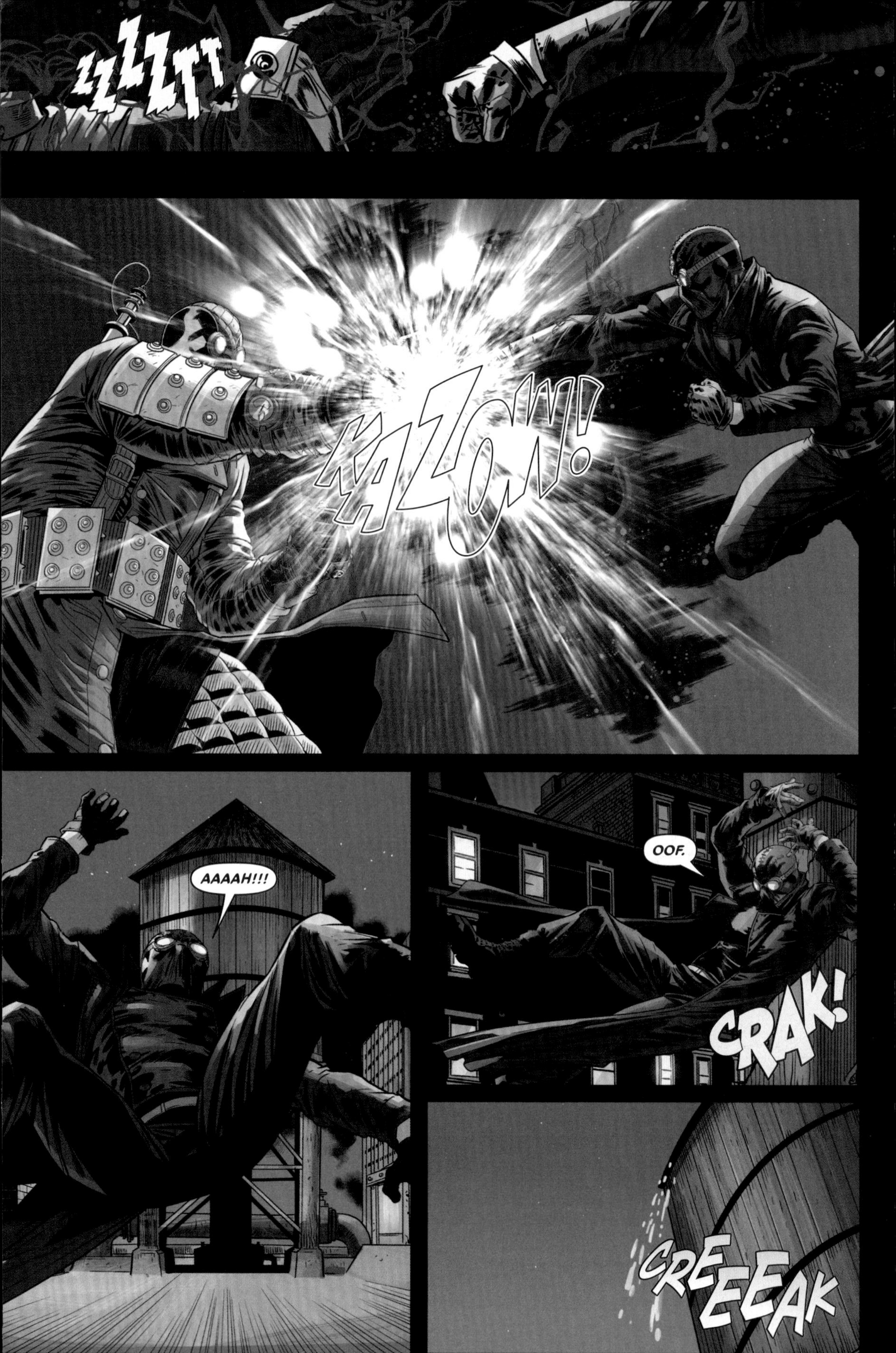
ZZZZZTT
KRAZOW!
AAAAH!!!
OOF.
CRAK!
CREEEEAK

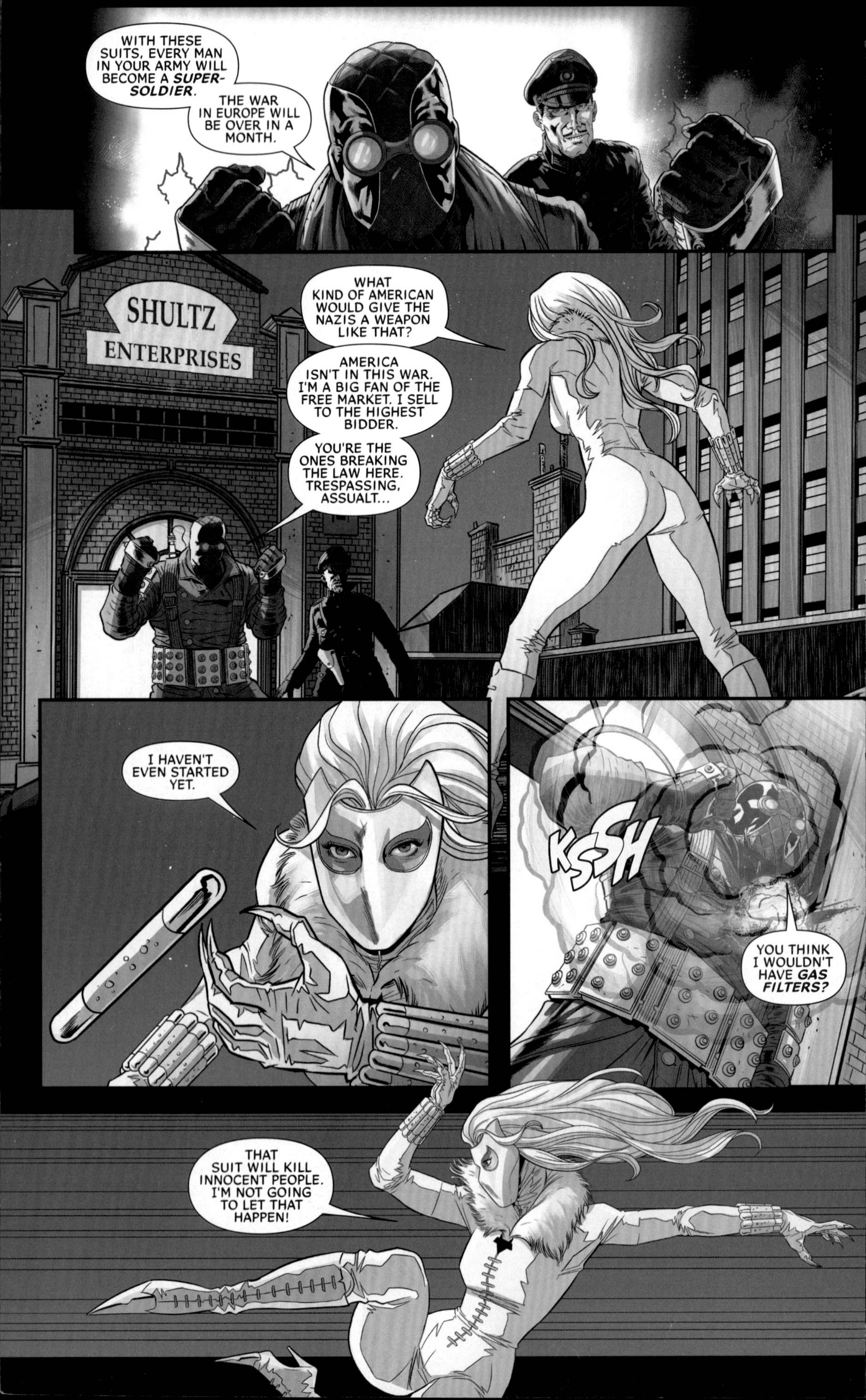
WITH THESE SUITS, EVERY MAN IN YOUR ARMY WILL BECOME A SUPER-SOLDIER.
THE WAR IN EUROPE WILL BE OVER IN A MONTH.
SHULTZ ENTERPRISES
WHAT KIND OF AMERICAN WOULD GIVE THE NAZIS A WEAPON LIKE THAT?
AMERICA ISN'T IN THIS WAR. I'M A BIG FAN OF THE FREE MARKET. I SELL TO THE HIGHEST BIDDER.
YOU'RE THE ONES BREAKING THE LAW HERE. TRESPASSING, ASSUALT...
I HAVEN'T EVEN STARTED YET.
KSSH
YOU THINK I WOULDN'T HAVE GAS FILTERS?
THAT SUIT WILL KILL INNOCENT PEOPLE. I'M NOT GOING TO LET THAT HAPPEN!

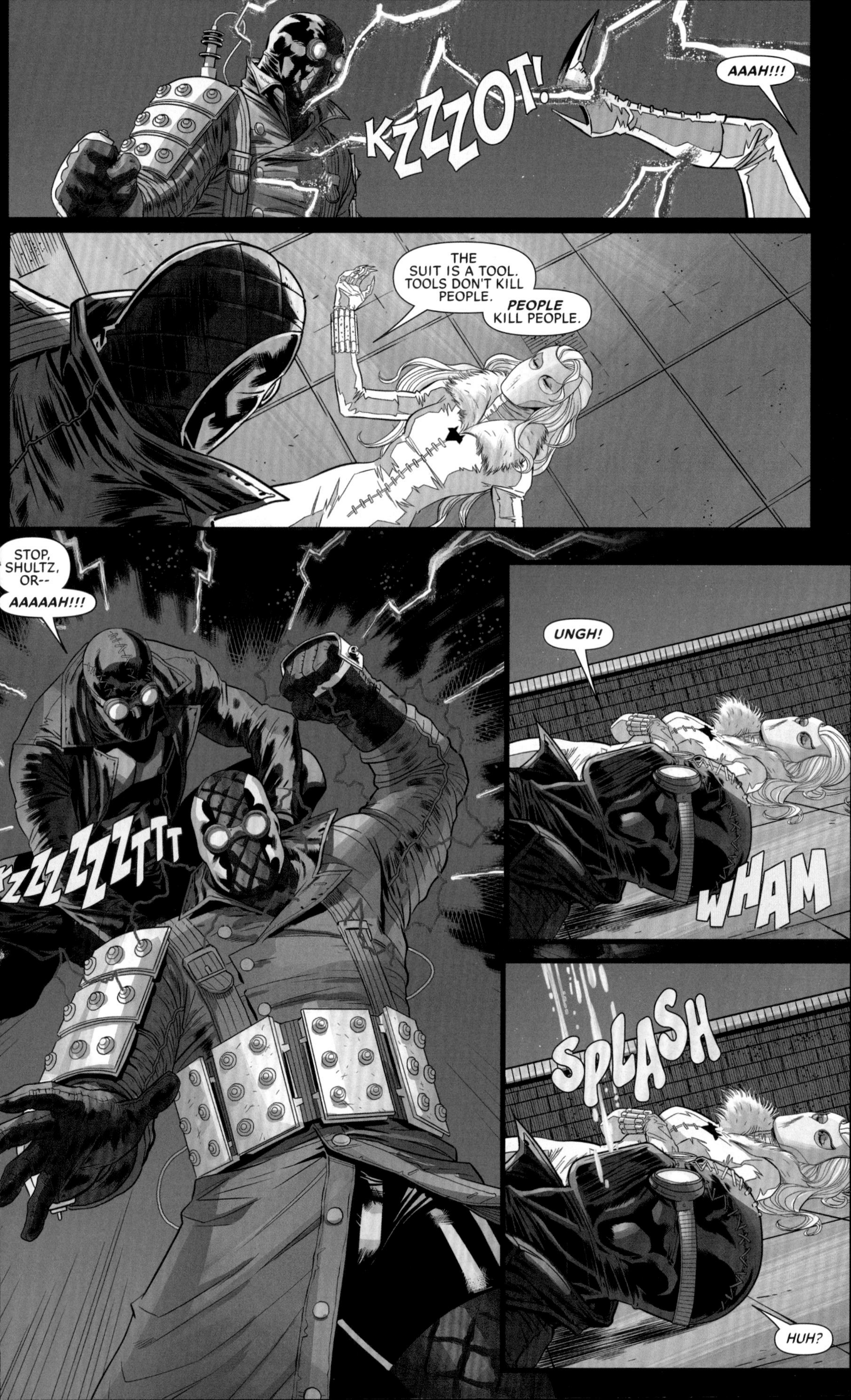
KZZZOT!
AAAH!!!
THE SUIT IS A TOOL. TOOLS DON'T KILL PEOPLE. *PEOPLE* KILL PEOPLE.
STOP, SHULTZ, OR-- *AAAAAH!!!*
KZZZZZZZTTTT
UNGH!
WHAM
SPLASH
HUH?

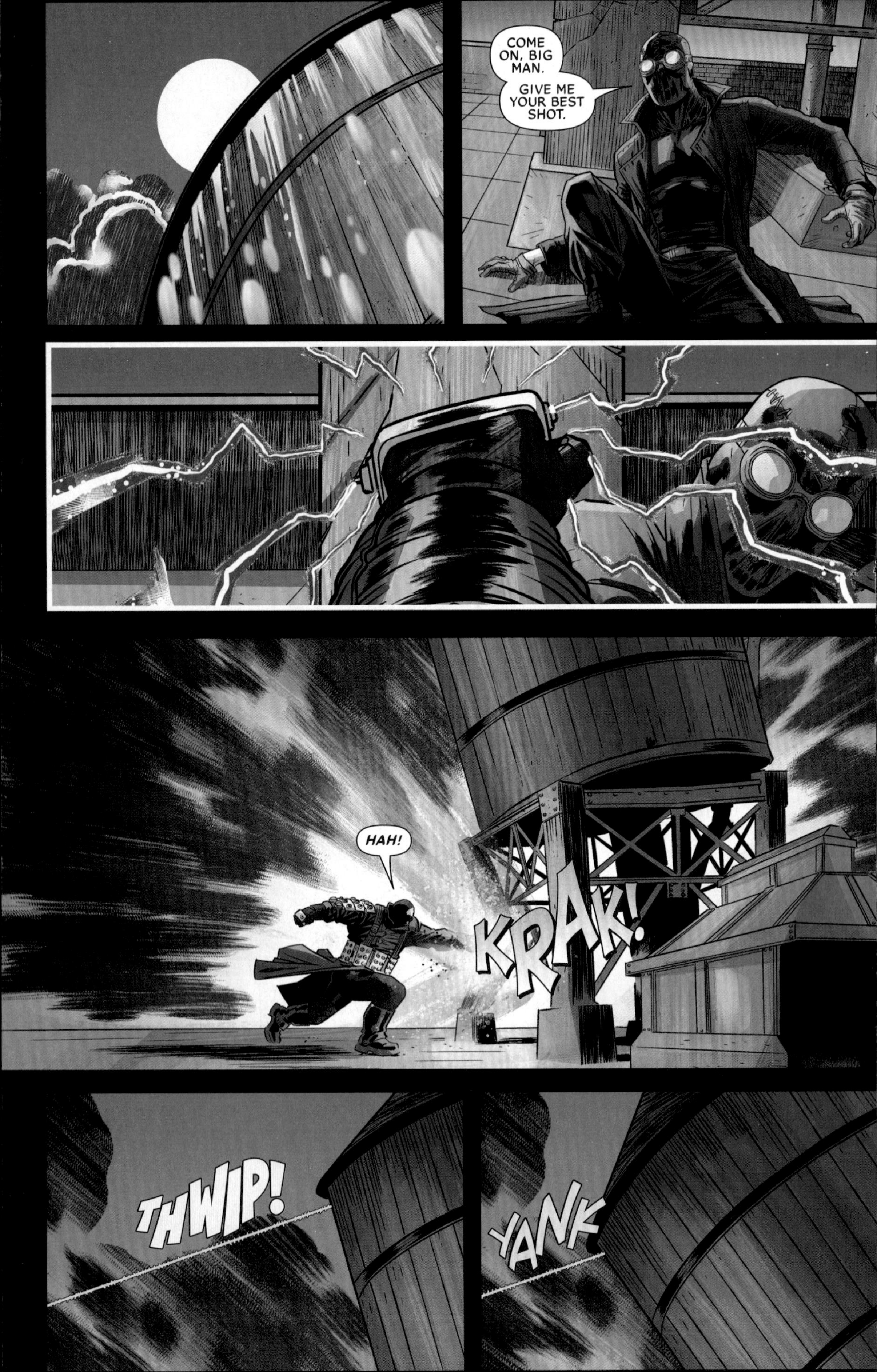
COME ON, BIG MAN.
GIVE ME YOUR BEST SHOT.
HAH!
KRAK!
THWIP!
YANK

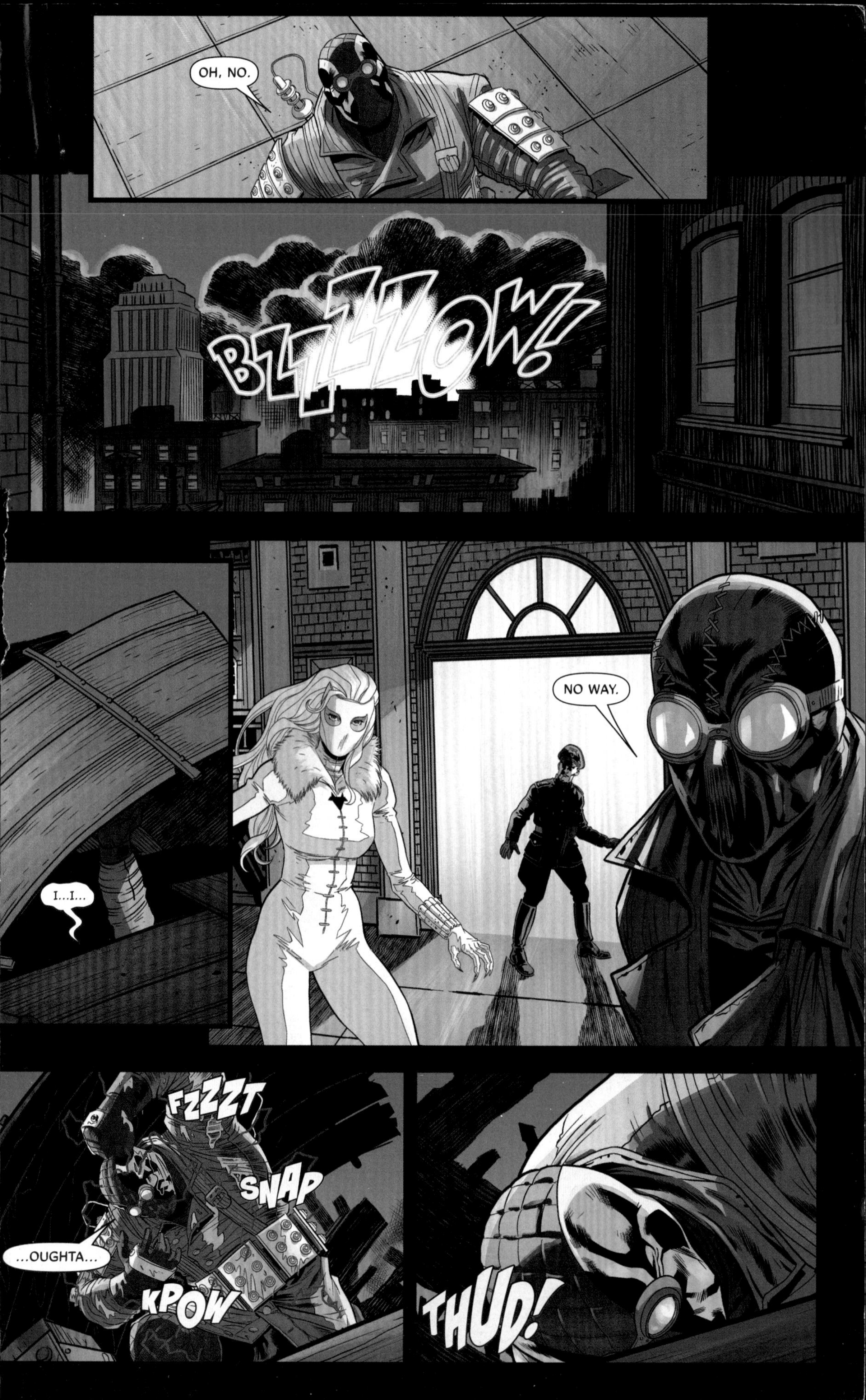
OH, NO.
BZZZZOW!
I...I...
NO WAY.
FZZZT
SNAP
...OUGHTA...
KPOW
THUD!

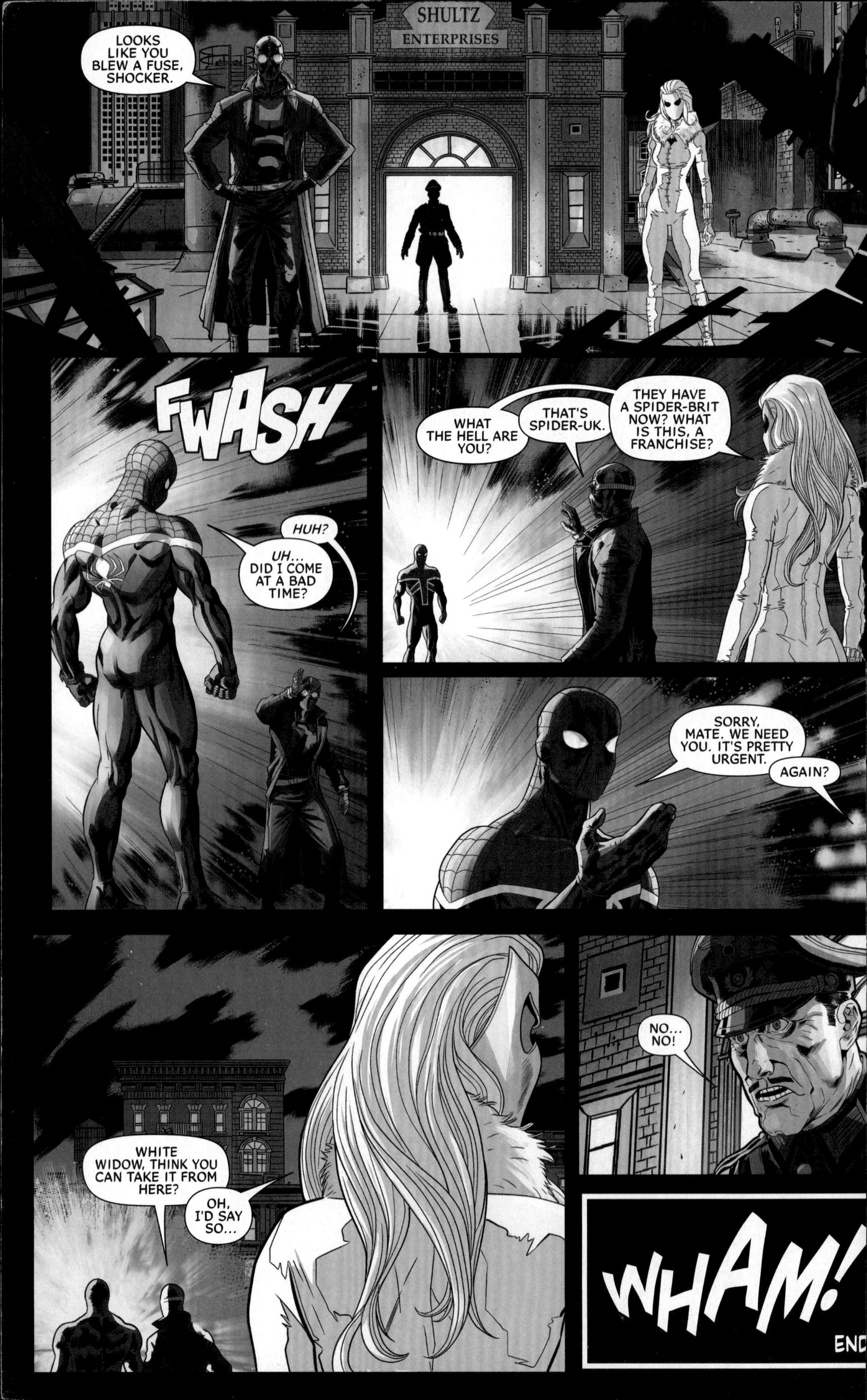
SHULTZ ENTERPRISES
LOOKS LIKE YOU BLEW A FUSE, SHOCKER.
FWASH
HUH?
UH... DID I COME AT A BAD TIME?
WHAT THE HELL ARE YOU?
THAT'S SPIDER-UK.
THEY HAVE A SPIDER-BRIT NOW? WHAT IS THIS, A FRANCHISE?
SORRY, MATE. WE NEED YOU. IT'S PRETTY URGENT.
AGAIN?
WHITE WIDOW, THINK YOU CAN TAKE IT FROM HERE?
OH, I'D SAY SO...
NO... NO!
WHAM!
END

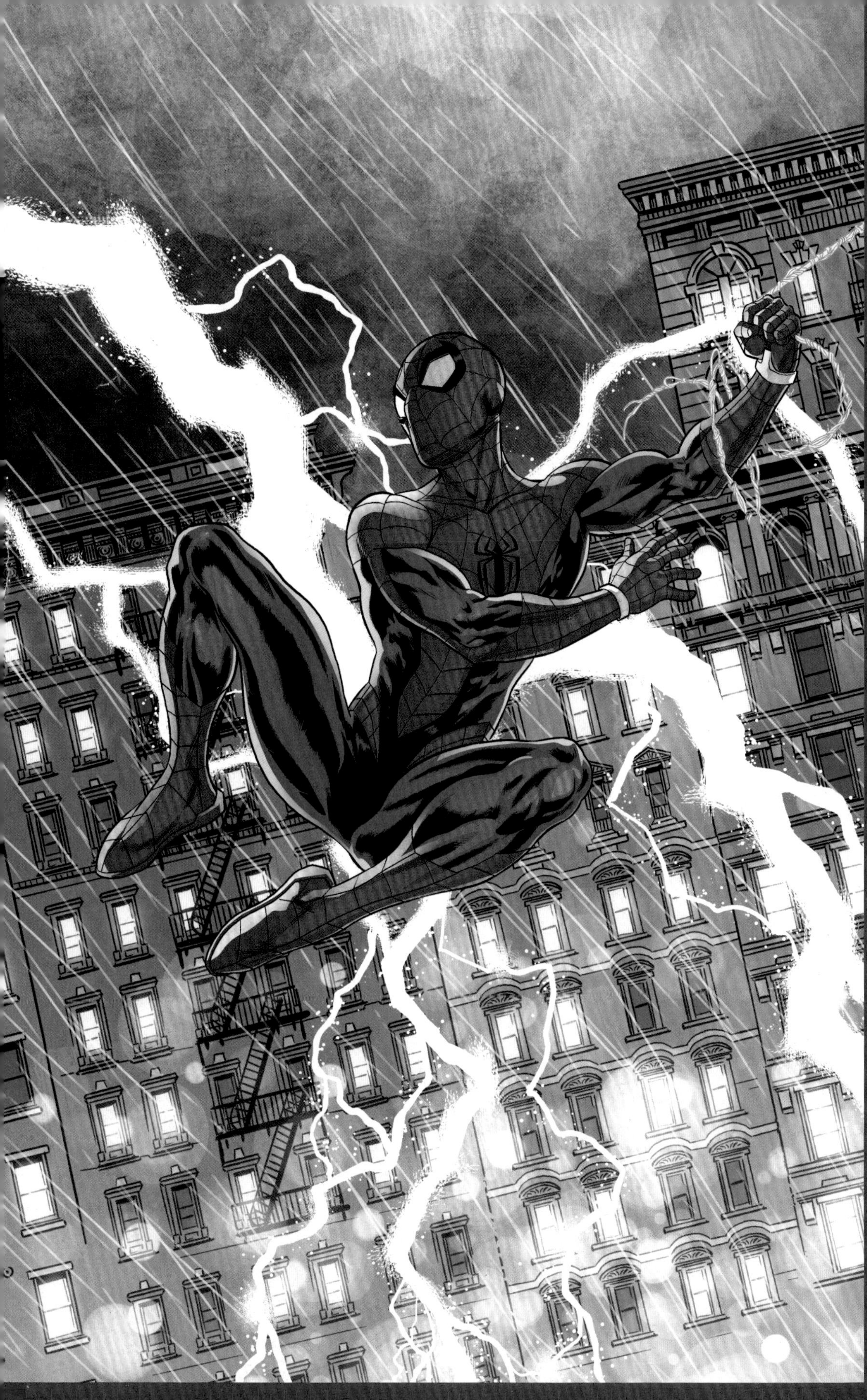

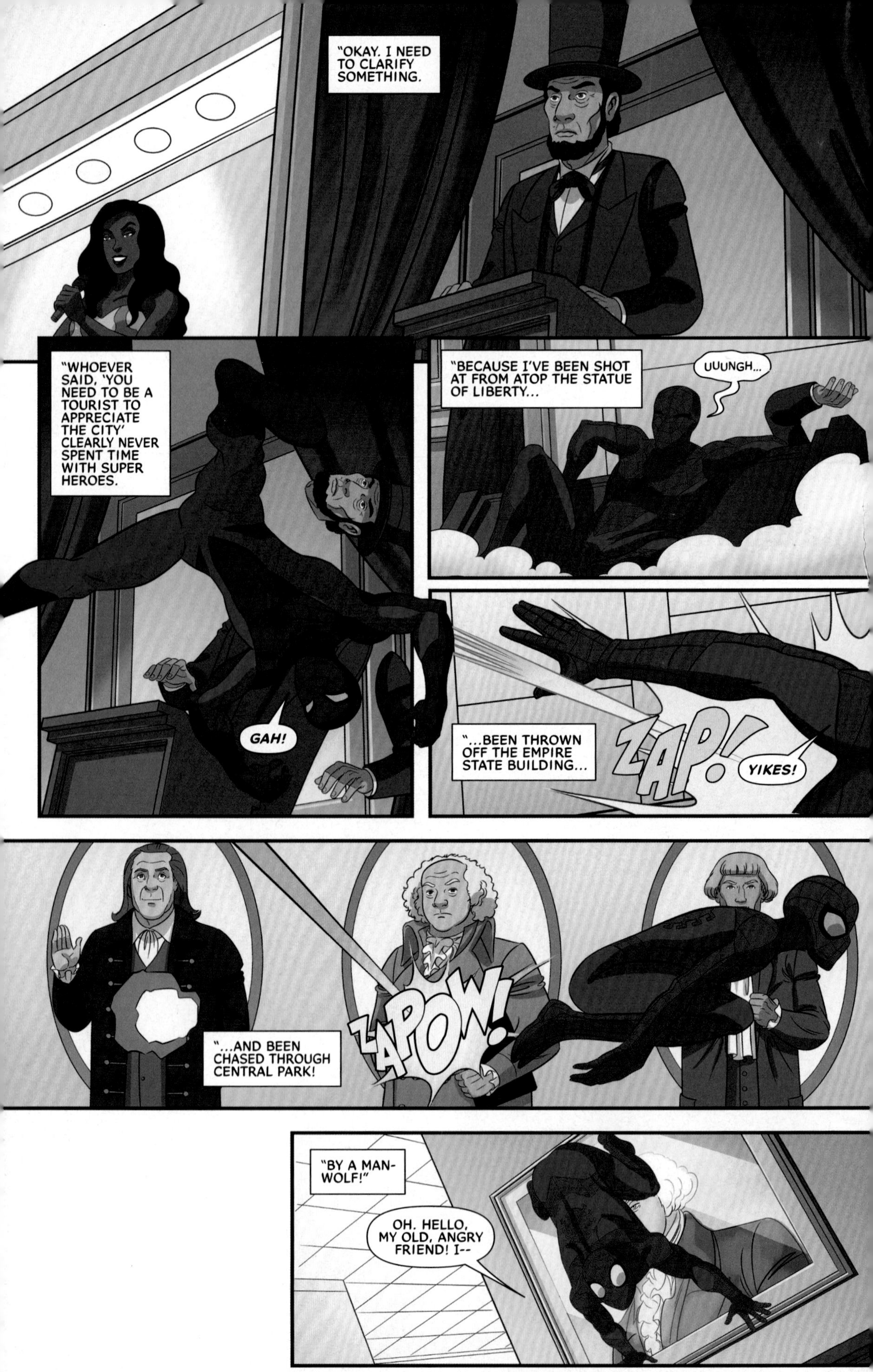
"OKAY. I NEED TO CLARIFY SOMETHING.
"WHOEVER SAID, 'YOU NEED TO BE A TOURIST TO APPRECIATE THE CITY' CLEARLY NEVER SPENT TIME WITH SUPER HEROES.
GAH!
"BECAUSE I'VE BEEN SHOT AT FROM ATOP THE STATUE OF LIBERTY...
UUUNGH...
"...BEEN THROWN OFF THE EMPIRE STATE BUILDING...
ZAP!
YIKES!
"...AND BEEN CHASED THROUGH CENTRAL PARK!
ZAPOW!
"BY A MAN-WOLF!"
OH. HELLO, MY OLD, ANGRY FRIEND! I--

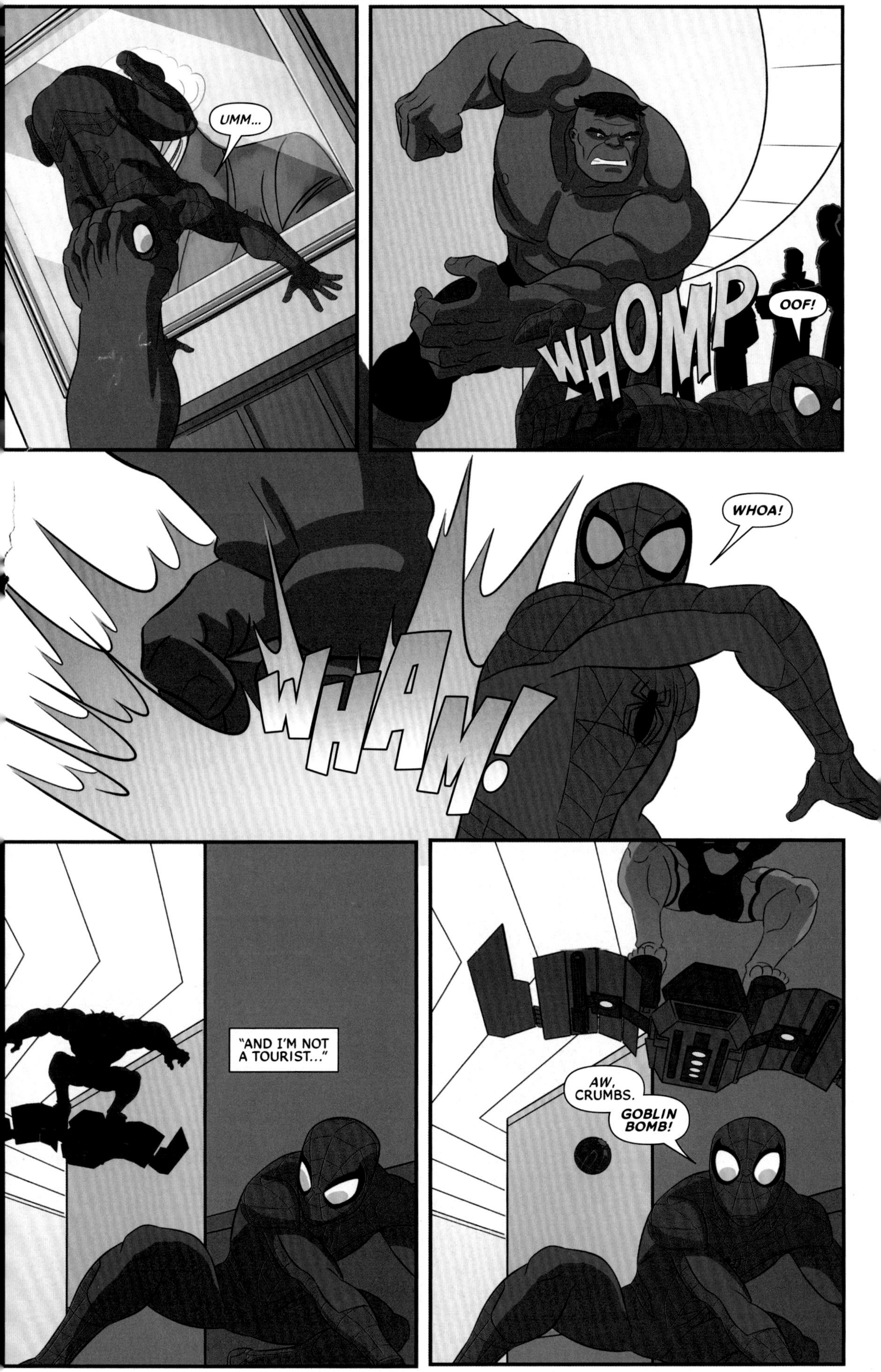
UMM...
WHOMP
OOF!
WHOA!
WHAM!
"AND I'M NOT A TOURIST..."
AW, CRUMBS.
GOBLIN BOMB!

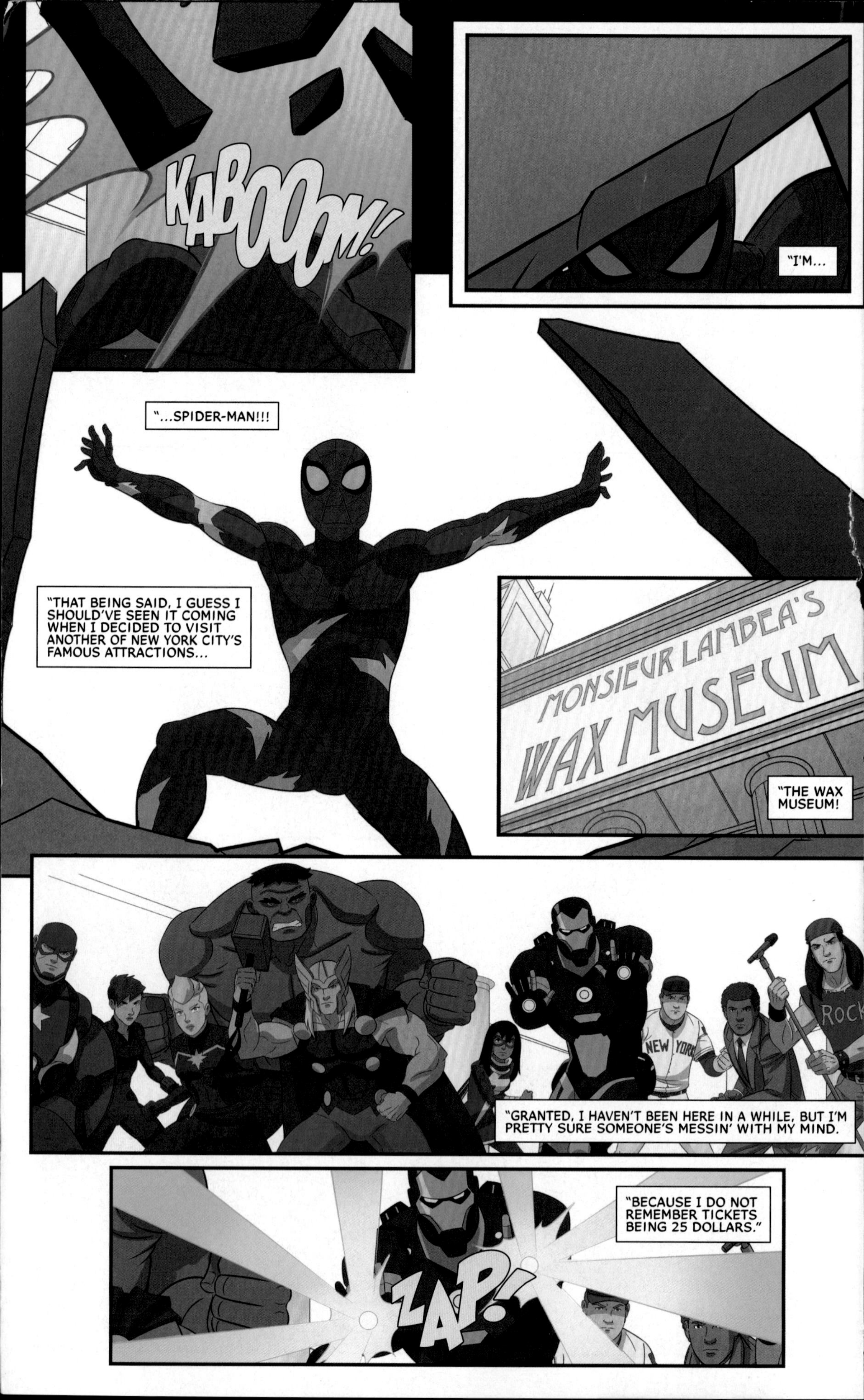
KABOOOM!
"I'M...
"...SPIDER-MAN!!!
"THAT BEING SAID, I GUESS I SHOULD'VE SEEN IT COMING WHEN I DECIDED TO VISIT ANOTHER OF NEW YORK CITY'S FAMOUS ATTRACTIONS...
MONSIEUR LAMBEA'S WAX MUSEUM
"THE WAX MUSEUM!
ROCK
NEW YORK
"GRANTED, I HAVEN'T BEEN HERE IN A WHILE, BUT I'M PRETTY SURE SOMEONE'S MESSIN' WITH MY MIND.
"BECAUSE I DO NOT REMEMBER TICKETS BEING 25 DOLLARS."
ZAP!

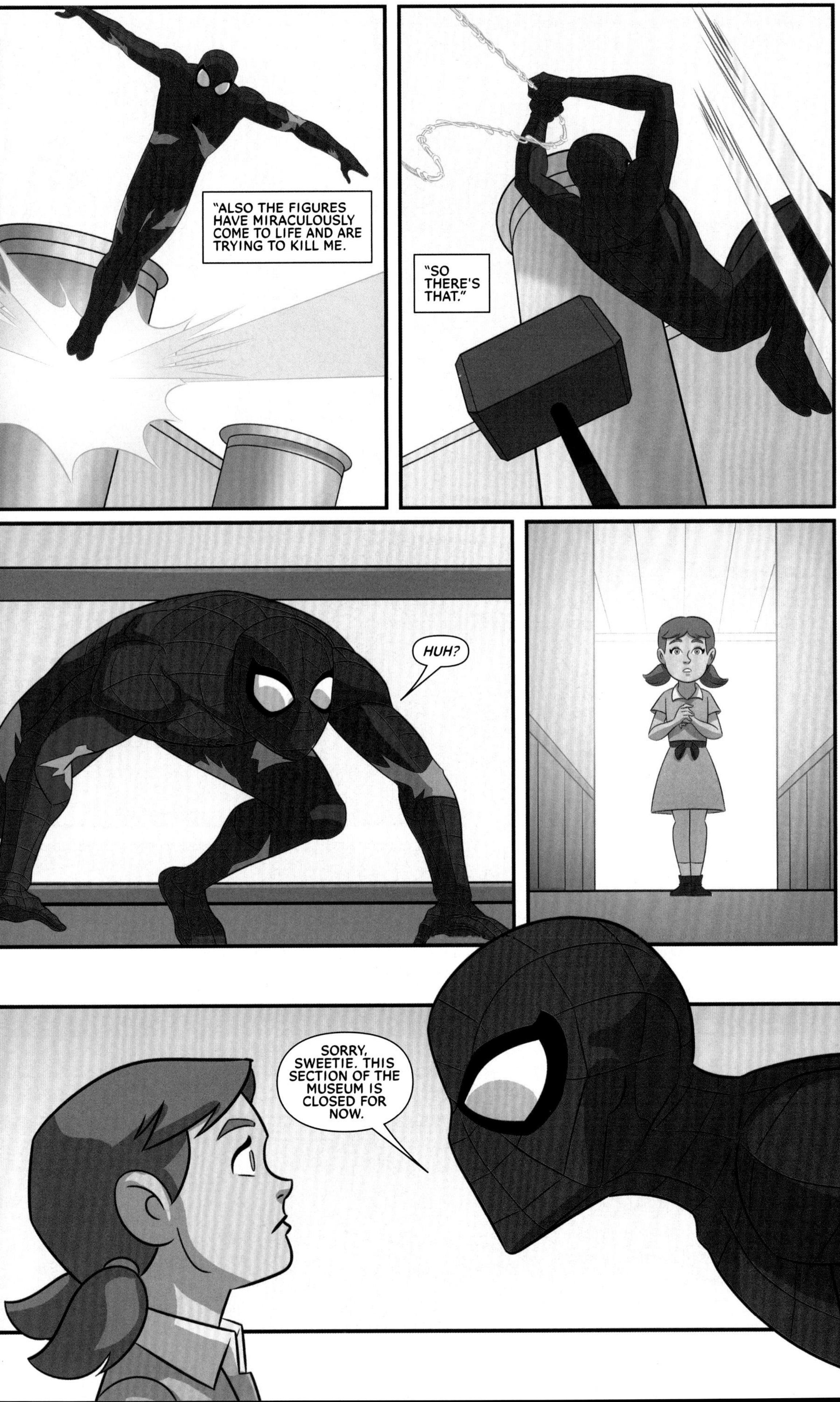
"ALSO THE FIGURES HAVE MIRACULOUSLY COME TO LIFE AND ARE TRYING TO KILL ME.
"SO THERE'S THAT."
HUH?
SORRY, SWEETIE. THIS SECTION OF THE MUSEUM IS CLOSED FOR NOW.

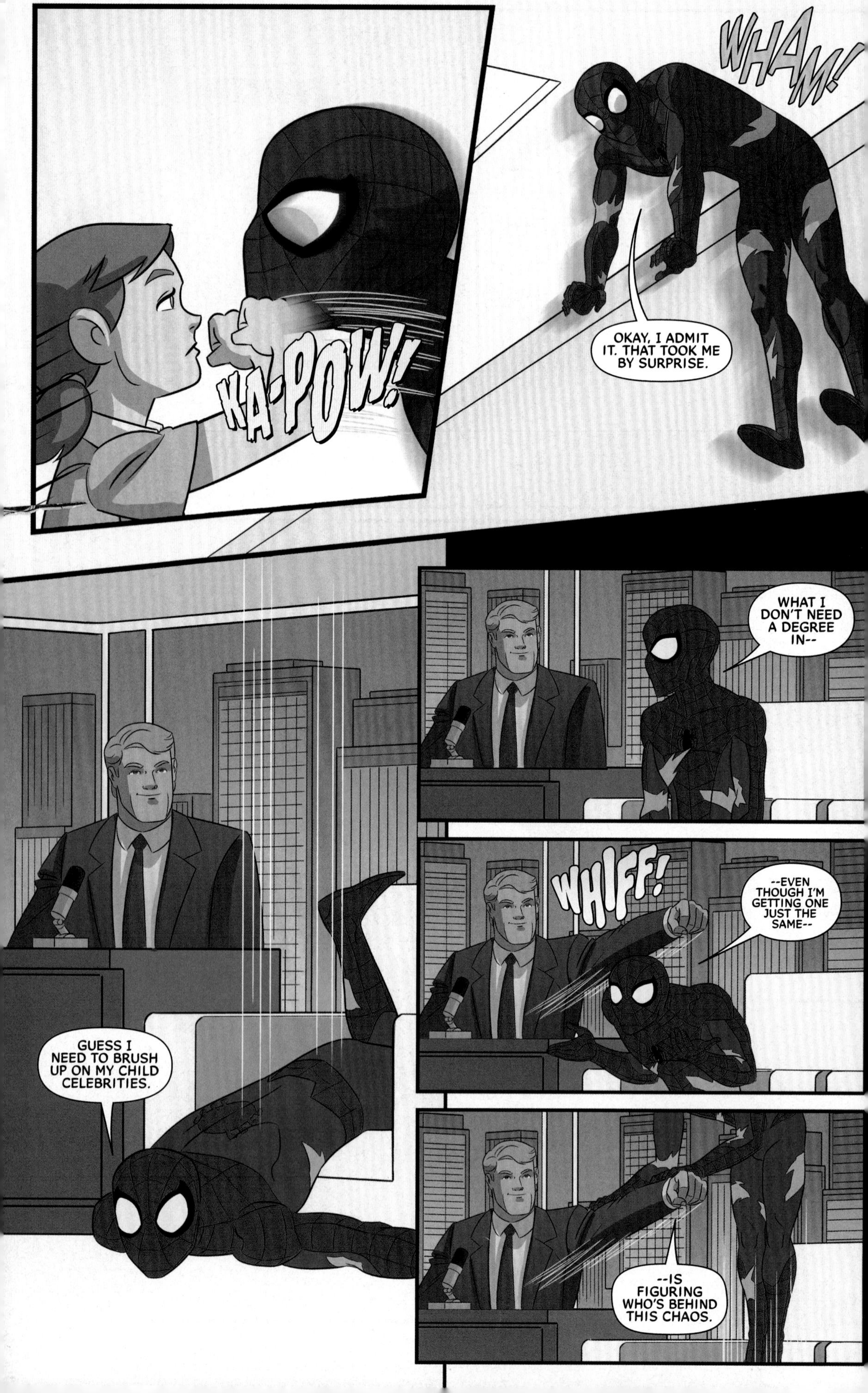
KA-POW!
WHAM!
OKAY, I ADMIT IT. THAT TOOK ME BY SURPRISE.
GUESS I NEED TO BRUSH UP ON MY CHILD CELEBRITIES.
WHAT I DON'T NEED A DEGREE IN--
WHIFF!
--EVEN THOUGH I'M GETTING ONE JUST THE SAME--
--IS FIGURING WHO'S BEHIND THIS CHAOS.

BECAUSE IF IT HAS ANYTHING TO DO WITH MANHATTAN OR A SENSE OF ILLUSION, IT CAN ONLY BE ONE OF TWO PEOPLE WHO HATE ME.

AND SINCE DAVID BLAINE AND I PATCHED THINGS UP, I'M GUESSING IT'S--

--MYSTERIO!

WHAT?

THEY GAVE HIM A WAX FIGURE!? HE'S NOT EVEN ONE OF MY MORE FAMOUS VILLAINS. I'D SAY HE'S... WHAT? 85TH, *AT BEST*.

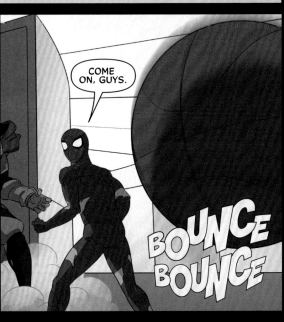
COME ON, GUYS.

BOUNCE BOUNCE

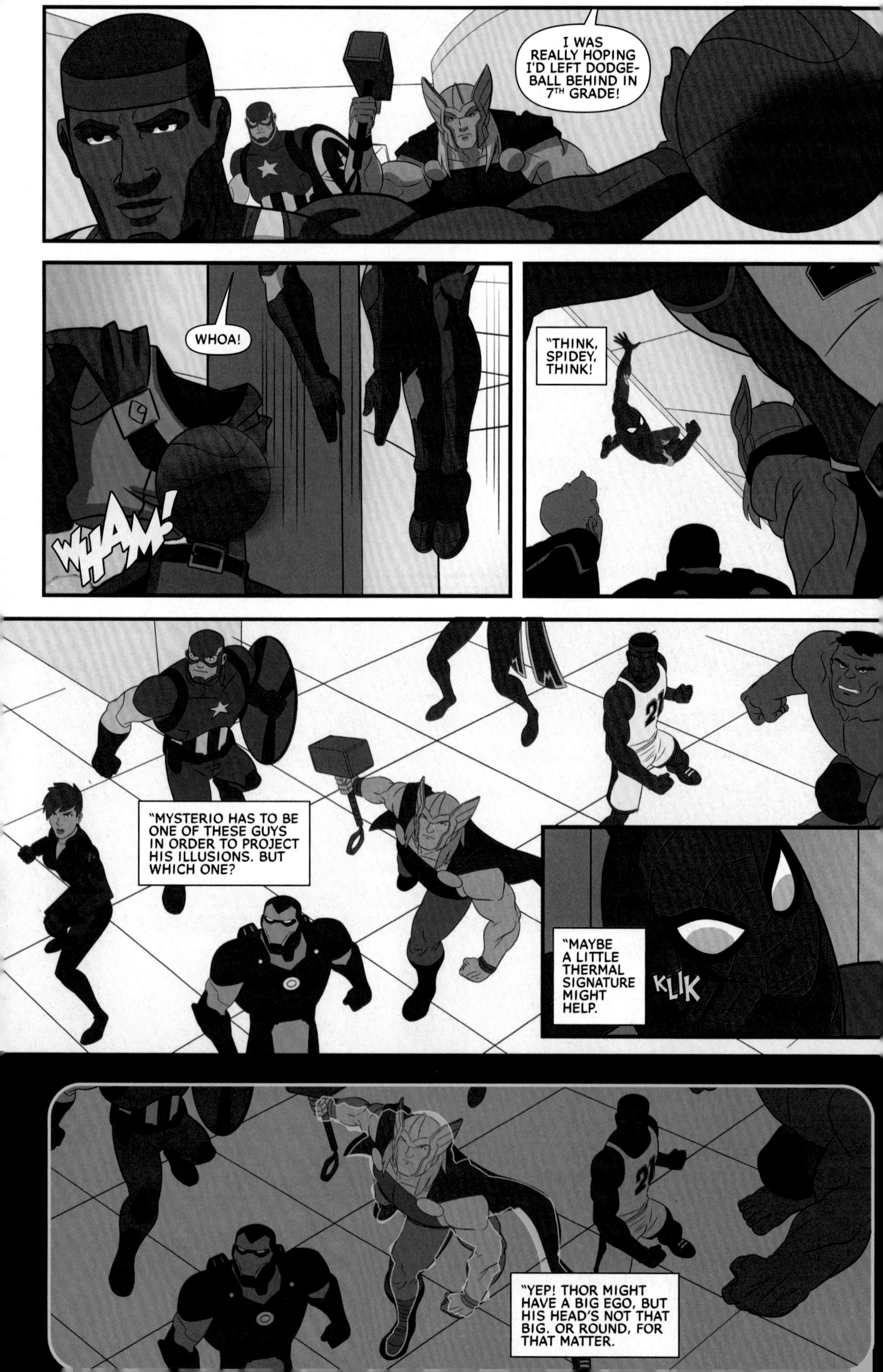
I WAS REALLY HOPING I'D LEFT DODGE-BALL BEHIND IN 7TH GRADE!
WHOA!
WHAM!
"THINK, SPIDEY, THINK!
"MYSTERIO HAS TO BE ONE OF THESE GUYS IN ORDER TO PROJECT HIS ILLUSIONS. BUT WHICH ONE?
"MAYBE A LITTLE THERMAL SIGNATURE MIGHT HELP.
KLIK
"YEP! THOR MIGHT HAVE A BIG EGO, BUT HIS HEAD'S NOT THAT BIG. OR ROUND, FOR THAT MATTER.

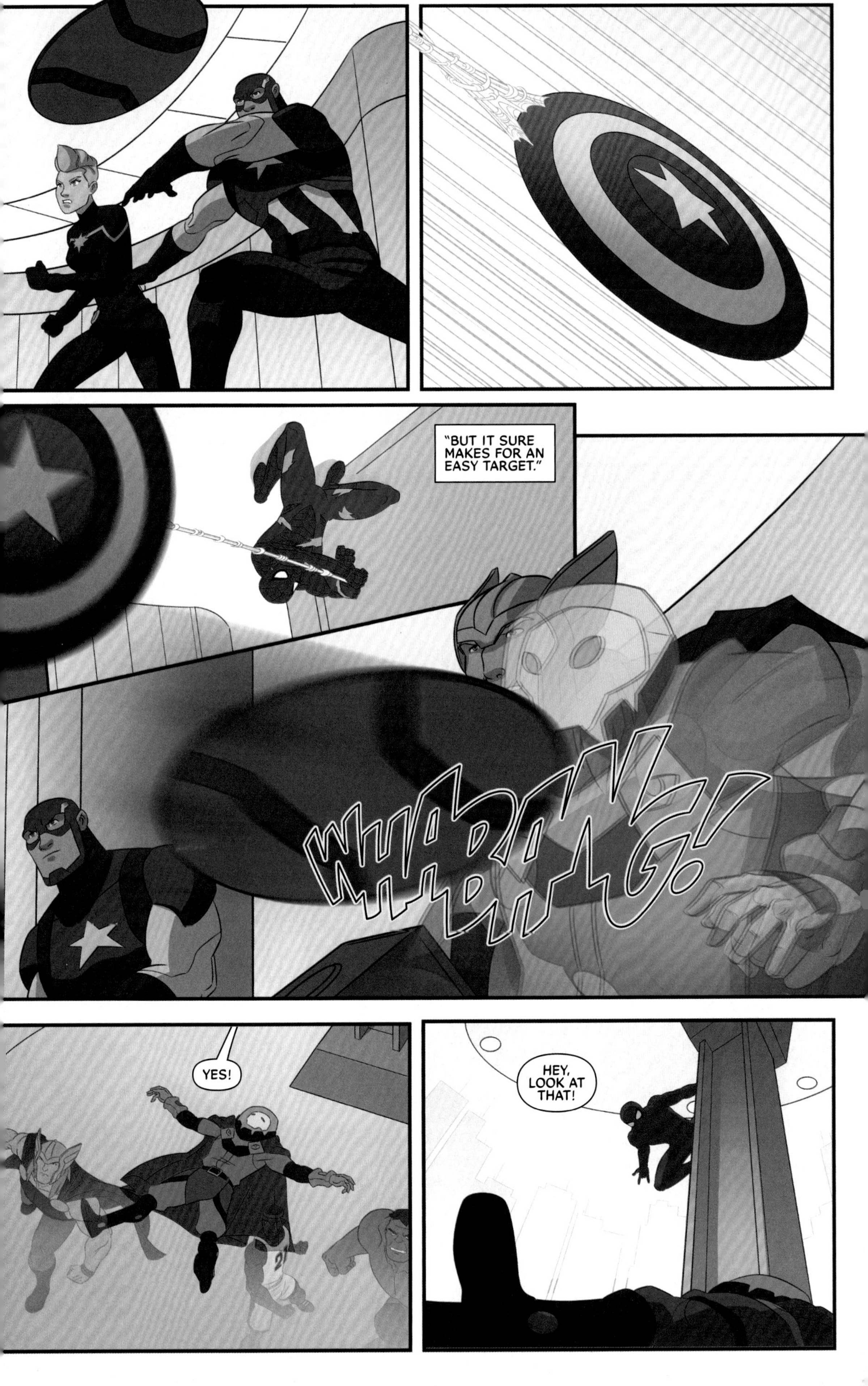
"BUT IT SURE MAKES FOR AN EASY TARGET."
WHAAANNG!
YES!
HEY, LOOK AT THAT!

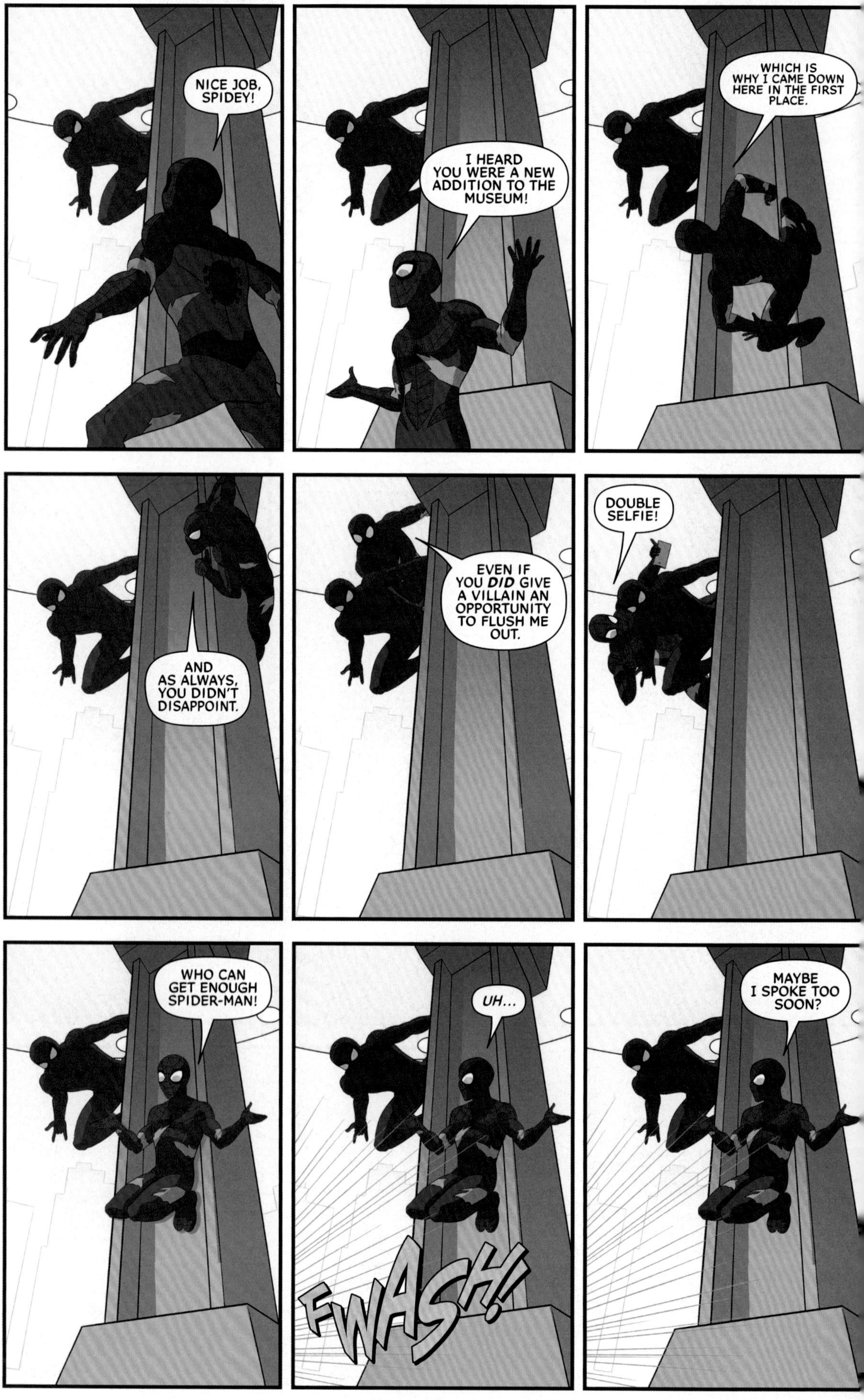

NICE JOB, SPIDEY!
I HEARD YOU WERE A NEW ADDITION TO THE MUSEUM!
WHICH IS WHY I CAME DOWN HERE IN THE FIRST PLACE.
AND AS ALWAYS, YOU DIDN'T DISAPPOINT.
EVEN IF YOU *DID* GIVE A VILLAIN AN OPPORTUNITY TO FLUSH ME OUT.
DOUBLE SELFIE!
WHO CAN GET ENOUGH SPIDER-MAN!
UH...
FWASH!
MAYBE I SPOKE TOO SOON?

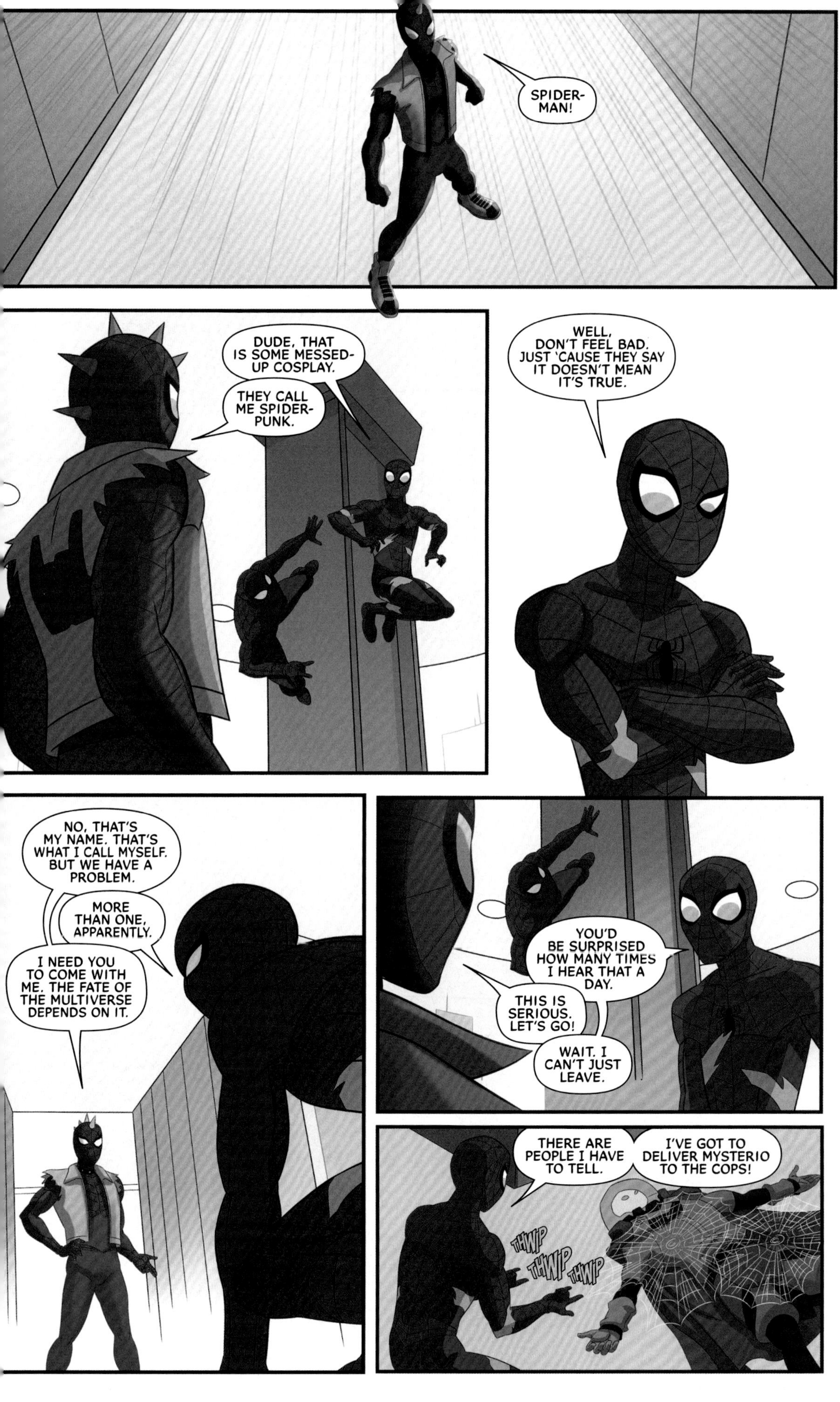
SPIDER-MAN!
DUDE, THAT IS SOME MESSED-UP COSPLAY.
THEY CALL ME SPIDER-PUNK.
WELL, DON'T FEEL BAD. JUST 'CAUSE THEY SAY IT DOESN'T MEAN IT'S TRUE.
NO, THAT'S MY NAME. THAT'S WHAT I CALL MYSELF. BUT WE HAVE A PROBLEM.
MORE THAN ONE, APPARENTLY.
I NEED YOU TO COME WITH ME. THE FATE OF THE MULTIVERSE DEPENDS ON IT.
YOU'D BE SURPRISED HOW MANY TIMES I HEAR THAT A DAY.
THIS IS SERIOUS. LET'S GO!
WAIT. I CAN'T JUST LEAVE.
THERE ARE PEOPLE I HAVE TO TELL.
I'VE GOT TO DELIVER MYSTERIO TO THE COPS!
THWIP
THWIP
THWIP

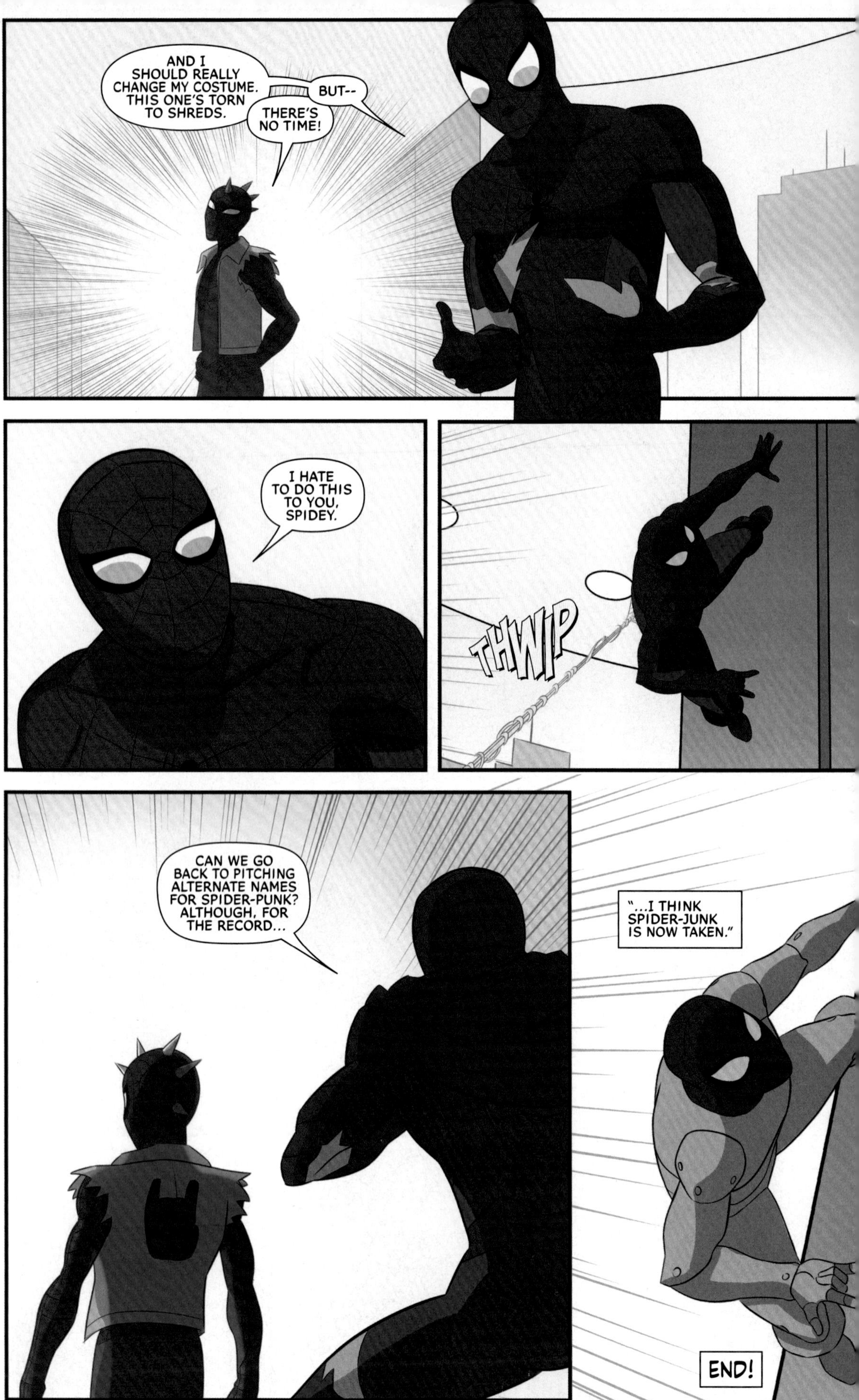
AND I SHOULD REALLY CHANGE MY COSTUME. THIS ONE'S TORN TO SHREDS.
BUT--
THERE'S NO TIME!
I HATE TO DO THIS TO YOU, SPIDEY.
THWIP
CAN WE GO BACK TO PITCHING ALTERNATE NAMES FOR SPIDER-PUNK? ALTHOUGH, FOR THE RECORD...
"...I THINK SPIDER-JUNK IS NOW TAKEN."
END!

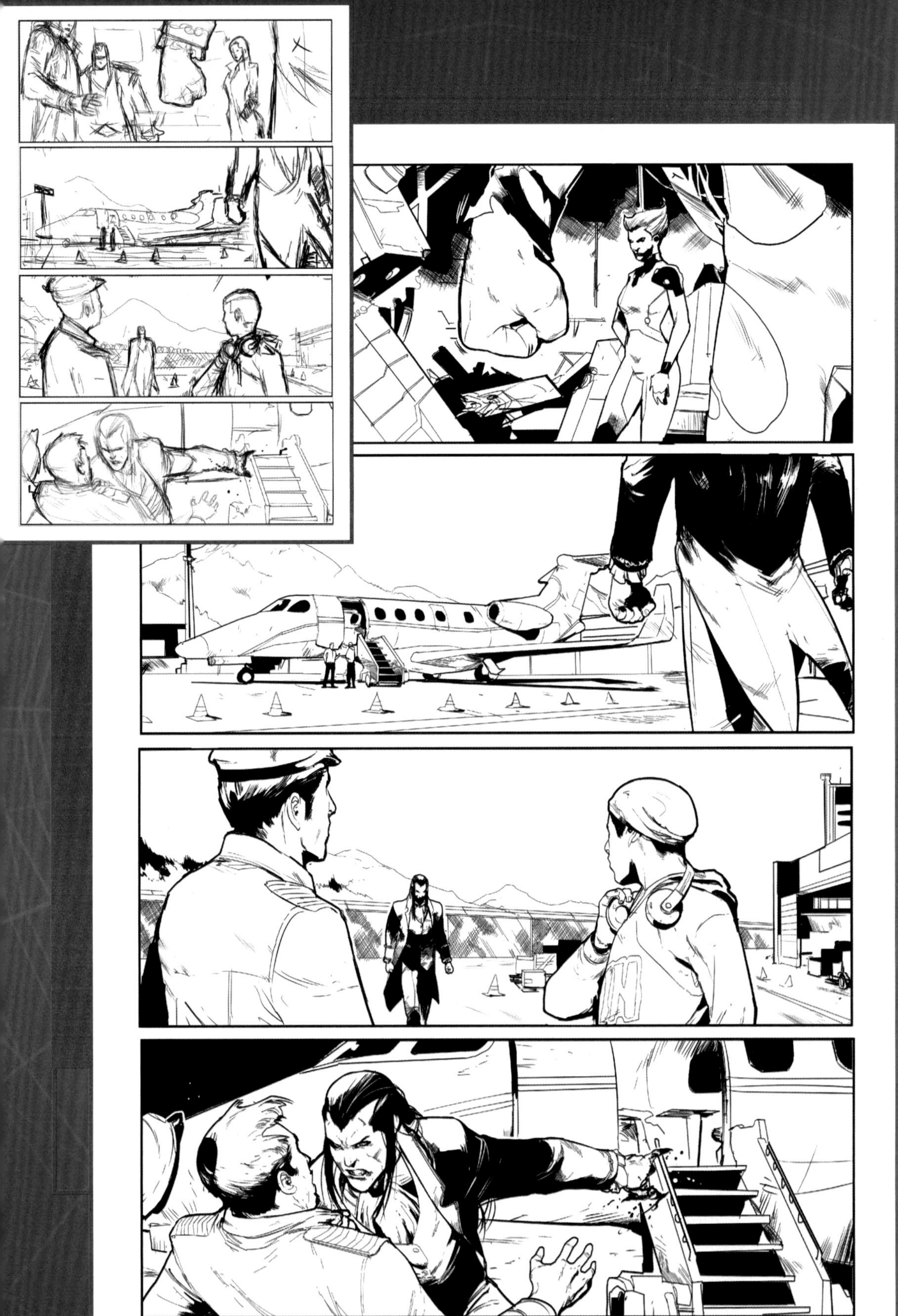

#311 PAGE 1 LAYOUTS AND INKS BY **JUAN FRIGERI**

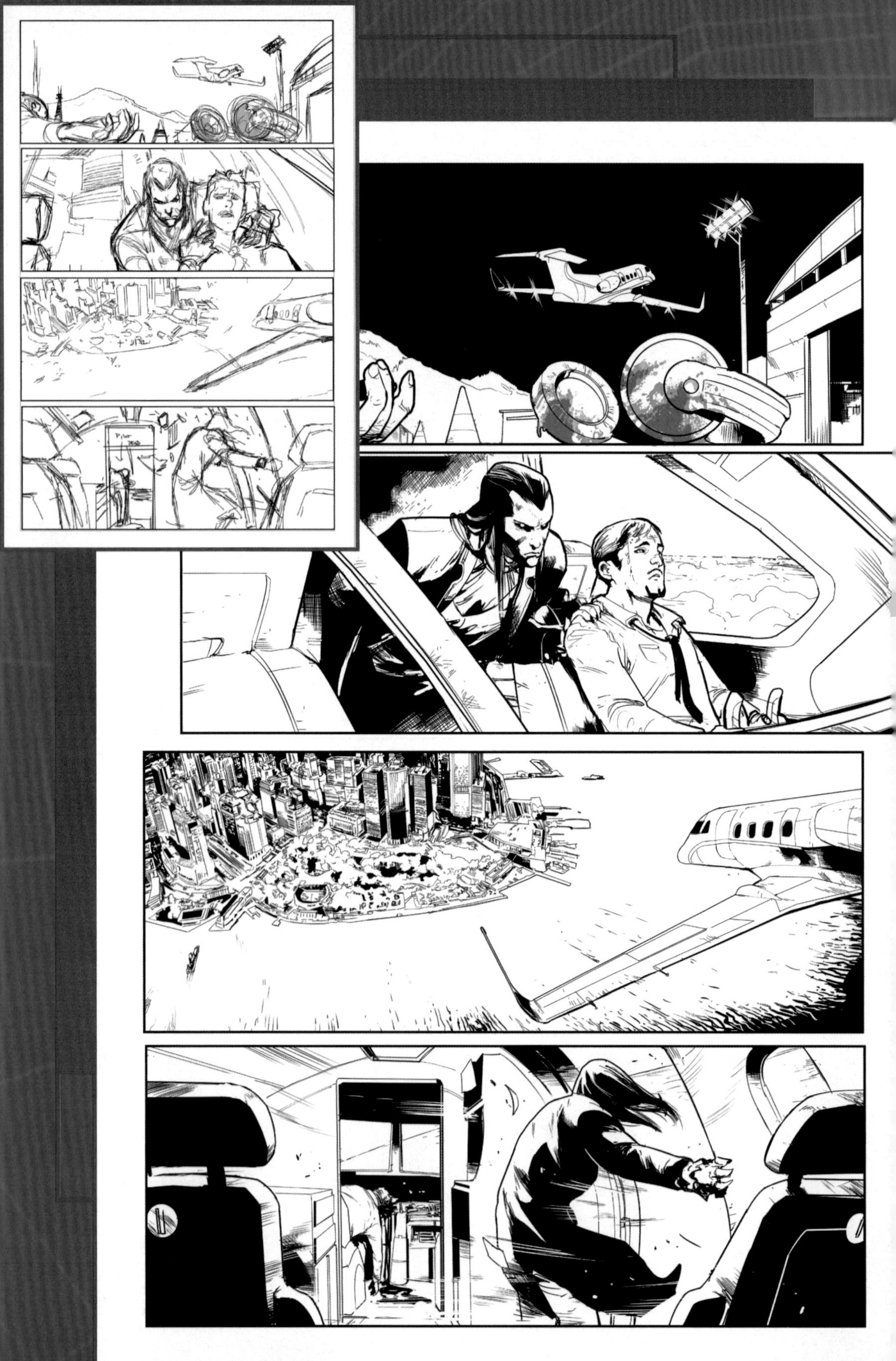

#311 PAGE 2 LAYOUTS AND INKS BY **JUAN FRIGERI**

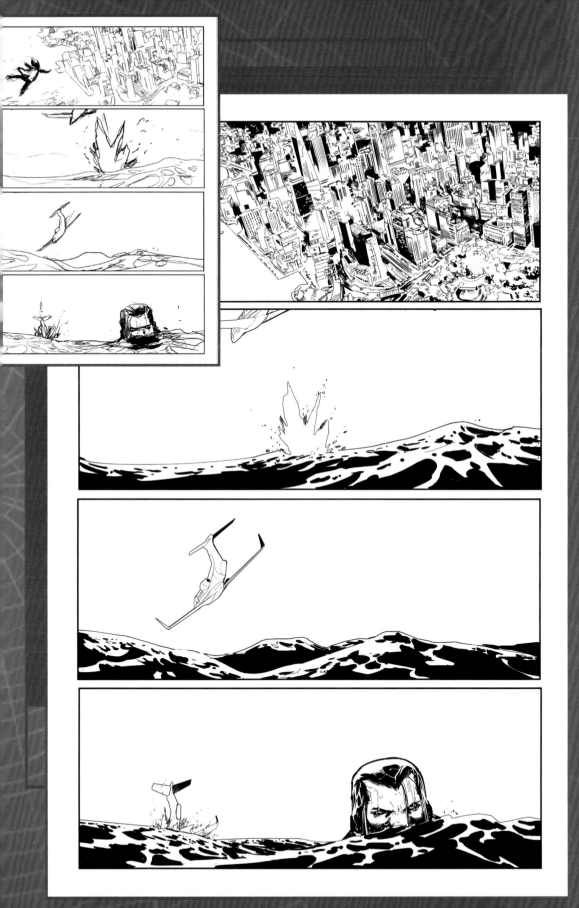

#311 PAGE 3 LAYOUTS AND INKS BY **JUAN FRIGERI**

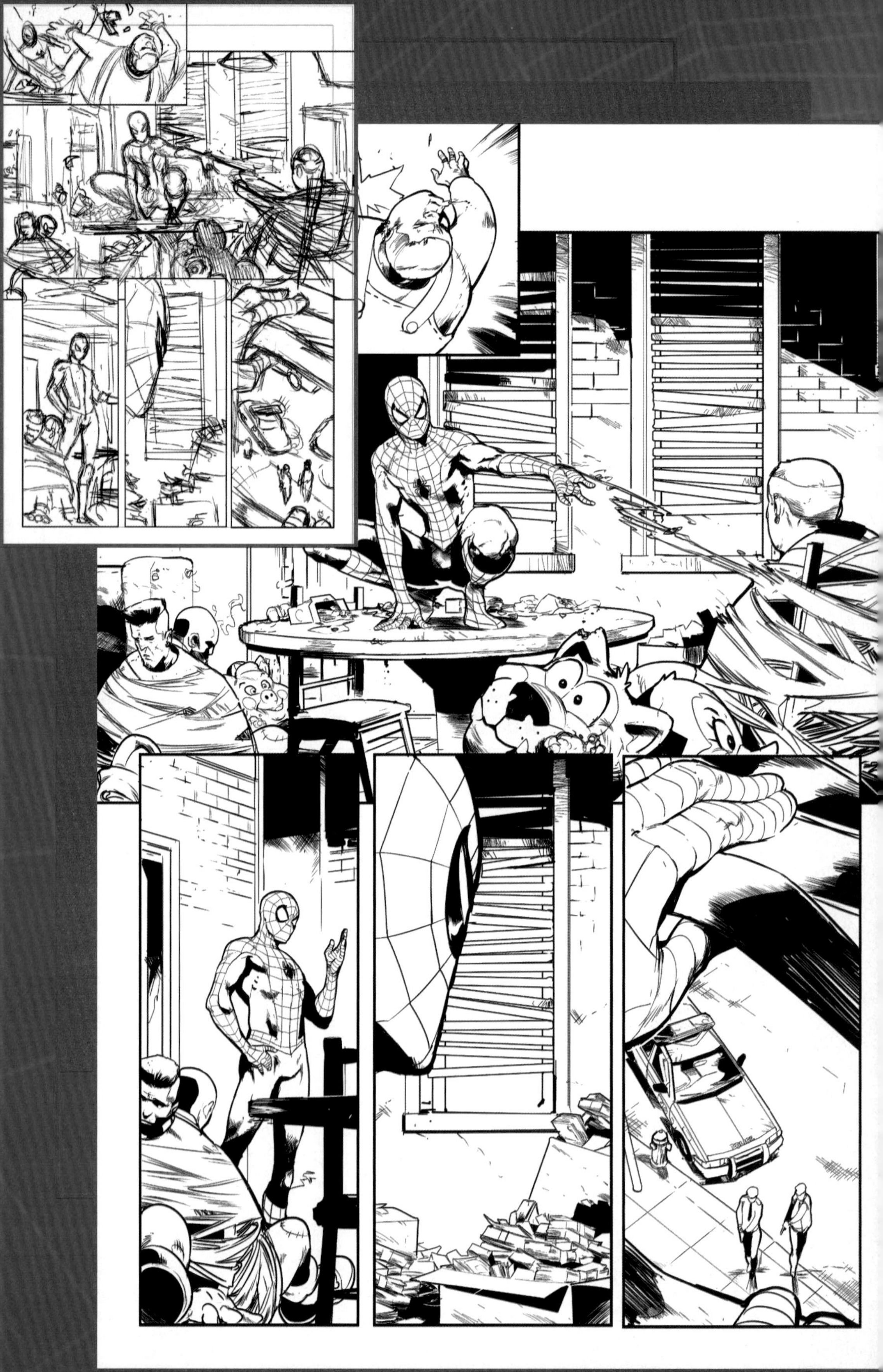

#311 PAGE 4 LAYOUTS AND INKS BY **JUAN FRIGERI**

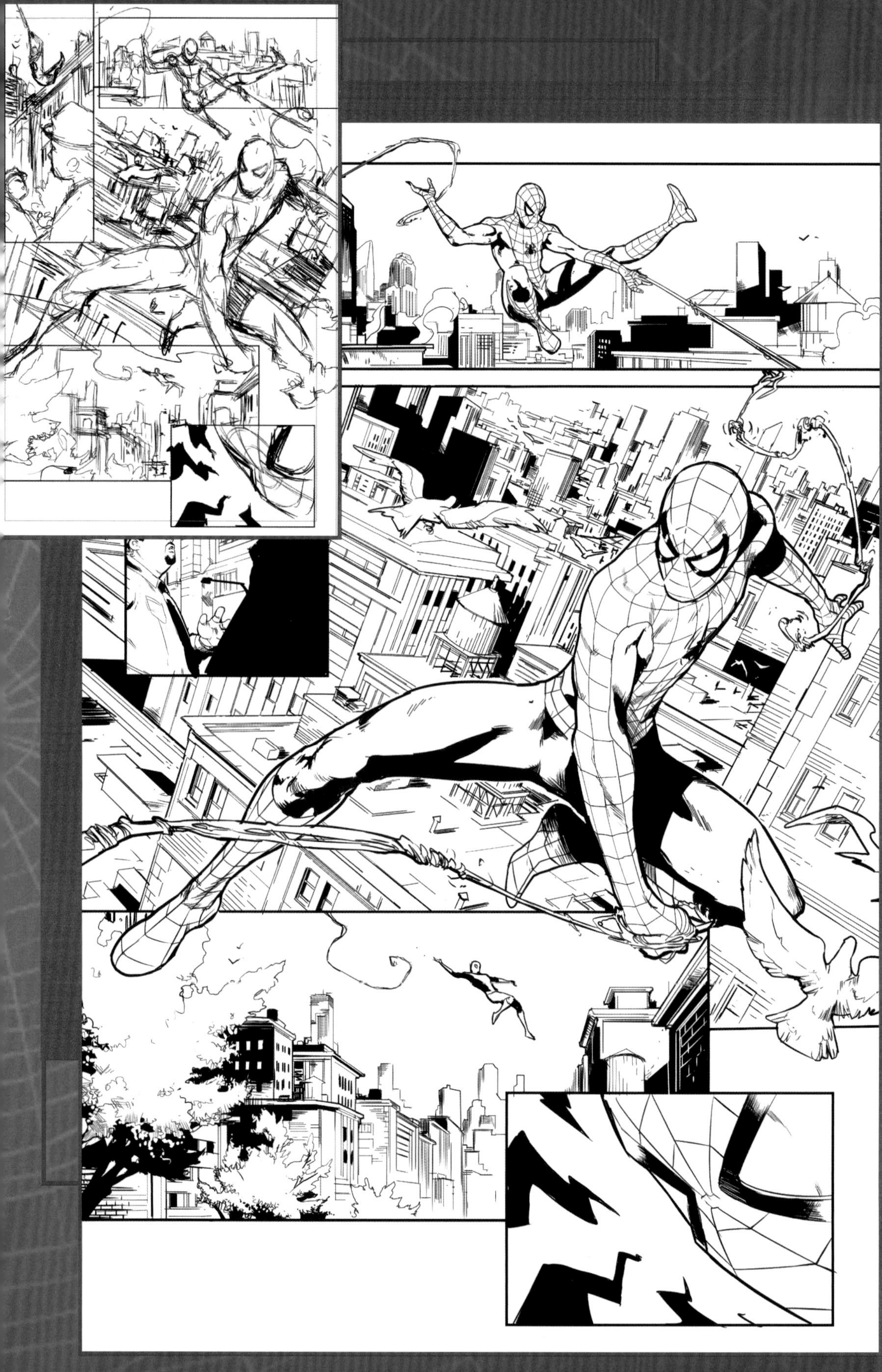

#311 PAGE 5 LAYOUTS AND INKS BY **JUAN FRIGERI**

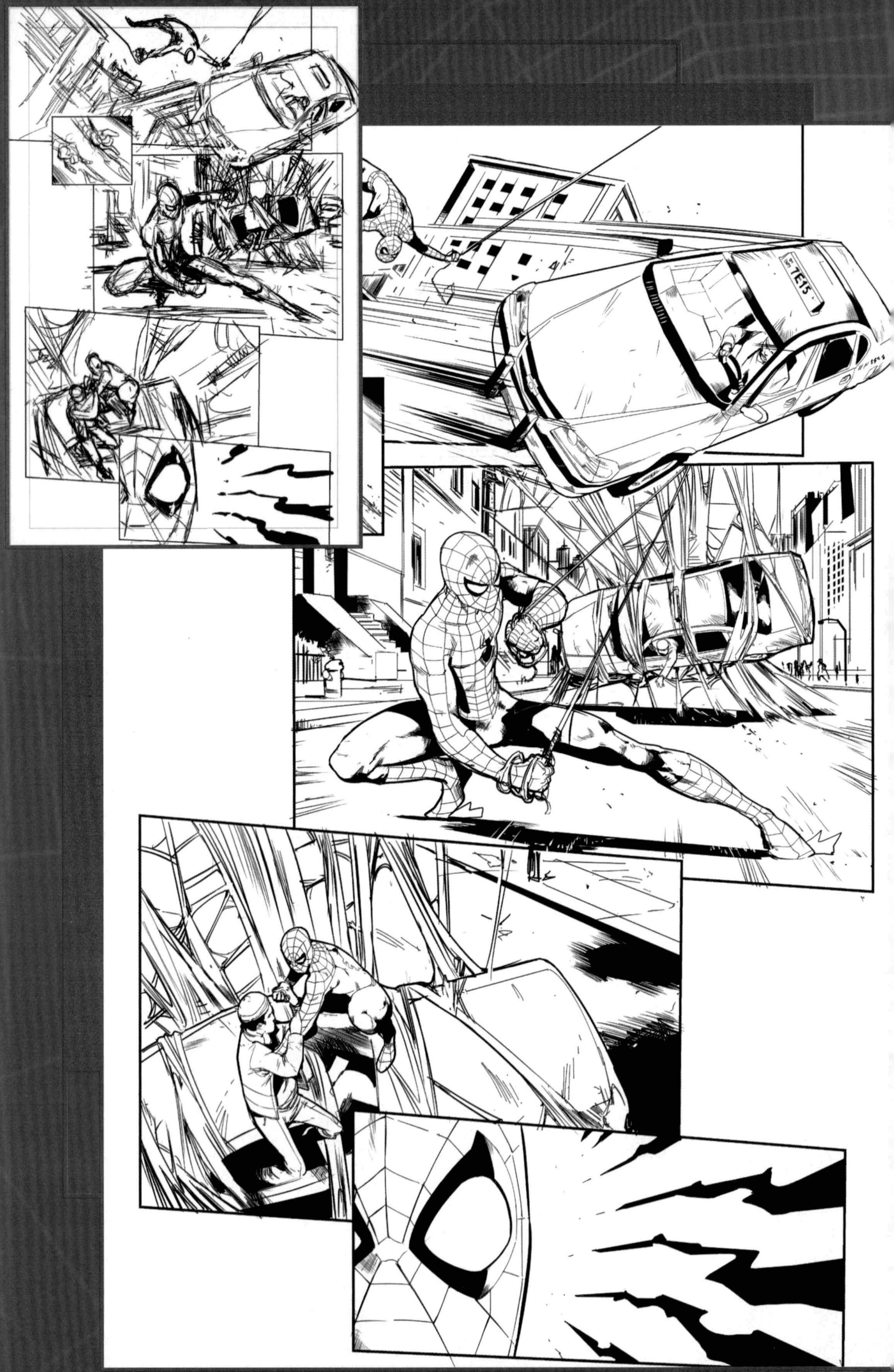

#311 PAGE 6 LAYOUTS AND INKS BY **JUAN FRIGERI**

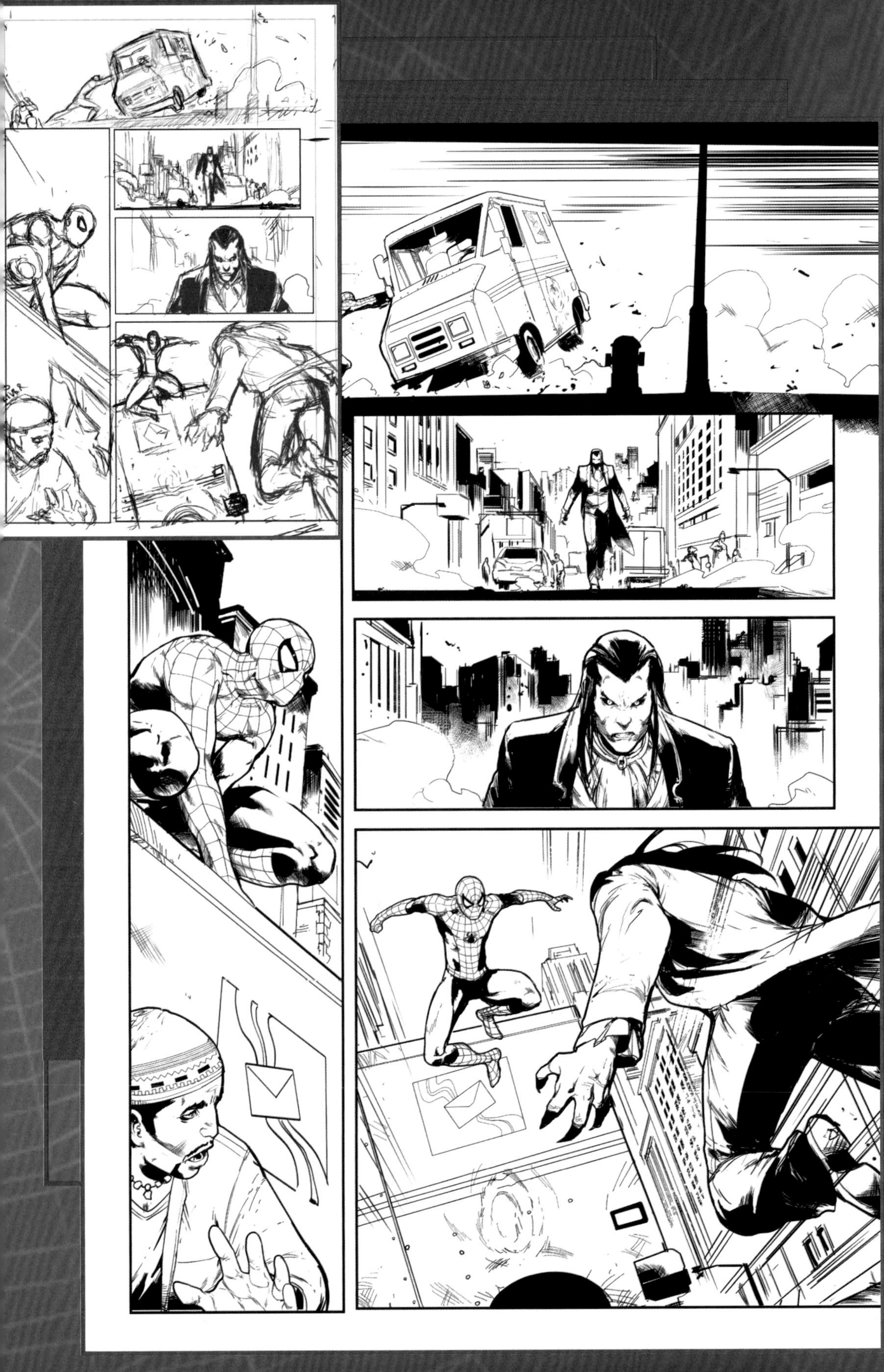

#311 PAGE 7 LAYOUTS AND INKS BY **JUAN FRIGERI**

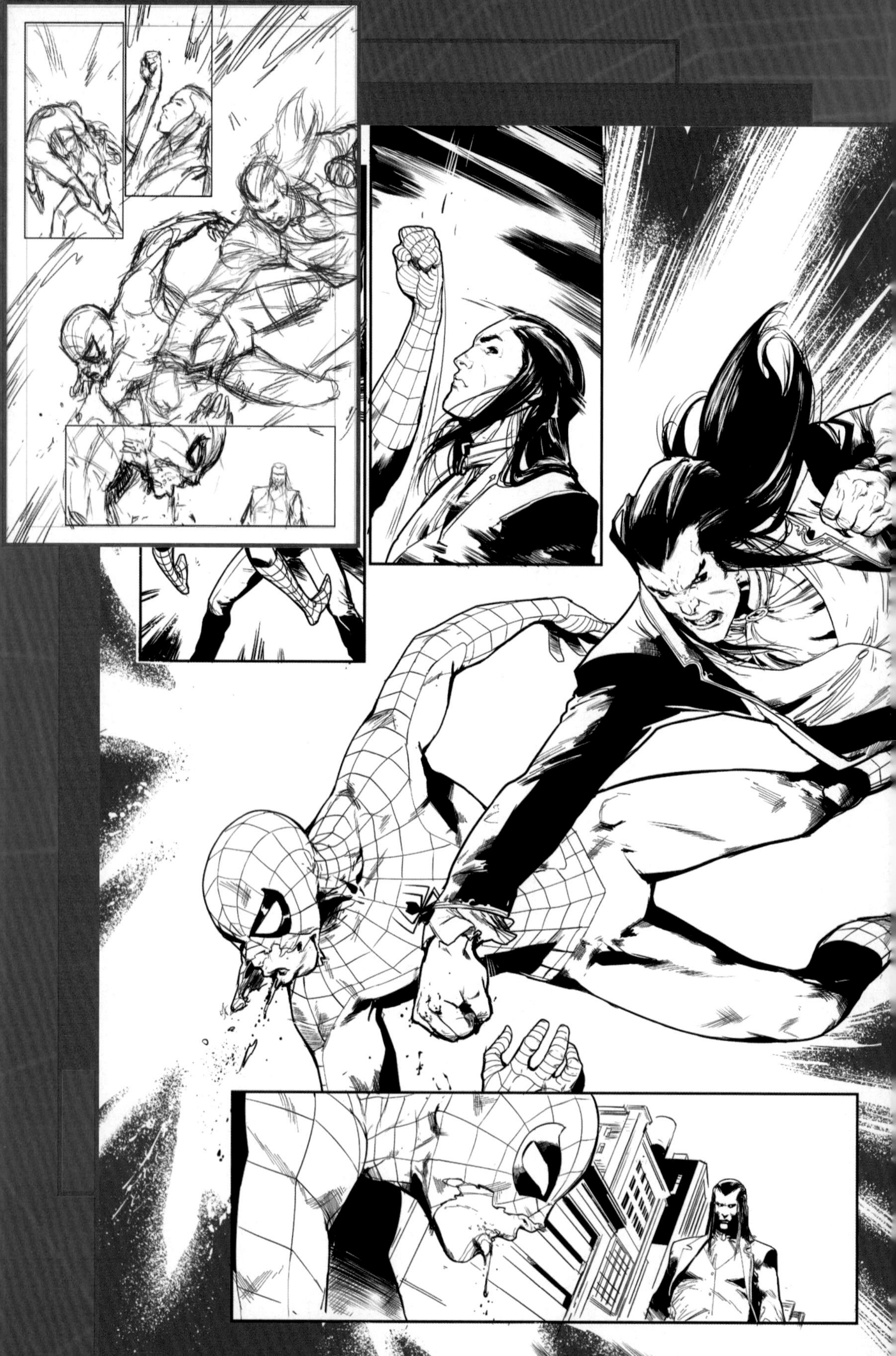

#311 PAGE 8 LAYOUTS AND INKS BY **JUAN FRIGERI**

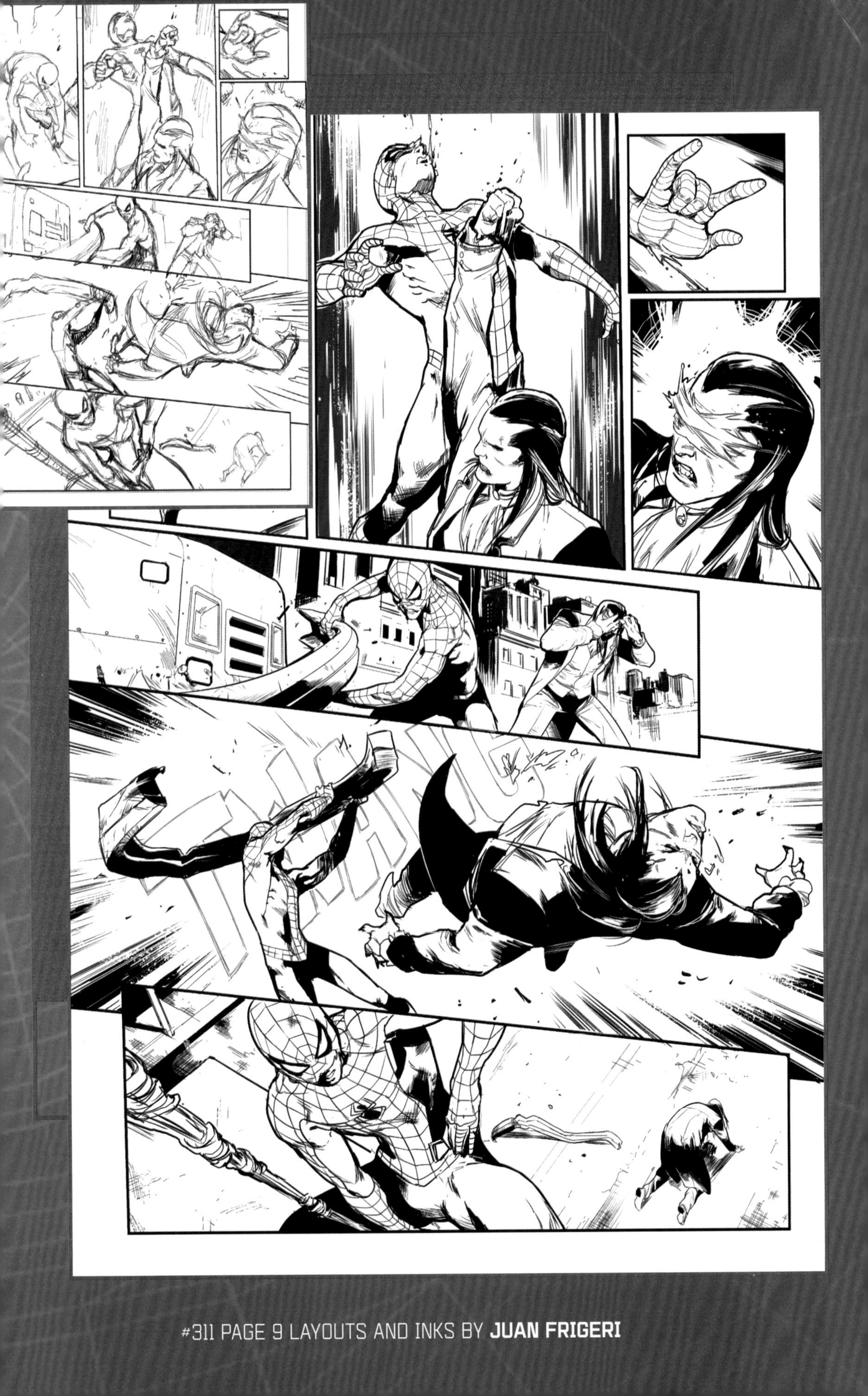

#311 PAGE 9 LAYOUTS AND INKS BY **JUAN FRIGERI**

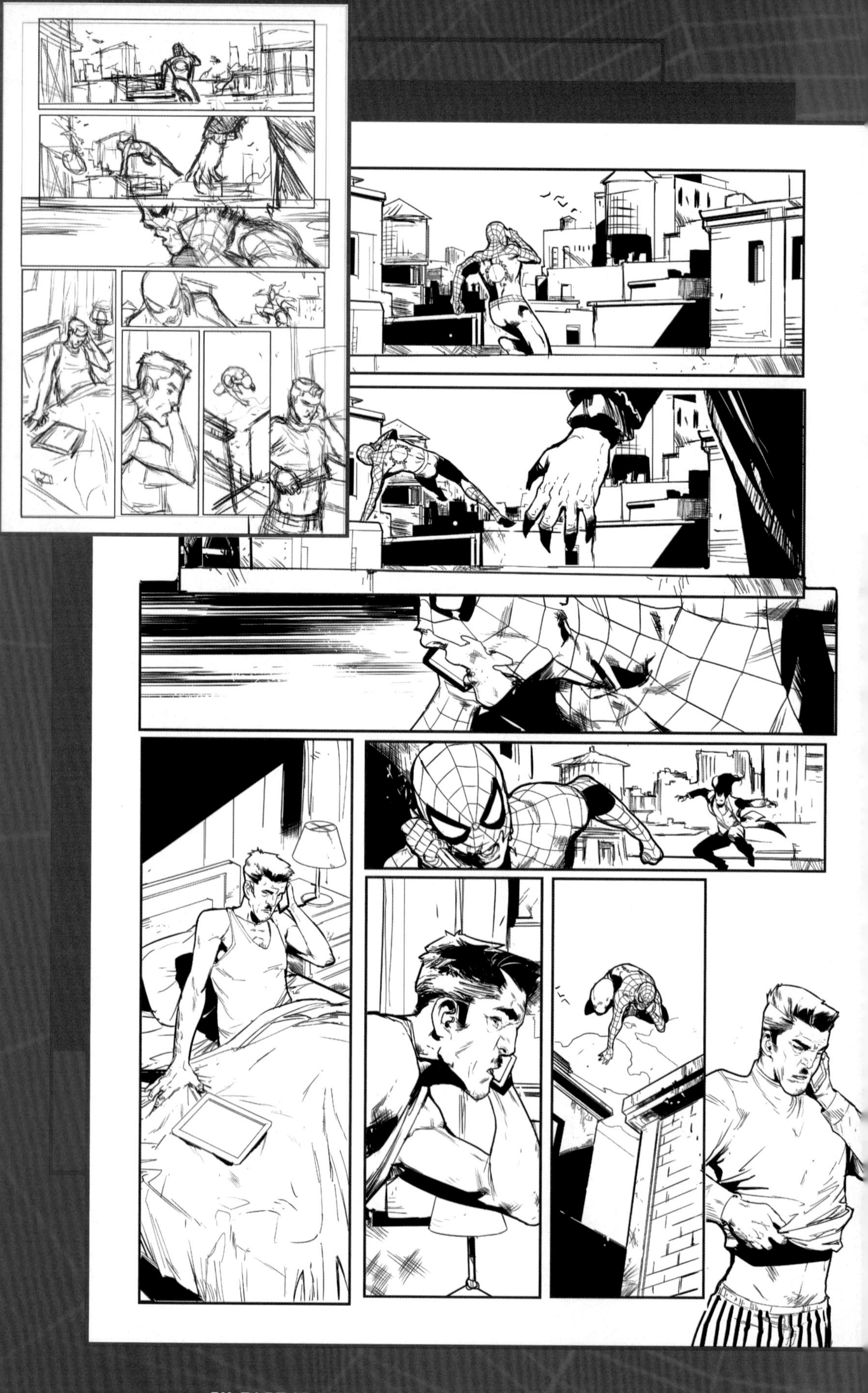

#311 PAGE 10 LAYOUTS AND INKS BY **JUAN FRIGERI**

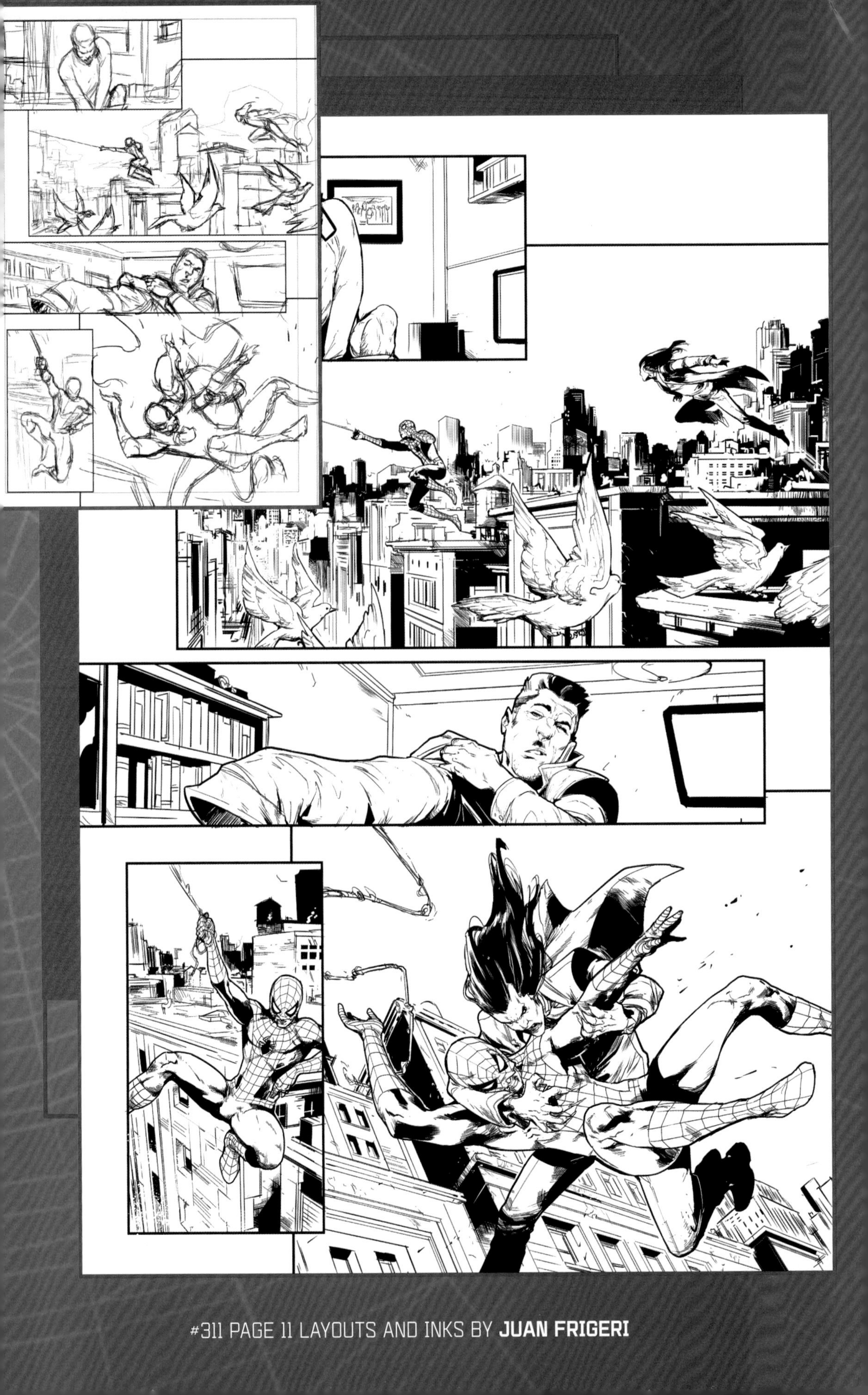

#311 PAGE 11 LAYOUTS AND INKS BY **JUAN FRIGERI**

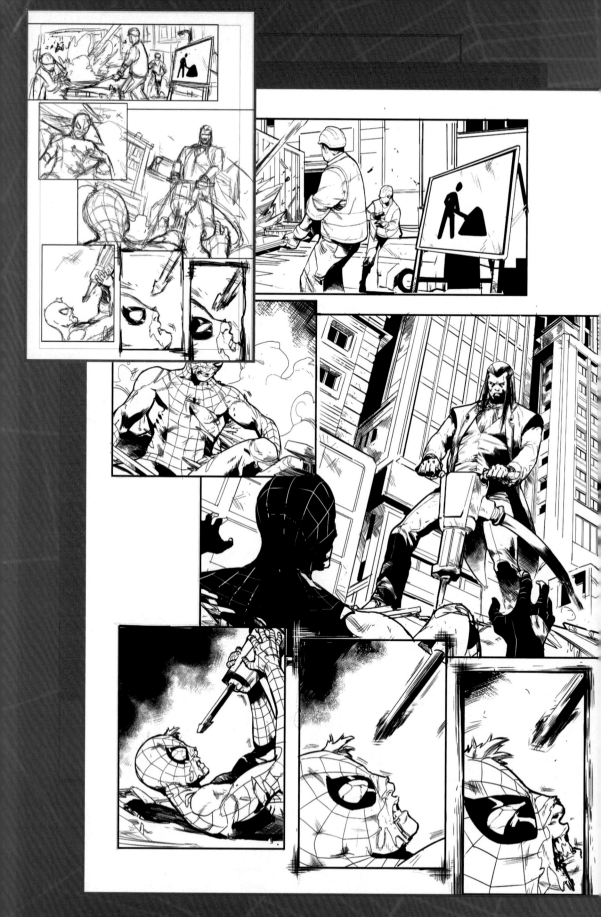

#311 PAGE 12 LAYOUTS AND INKS BY **JUAN FRIGERI**

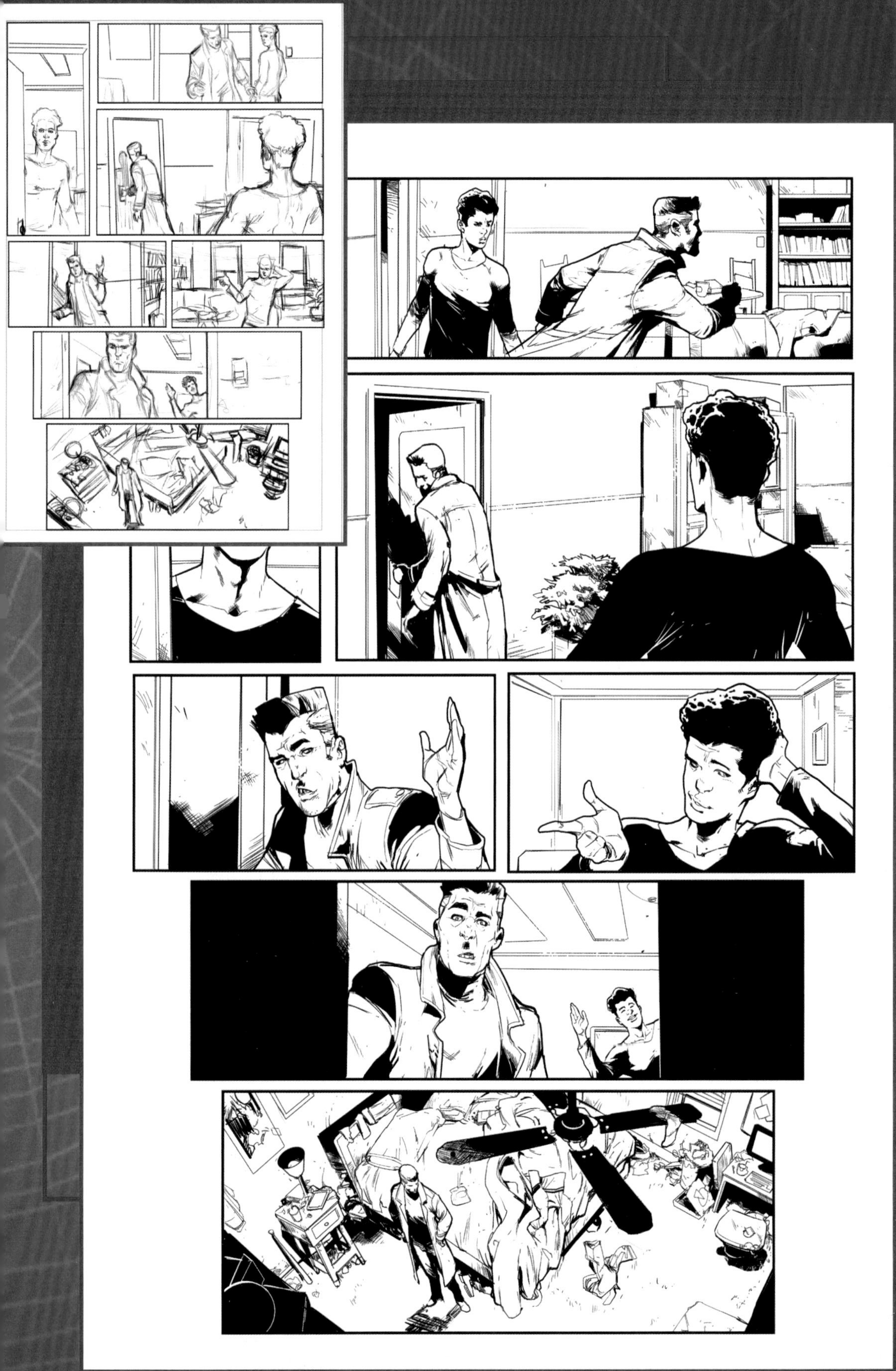

#311 PAGE 13 LAYOUTS AND INKS BY **JUAN FRIGERI**

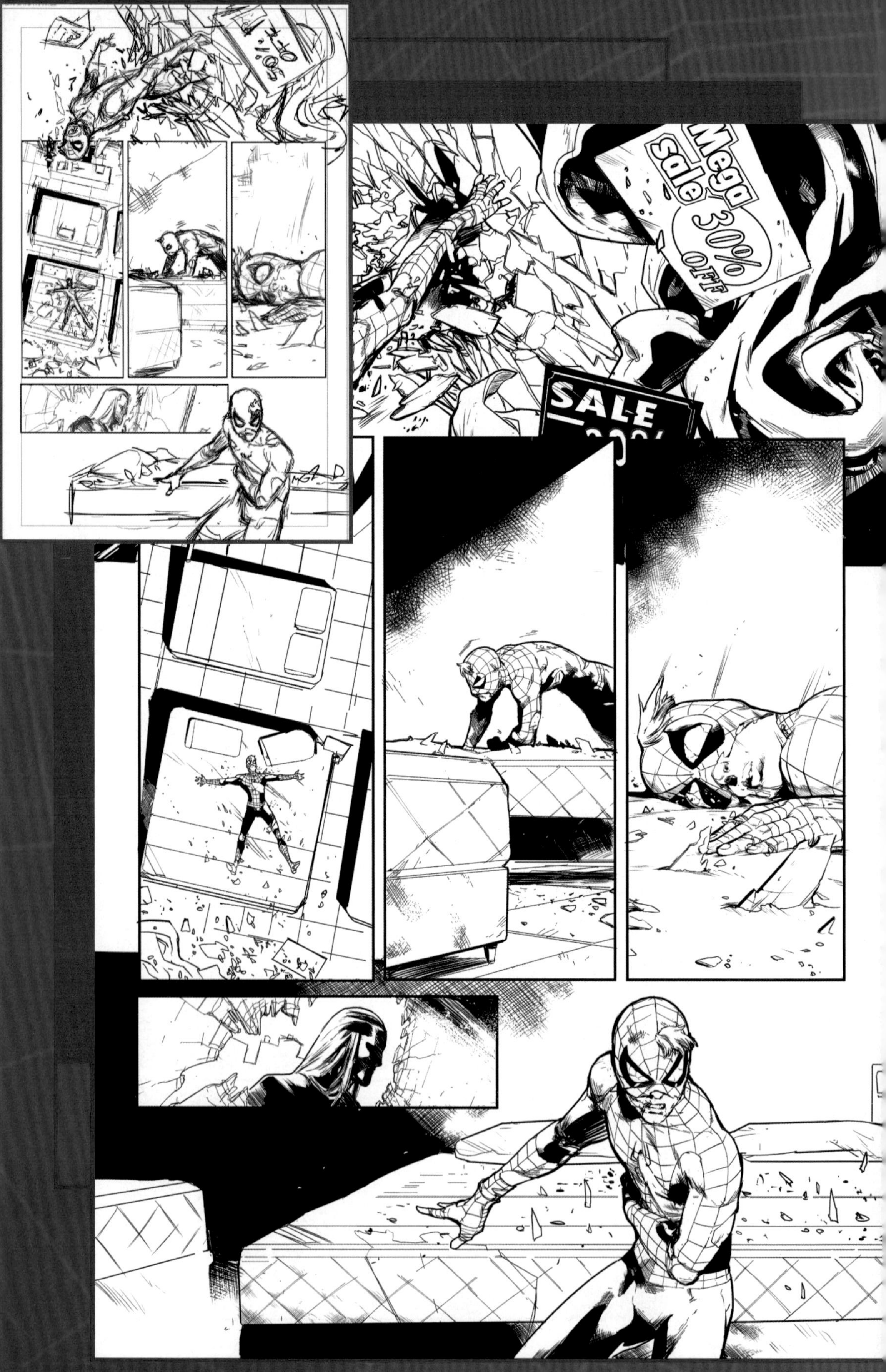
Mega Sale 30% OFF
SALE

#311 PAGE 14 LAYOUTS AND INKS BY **JUAN FRIGERI**

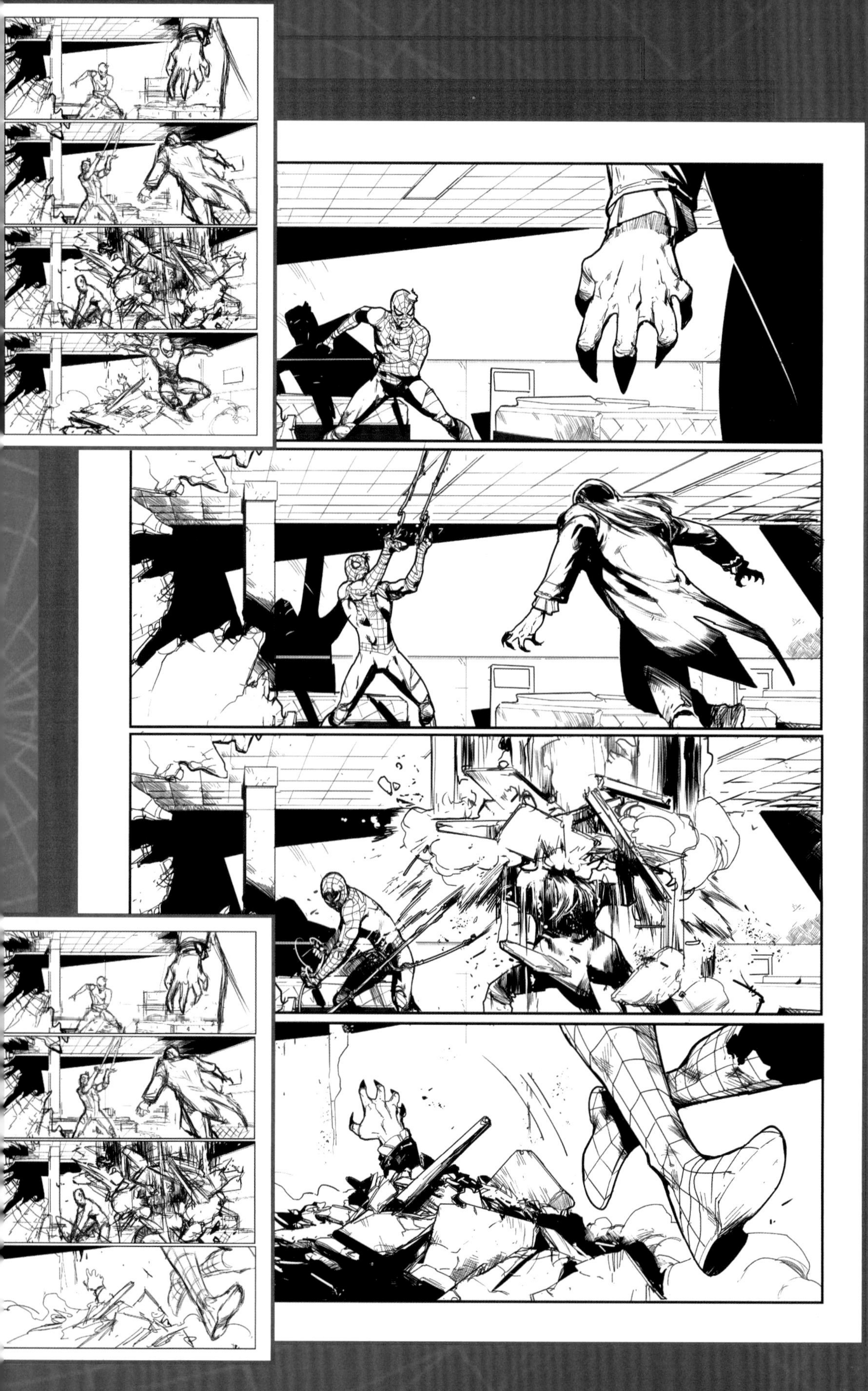

#311 PAGE 15 LAYOUTS AND INKS BY **JUAN FRIGERI**

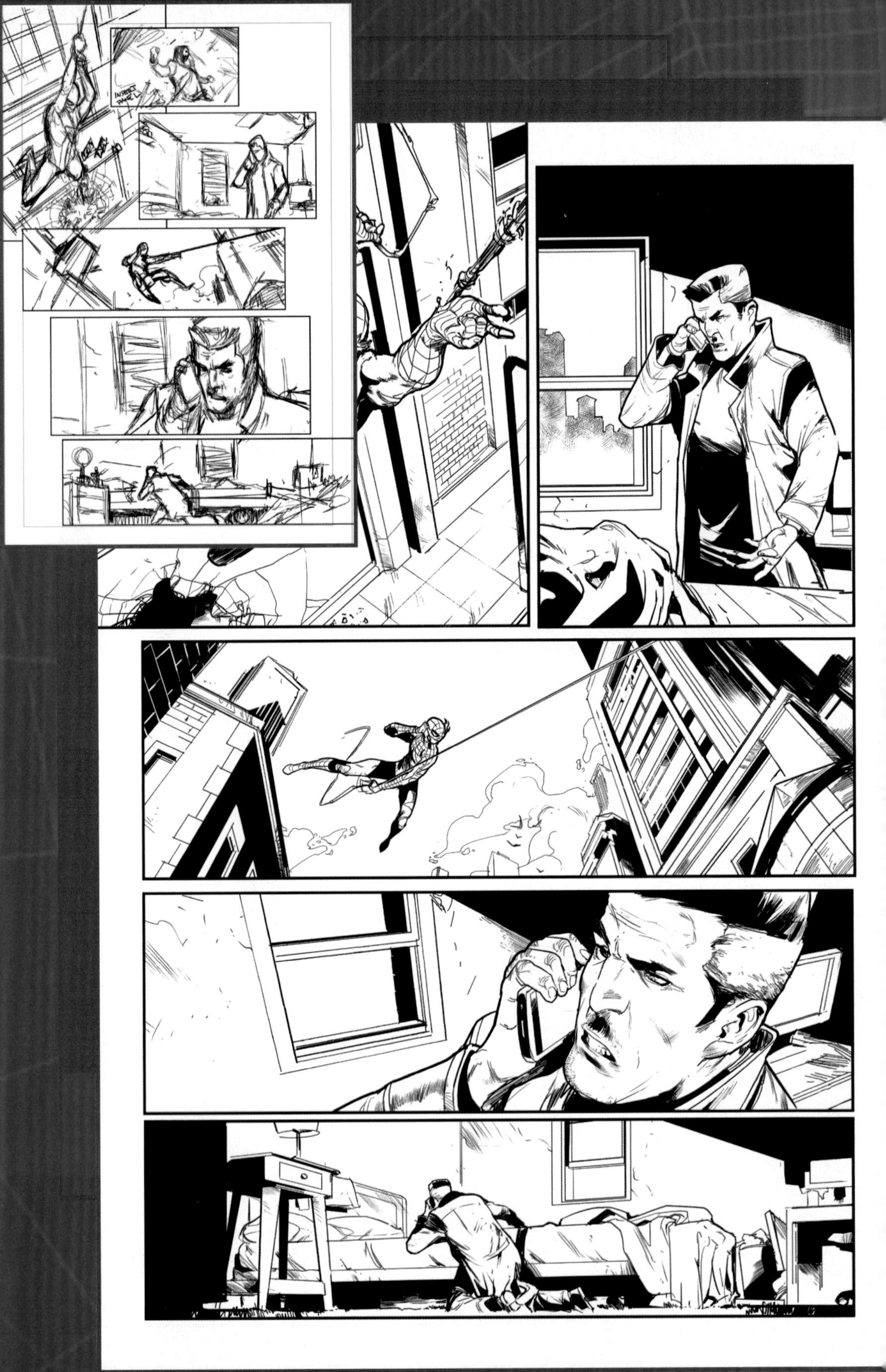

#311 PAGE 16 LAYOUTS AND INKS BY **JUAN FRIGERI**

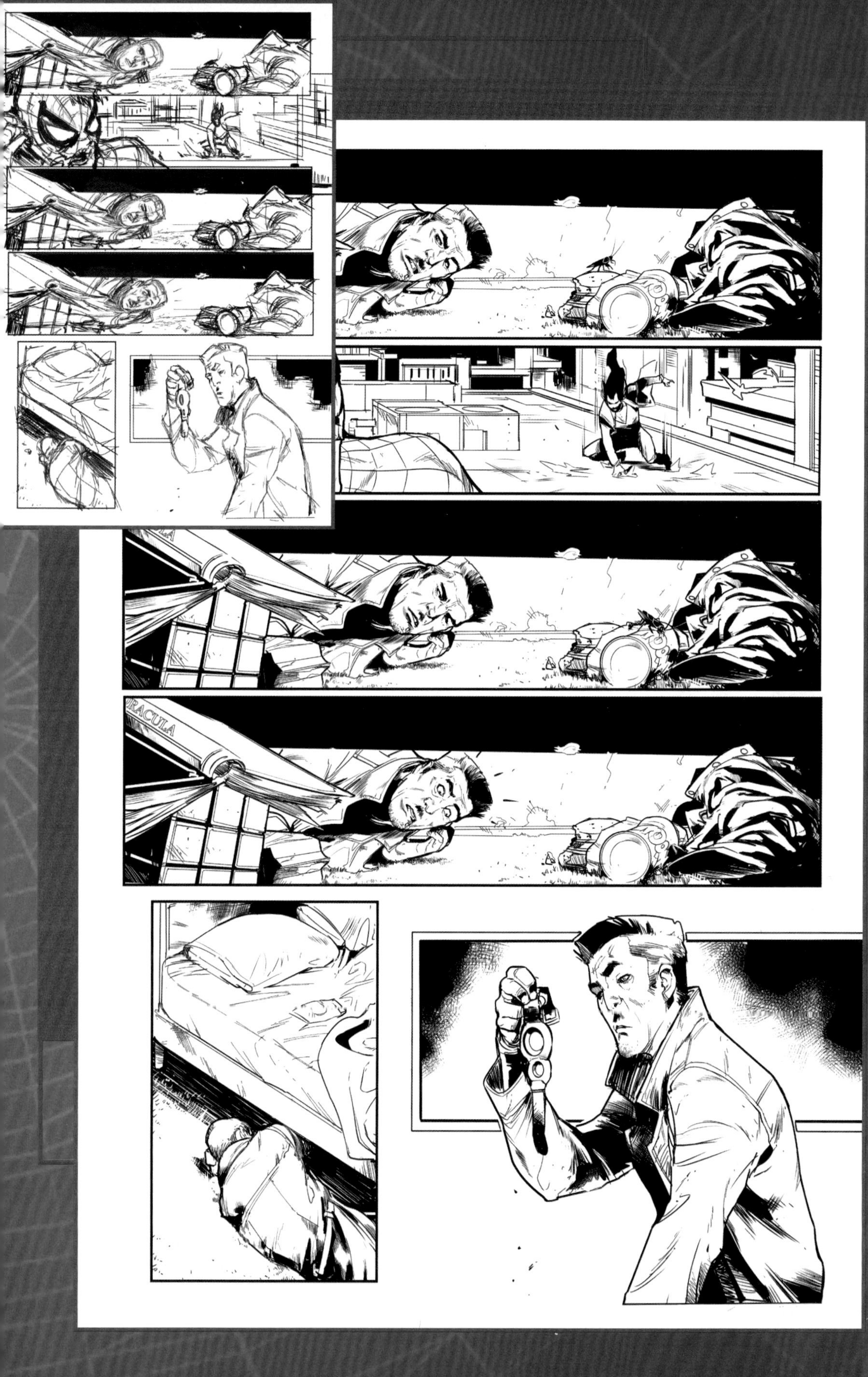
DRACULA

#311 PAGE 17 LAYOUTS AND INKS BY **JUAN FRIGERI**

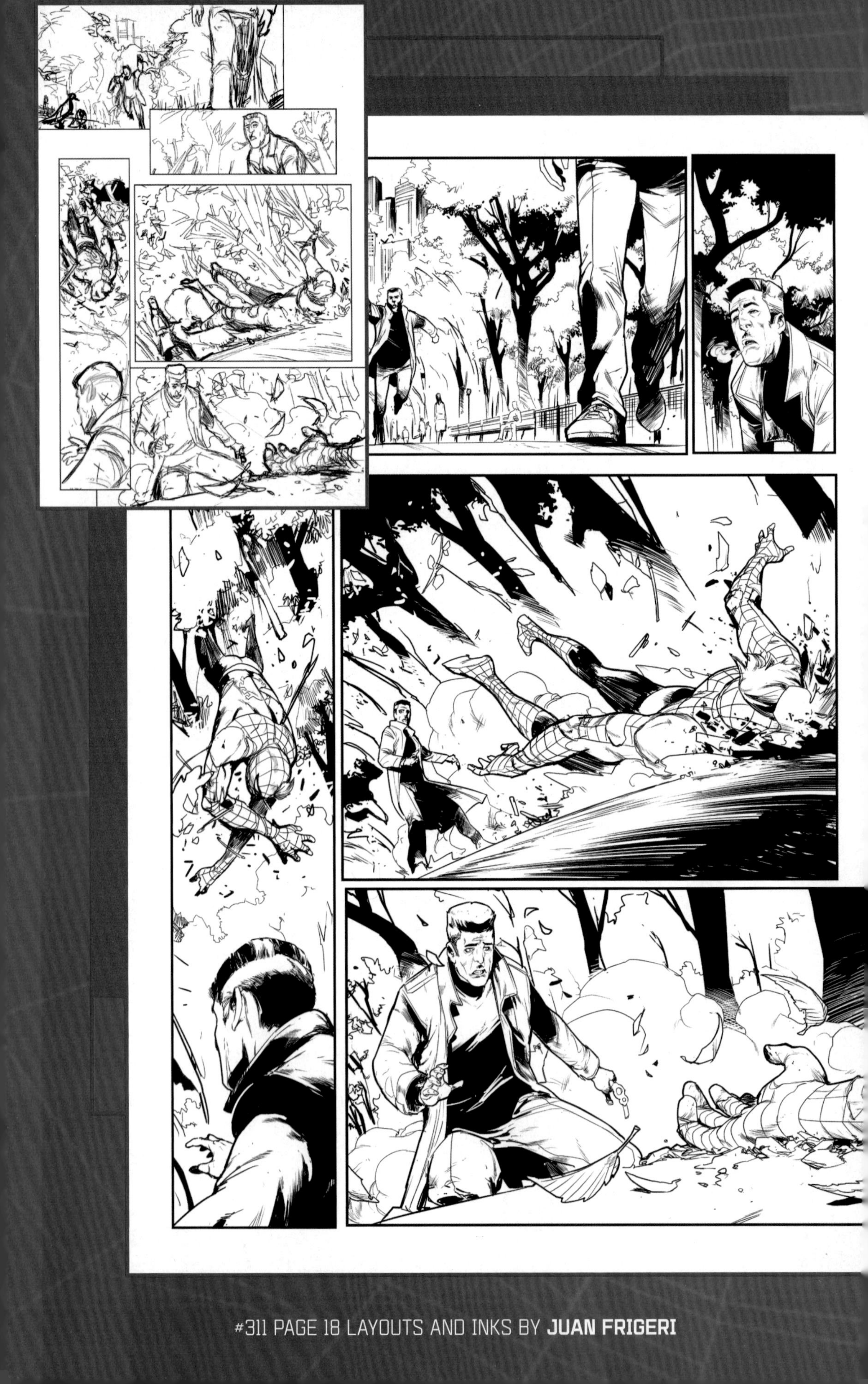

#311 PAGE 18 LAYOUTS AND INKS BY **JUAN FRIGERI**

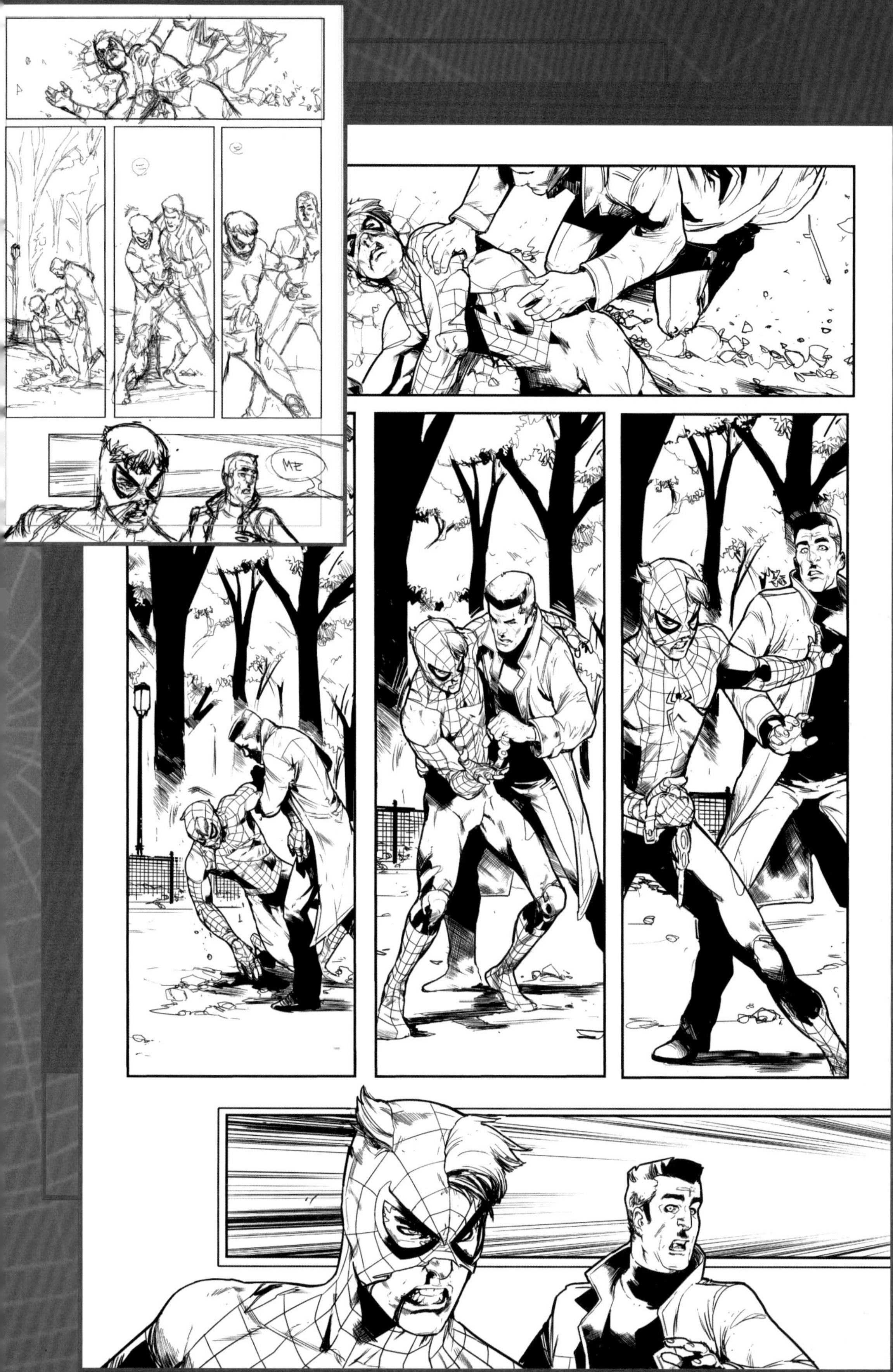
ME

#311 PAGE 19 LAYOUTS AND INKS BY **JUAN FRIGERI**

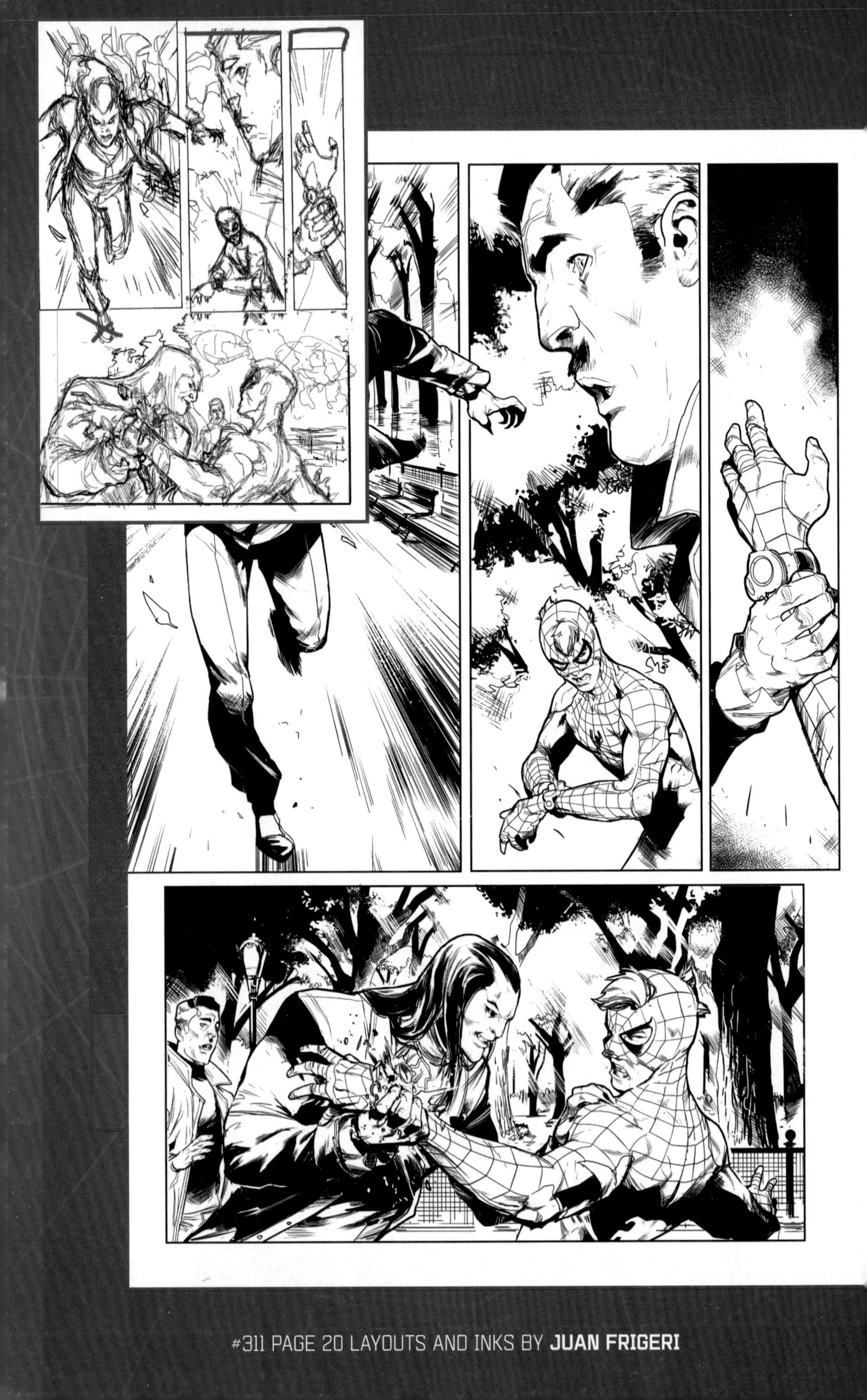

#311 PAGE 20 LAYOUTS AND INKS BY **JUAN FRIGERI**